THE WILD MUSE

The poetry of Annette von Droste-Hülshoff, with translations into English

MARION TYMMS

THE WILD MUSE

The poetry of Annette von Droste-Hülshoff, with translations into English

MEMOIRS
Cirencester

Published by Memoirs

1A The Wool Market Cirencester Gloucestershire, GL7 2PR
info@memoirsbooks.co.uk www.memoirspublishing.com

First published in England, 2013

Book jacket design Ray Lipscombe

ISBN 978-1-86151-091-4

Printed in England

For Ralph, without whom I should probably not have embarked on this project, and for Jo, without whom I should certainly never have completed it, with love and gratitude.

CONTENTS

INTRODUCTION

CHAPTER 1 - Events and influences in the early life of Annette von Droste-Hülshoff

CHAPTER 2 - The 1838 edition of her work

CHAPTER 3 - 'The Spiritual Year'

CHAPTER 4 - Levin Schücking and the flowering of Droste-Hülshoff's poetic genius

CHAPTER 5 - A selection of the poems of Droste-Hülshoff in English translation

Annotated bibliography

Index of poems translated

German titles of poems translated

Poems from 'The Spiritual Year' translated in this volume

INTRODUCTION

Few people asked to name some German poets of the 19th century would immediately think of Annette von Droste-Hülshoff, although most German speakers who have undergone a fairly traditional education or grown up in an averagely well-informed home environment will have come across her. They are likely to know her name and perhaps a few of her poems, and very probably her remarkable *Novelle, Die Judenbuche*, which has also established her as a familiar figure through its inclusion in the syllabus of British schoolchildren learning German, and more widely, through a number of translations. The past few decades have seen a rise in scholarly interest in her, in both Germany and England. This is due in no small measure to the work headed by Winfried Woesler in producing the definitive edition of her complete works, the *Historisch-kritische Ausgabe*, the publication of which by Niemeyer was finally completed in 2000 after 22 years of collaborative effort on her work and letters. At the same time, Germanists were turning their attention to her in their pursuit of women writers of that period, but she remained elusive to non-German speaking scholars and has even now not attained anything like international status. There are many explanations for this relative obscurity, and they do not all relate to the question of language.

Rather does her current isolation reflect the position she held during her lifetime, and no one was more conscious of this than

Droste-Hülshoff herself. It is always tempting to link the life of a creative artist with his or her work, and this is quite appropriate in her case, particularly as we are in possession of substantial information about the external details of that life. When it comes to her inner life, there is a vast amount of material contained in letters to and from this prolific correspondent, and the work itself is rich in clues. Even so, and when all this is taken into account, one is left with something of an enigma, for this is a woman who emerges as a mass of contradictions in many respects, sociable and open, yet almost crippled by her introspection and guarded in what she chooses to disclose. The examination of her work, with its wide range and rich textures, is likely to lead to fascination coupled with the recognition of inscrutability and a fathomless puzzle. Not for nothing is her work as a whole anything but a whole, but punctuated with fragments and gaps, tightly bound to time and place, yet eluding all attempt to limit her or to impose a category on her.

It is true that she belongs chronologically to the age of Goethe (1749-1832), that she shares the year of her birth (1797) with Heine and overlaps with Eduard Mörike (1804-1875), but she has little in common with these great figures of German poetry when it comes to content or style or poetic manner, although, that being said, it must be admitted that each is distinctive in his own way and quite distinct from the other two. Critics have chosen to point out that she bridges German Romanticism and the movement classed as Realism, but although her lifetime, albeit short, broadly spans these two periods, she belongs properly to neither, even if features of her work suggest a connection in thought or manner on fleeting occasions. Most scholars would throw doubt on the wisdom of assigning anyone conclusively to a specific 'movement' or even to categorizing any creative writing in the way that this implies, but in the case of Droste-Hülshoff, this is particularly unsatisfactory, since she is herself so fluid, and so little defined by type.

If one looks at the facts of her life it is not hard to see why her least perceptive, or indeed frankly uninformed, critics arrive at a view of her as a parochial figure, who, unlike many of her literary contemporaries, did not travel widely but seems to have contented herself with the life of an aristocratic lady, deeply rooted in the landscape and traditions of her native Westphalia and her adopted home in the south of Germany, where she spent a large part of her last years and died without much comment from a largely indifferent public in 1848, when Europe was in a state of uproar and change was brewing on all sides. This is no international figure at the heart of political and artistic developments but someone who seems deliberately, almost perversely one might say, to eschew the influences and contacts which, on the face of it, must have been available to her. The Droste-Hülshoff family was well connected and respected; visitors came and went; conversation was lively and encouraged, but the young Annette appears to have enjoyed a more domestic companionship, her warmth and hospitability counteracted by an aloofness and awkwardness which was often referred to and which possibly, to the end of her life, militated against easy social exchange. Against that, however, one can speak of the depth of the relationships which truly mattered to her, with her immediate and large extended family, and with the handful of close friends to whom she remained devoted. They clearly saw aspects of her personality which were concealed, perhaps even deliberately, from a wider circle.

The explanation for such remoteness is not hard to find. The life of an intelligent woman of her class, possessed of a lively mind and a voracious appetite for knowledge, must have been stifling. Her father, with whom she had the closest bonds, died when she was relatively young, but not before he had encouraged in his younger daughter a love of nature. This manifested itself in her not so much as the avid spirit of the collector of flora and fauna which filled his study, but as a kinship with natural things, animals and plants, and a response to landscape, the elements and the importance of the changing seasons and times of day, all of which she evokes with unique skill and power in her work. It is his mark that rests on her, rather than the inhibiting impact of her mother, who assumed responsibility for an education which was apparently lacking in the breadth and imaginativeness to which the highly original young woman would undoubtedly have responded.

Nor did Therese von Droste-Hülshoff oversee the social development of her daughter or nurture the artistic tendencies which were very soon apparent in her. Annette appears to have retained for her mother, who survived her, the ties of affection and duty, but no profound understanding of psychology is needed to select two features of the relationship which strike one as startling, even shocking. She relates how, when she gave to her mother the first manuscript of the cycle of religious poems known as 'The Spiritual Year' (*Das Geistliche Jahr*), Therese read it with some emotion, said nothing, and put it away without comment. When she came to the point of wishing to publish some of her early writings, she had to seek the permission of her mother to do so, and to go against the discretion normally demanded of a young woman attempting such an outrageous action by revealing her name, rather than taking refuge in the at least partial anonymity of her earlier publications. Much later, when she had entered into the emotional relationship with Levin Schücking which was destined to effect such a change in her, both personally and as a poet (see below, pp. 80-100), she urged him to refrain in the letters addressed to her in Münster (where she still lived with her mother) from using the 'du' form which betrayed the nature of the bond between them, in favour of the formal 'Sie'. Small wonder that this friendship, like the earlier confused one of her late teenage years (see pp.10ff below) was doomed to misunderstanding and failure!

All this leads to the impression of a woman inhibited by circumstances and almost stunted in her emotions, but her work could hardly be more different. In almost all of it, from her earliest ventures through a wide range of experiments, often left in a fragmentary state, to the majestic poetry of her last years, what is most apparent is the passion of a woman who writes with conviction and power of emotions deeply rooted in her mind and her soul.

In his article in the *Times Literary Supplement* of 19 March 1954, J. M. Cohen, ostensibly reviewing the single-volume edition of a substantial selection of Droste-Hülshoff's work by Clemens Heselhaus, published by Hanser Verlag, introduces her to a public which may not even have known her name, still less her work. This must have been a ground-breaking contribution at a time when very little of her work other than *Die Judenbuche* was available in English translation, and it would be ten years before Margaret Mare's useful and very thorough introduction appeared. Even today, access to much of her poetry is denied to potential readers with no knowledge of German, a gap which the present volume seeks to fill, though always with the reservation that a translation can only ever be second best to a reading in the original language and that this must inevitably be more the case with poetry than with prose. Cohen's article provides a comprehensive introduction, although, with the many quotations in German and the implied assumption that his readers are familiar with the literary background, it is aimed first and foremost at Germanists. It is packed with perceptive and sensitive insights and in all provides a stimulating source of information about this enigmatic writer and her context. Particularly striking is the title of the article – 'The Disciplined Romantic' – which begs questions not necessarily answered in the article itself, but already exposing her contradictory nature.

Throughout her creative life, Droste-Hülshoff was clearly deeply committed to her writing, correcting and revising her versions and, significantly, abandoning projects when she was uneasy or dissatisfied with them. Although she appears early on to have been drawn to writing, her youthful efforts are largely derivative, rooted in the literature doubtless available to her in the educated but fairly traditional household in which she grew up, but without much actual guidance in literary tastes. A young girl of her class and eager thirst for knowledge growing up in a period of great activity in literature in Germany can hardly have failed to know the works of Goethe (1749-1832) and Schiller (1759-1805), who were dominating the literary scene, but their influence on her writing is impossible to pinpoint. The impact of figures who are included under the generalized heading of 'romantic' writers (Novalis, Tieck, Arnim, Wackenroder) appears likewise almost negligible. The brothers Grimm and A. W. Schegel, who visited her home and with whose work she must have been familiar, have left no discernible traces in the writing of a young woman who seems to have picked her way through any material which may have been accessible to her, though in a desultory fashion. It is relatively less well known names –Hölty, Bürger and even Fouqué - who come to mind if one searches for signs that the young Droste-Hülshoff was really influenced by anyone.

However, her cycle of religious poems *Das Geistliche Jahr* does show echoes in language and thought of poets of an even earlier age, figures of the stature of Andreas Gryphius (1616-1664) and Angelus Silesius (1624-1677), whom she honours to the point of actually copying him in a poem later in her career. For the most part, these are passing echoes, for Droste-Hülshoff is essentially herself and stands alone as an artist, just as close acquaintance with her as a person – gleaned above all from her copious letter-writing – reveals a solitary life, despite the enthusiasm with which she obviously entered into the lives of the many people she encountered.

Another interesting feature of her writing is that it took a very long time – most of her adult life, in fact – for her to settle to the genre of poetry which was her real artistic environment and which brought her the gradual and somewhat reluctant acknowledgement she enjoys today, though this, it must still be stressed, is not widespread. If she is sometimes claimed as Germany's greatest woman poet, this is not in the face of very much obvious competition, and it also doubtful whether it would be an accolade that would greatly please her. Yet again there is something of a contradiction: she is a substantial poet who happens to be a woman, and one could make a case for saying that there are elements in her work which derive from her gender and which can be attributed to the life she led as a young woman of her class in the restricted society of a modestly-sized but culturally-lively town in Germany. Over and above that, however, and although she sometimes kicks against the restrictions she perceives, and even at times takes on the persona of a man in her writing, she is more concerned with her role as a poet and a human being, writing for fellow human beings who share her experiences and not least her sufferings.

In a poem as early as that for the Fifth Sunday in Lent of her cycle of religious poems which, for some though not all of her critics, constitutes her most significant achievement, she writes of her belief that her poems will live on long after her death:

> My songs will live,
> long after I have disappeared.
> Many a one will tremble before them
> who has felt as I do,
> whether another has offered them,
> or my own hand.
> Behold, the songs were allowed to live,
> but I disappeared.

These are striking words from a young woman barely twenty, and they reflect two important features of her life and her work: that she had a deep sense of her vocation as a poet, and that she was already aware that she belonged not to her own age, but to an undefined future, when her message would reach kindred spirits. A similar thought is expressed many years later in a letter to Elise Rüdiger, a close friend and confidante, increasingly so towards the end of her life: "I cannot and do not wish to be famous *now*, but after a hundred years I should like to be read, and perhaps I shall succeed in that, for basically it is as easy as Columbus's trick with the egg, and merely demands the sacrifice of the present." (Letter of 24 July 1843.)

The two statements frame her creative life, the one the expression of her hope for the importance of the cycle which would preoccupy her for most of her adult life, and the other her deeply held conviction that she had a genuine vocation and a place in a broader artistic context.

It is in her poetry that Droste-Hülshoff achieves her stature, but this is after she has tried her hand at other literary forms and dabbled in her youth in writing verse which gives little indication of the heights she will later reach. This is for the most part childish and derivative verse, but then she was a child and, though prompted to write from a very early age, tied to patterns derived from her own, restricted, reading and to material inspired by family events – very much 'occasional' poems – and decidedly pious musings based on thoughts embedded in her strict Catholic upbringing. When she branched out, it was into something quite different in form and content; the young Annette worked eagerly for some time on a piece of tragic drama, *Berta*, destined to remain uncompleted and almost certainly way beyond her potential at that time, and possibly beyond her artistic taste at any time. A second attempt at narrative writing was more successful, and she herself was more committed to a romance in verse entitled *Walter*, doubtless inspired by chivalrous epics and owing something at least to her romantic precursors in its content and manner. She completed it in six cantos, which from time to time point forward to the dramatic achievements of her later career, when in powerful ballads she would excel in evoking atmosphere and suspense. For now, however - and she was still barely out of her teenage years – these positive features were often marred by sentimentality and immature exuberance. They might merit the description 'romantic' in certain respects, but the control of form and subject matter of later years was barely even hinted at: there was no sign of the 'discipline' which would prevail at a later date.

At this point, when she was experimenting and becoming acquainted with her artistic strengths - with characteristic honesty despite the enthusiasm displayed in her letters - she tried her hand at the only novel she ever attempted, *Ledwina*. This, however, also remained a fragment, though an interesting one which betrays much that is truly Droste-Hülshoff. It is undeniably at least partly autobiographical, its central figure the ailing and highly introspective Ledwina, with her profound sense of isolation both physical and emotional. Droste-Hülshoff abandoned her work on it, again after some years of diligent commitment to the project. However, these were years when she was turning to other ideas also, and most significantly for the picture of her whole career, making headway with the work which would occupy her for most of the rest of her life, the series of religious poems originally intended for her devout step-grandmother but increasingly evolving into the powerful and very revealing 'Spiritual Year'. (See below, pp. 30-79)

It was also a poignant time in her personal life, focused on the confused experience of a strange double attachment to two young men with whom she believed herself romantically linked, and the devastation caused by the breakdown of the relationship with both. The end of her friendships with Heinrich Straube and August von Arnswaldt left her, at 23, emotionally exhausted and consumed with negative thoughts, in which guilt and self-accusation dominated. These appeared to exceed any sense of embarrassment and humiliation, and even the bitterness she undoubtedly did feel, and express, towards those in her circle who she thought had colluded against her and judged her without knowing the full story. This period of her life –and her letters at that time leave no doubt of the impact upon her – was compounded when, in 1826, her beloved father died, making a huge change in her domestic life inevitable. With the succession of her brother to the title and estate, she moved with her mother to a much less imposing country residence, the Rüschhaus in remote countryside outside Münster, which remained her home until, ailing and aware of her solitariness, she spent large periods of her last years in a very distant region of Germany, in Meersburg, on Lake Constance.

It is impossible not to link Droste-Hülshoff with these two very distinct parts of Germany, because they have a marked impact on the content and essence of her writing, not necessarily because she is actually describing them, but because she is herself so much in tune with their respective qualities. She remained deeply rooted in the history and culture of her original homeland, continuing to write about it throughout her life, yet she found in the adopted environment of her last years a different inspiration. Some of her last poems – and many critics would say her finest ones – are imbued with a new vigour and a completely different tone. It is indeed possible to speak of a release, a freedom and a new confidence pervading her work as she approaches the end of her all too short life, and to wonder where these things would have taken her in the future denied to her. Almost certainly they would not have led her into the mainstream of developing trends in German literature, for this was a woman destined to remain aloof in artistic and almost certainly also in personal terms. One returns, then, to the enigma of Droste-Hülshoff, and to the contradictions observed throughout her life by those close to her, by her literary critics, and by herself.

By now there are plenty of scholarly commentaries and interpretations at the disposal of those who would seek to understand something of this fascinating figure, and this book does not set out to add to them. Its purpose is quite specific: to make the lyric poetry of Annette von Droste-Hülshoff available to readers without a knowledge of German and invite them to enjoy a remarkable poet who would otherwise remain closed to them. This is simultaneously a modest intention and an act of extreme arrogance. It will always be difficult, not to say impossible, to capture great literature in a language other than the original, and this is very much the case with this poet, who was so adept at conveying the nuances of language in a diction very much her own, belonging to a time and a place very familiar to her, but which, to those who struggle with it two hundred years later, often appears alien and sometimes even defies comprehension. In this enterprise, which occasionally seems doomed to failure, one can rely, in the case of Droste-Hülshoff, on the woman herself and on the abundant guidance she provides, whether consciously or otherwise, to a personality and a lifetime which, for all its contradictions, are surprisingly consistent and revealing.

Thus this selection of some of her poems rendered into modern English is accompanied throughout by references to the stages in her personal life, the relationships which exerted an influence at every turn, by cross-references to language and thought within her poems, and to that fund of information at hand in her copious lifelong letter writing. If, at the end of all this, the reader is encouraged to pursue the scholarly literature on specific issues, then the purpose of this volume will perhaps be served and Droste-Hülshoff's hope that she would be known, not during her own lifetime, but many decades after her death, will be just a little closer to fulfilment.

All translations from German in this volume are my own.

CHAPTER ONE

EVENTS AND INFLUENCES IN THE EARLY LIFE OF ANNETTE VON DROSTE-HÜLSHOFF

The major events of Annette von Droste-Hülshoff's life, identifiable turning points which are reflected in her subject matter and the way she treats it, are just as important for an understanding of the lyric poetry of her work as the specific regions of Germany with which she is associated. Her work is extraordinarily personal. Its principal themes recur, though the context changes, and the consequence is an unusually compact *œuvre* inseparable from the experiences of a lifetime which was tragically short yet lived with intensity and emotional depth from beginning to end.

Her critics and her editors, both during her lifetime and after it, have taken differing views about the best way to present her work, essentially whether to adopt a chronological approach or a thematic one, and the present volume chooses a compromise in this as in other respects. At the heart of this decision is the recognition of the sheer concentration of her work, and of the fact that it simply cannot be separated from her as an individual enigmatic and challenging, self-analytical and demanding, and ultimately, much as one might wish it to be otherwise, rarely at ease with herself.

The person who probably knew her best, as a human being and an artist, was the writer and critic Levin Schücking, with whom she had a rather brief but very significant friendship towards the end of her life. The nature of this friendship has been much discussed, but suffice to say here that, for her, its significance was immensely important (see below, pp. 80-100), and posterity is indebted to Schücking for the *Lebensbild* ('Picture of a life') which accompanies his early editions of her poetry. He published it fourteen years after her death, and he admits that some of his early recollections, particularly of his first meeting with her when he was a fifteen-year-old schoolboy, are coloured by his youth and the undoubted awe he felt at meeting for the first time this woman who was much older than himself and way beyond him in background and experience.

One extract stands out in particular and may serve here to express the essential personality of Droste-Hülshoff:

For that was precisely the peculiar quality of this character which combined within itself apparently contradictory features: lyrical power, the depths of a truly feminine sensitivity, all the heartfelt gentleness of a poetic soul, and yet at the same time the sceptically probing urge for knowledge and the capacity for cool, critical thought. It was the peculiar quality of this character that its greatest strength was concentrated in her incisive knowledge of human nature, in her brilliant judgement of the world and its circumstances, in her calm, clear gaze that appeared to see into all the hidden layers of the heart.

The middle-aged Levin, looking back now at his privileged acquaintance with her, manages to convey so much that can enhance the understanding of her work, and indeed it is not least among his contributions to her reputation that he understood the complexity of her nature and was able to present her at this time (1862) to a public which was only just beginning to appreciate her, or even to comprehend that there was anything to appreciate.

If, however, one goes back to the beginnings of Annette's emergence as a poet of substance, one finds a poem which, likewise, conveys her very essence and surprises us with what it reveals of her future development. It is used here to set the tone for this selection of her lyric poetry and to demonstrate the direction she was to take. Its very title, 'Unruhe', expresses one of her prevailing moods and her capacity to transcend the personal in a statement of universal concern:

Restlessness (1816)

Let us rest here on the shore for a while.
The rays of Phoebus play upon the sea.
Can you see over there the white armies of pennants?
The boats are all set for their journey to the distant land.

Ah, how uplifting it is to delight
in the infinity of the ocean!
There is no longer any thought of size and space
concealed as a goal for our dreams.
We must not shrink from imagining it
as immeasurable as eternity.

Who has fathomed the limits of the sea,
how far it drives the foaming wave?
And who its depths when the heavy plumbline
comes up unsatisfied
and the anchor provides no stability
in the wild sea?

"Would you not like to travel in circles
with the intrepid sailors on the infinite plain?"
Ah, I should like to fly like a bird,
to go with the bright pennants,
far, far, where no footstep ever sounded,
no human voice ever echoed,
no ship ever cut through the fleeting pathway.

And onward still, endlessly, eternally new,
to hurl myself free and unfettered, full of joy,
through alien creations –
ah, there is a thudding and a glow in my heart!

Restlessly I am driven from side to side in my narrow life,
with place and time pressing down upon me.
The fearful striving of the soul is called freedom,
and in my breast eternity resounds.

Quiet, quiet, my foolish heart!
Will you eternally long in vain,
eternally pour forth in fruitless agony
tears battling with the impossible?
To be sure, the earth can offer much pleasure,

and every moment precious joy.
So still, my heart, your fervent trembling:
in truth there is in life so much that's good,
such sweet desire, but ah! so seldom happiness.

For only rarely does a man enjoy the pleasures
that blossom all about him: they vanish unperceived.
Be still, my heart, and learn to acquiesce.
Does the bright ray of Phoebus which plays gently shimmering
upon the waves bring you no joys?

Let us turn home from this damp shore!
It does no good, my friend, to stay here.
My dreams press heavily upon me;
from far off come the sounds like songs of homeland,
and the old restlessness returns –

let us turn home from this damp shore:
you wanderers on the waves, fare well!

They try to tie us to our firesides,
and call our yearning dreams and foolish hopes,
and yet the heart, that tiny speck of earth,
has room for all creation!

This is Annette at eighteen years old, and it stands out among most of the work she was producing at that time for its maturity of thought and, certain clichés aside, her command of poetic language and expression. It could well have been written by her thirty years later. It is chosen to stand at the beginning of this selection of some of her most representative poems which will, it is hoped, demonstrate in turn the coherence of her work and the impossibility of separating her creative achievements from her biography. Events and experiences helped to shape her, of course, but they did not really define her as a person or as a poet: the ingredients of both are already there in this assured poem. She enclosed it in a letter of February 1816 to her friend and mentor Anton Matthias Sprickmann, a lawyer almost forty years her senior who had introduced her to the world of literature. Although his own literary achievements were unremarkable, he was well read and had connections which opened up important new avenues for the young Annette, who valued his advice and confided in him the plans and aspirations she was already forming. She also admitted in the letter that the poem, written some weeks previously, reflected her troubled state at that time.

There is other evidence from these months that she was experiencing the first major illness of the many that would dog her for the whole of her life. Some of the symptoms were physical

- breathlessness, problems with her eyes and her heart - but there were also signs of acute depression and what she describes in her letter as 'almost feverish restlessness'. Although this severe affliction had abated by the time she was writing to Sprickmann, and she dismisses it somewhat flippantly as due perhaps either to over-adherence to the advice of her doctor or her outright refusal to follow medical advice, it is clear that this poem, with its echo of that same word *Unruhe*, expresses a state of mind and a tendency which would be important aspects of her personality throughout her life.

It is a very personal poem, speaking of the closeness she felt to nature and the elemental power of the sea and their capacity to bring relief and calm, yet at the same time of her frustration and sense of isolation, and her yearning to surrender to those same powers in order to achieve the freedom she craves. This young woman was already deeply conscious that the social and domestic environment to which she was bound, and to which all her life on one level she acquiesced, was a crippling force which threatened her deepest passions and her creative urge. It says much for the trust she had in Sprickmann that she felt able to confide such intimate emotions to him, although it surely speaks for his own sense of inadequacy in responding that he took a whole year to reply, and that when he did, although he told her that he regarded this piece as among the very best work of hers he had seen, he admitted that he no longer had it to hand since it was tucked away among his treasured possessions. Like most of the truly important and formative relationships of Droste-Hülshoff's life, this one played a role for a time but then left her alone and largely without resolution.

The friendship with Sprickmann is the first in a series of really quite puzzling associations recorded throughout her life and accompanied by periods of intense correspondence. Almost certainly Sprickmann and his wife felt drawn to this unusual young woman, and he in particular glimpsed an artistic talent which went unrecognized by her family, whose members seem to have been aware that she had some very unusual qualities but were at a loss to understand them or to encourage them. The fact that she confided her confusion and her sense of isolation, as she does in this poem and the long accompanying letter, to an outsider, already speaks for the solitariness she felt from her earliest years and particularly for her awareness that she did not belong within the social environment and family background which, on the face of it, she embraced with warmth and generosity. There is absolutely no suggestion that Sprickmann was anything more than a concerned much older man, genuinely committed to fostering the extraordinary mental and creative powers he discerned in her, but the address to the 'friend' who is accompanying her on the walk by the shore in 'Unruhe' and is apparently the recipient of these heartfelt reflections is echoed in the same address to him in the body of her letter. Mentor he may have been, a wise and learned confidant, but she also felt sufficiently close to him on a purely human level to entrust him with her anguished thoughts about something which was already troubling her and would continue to trouble her to the end: where she fitted in and what she should do with the peculiar gifts she must have known she possessed.

The final strophe of this remarkable poem moves it into a different sphere, when she appears to be speaking not just for herself, but for a broader group of human beings. It is easy enough to interpret this cry of frustration as an early feminist appeal for release from the bonds of social convention, symbolized in home and hearth, but it is more than that, for what she feels, at the close of the poem and throughout it, are the stifling effects of convention and the desire to abandon herself to broader experience and the burgeoning awareness of her creative destiny.

The theme of restlessness was to accompany Annette von Droste-Hülshoff throughout her life, and it was a feeling that concerned her again in a letter to Anton Matthias Sprickmann in February 1819, when she was trying to explain to him the sensations which sometimes overwhelmed her and which she recalled vividly from her early childhood. This extraordinary passage in a very long letter, again to this much older friend, lets us into secrets of her life and deepest emotions which she seems to have concealed from her family, notably from her mother and her sister Jenny who, for all their mutual loyalty and affection, were strangely distant from her and almost certainly incapable of understanding her at the level she craved and rarely, if ever, found. The relevant passage is offered here in its entirety, precisely because it seems to offer a key to her personality which in turn illuminates her development as a poet and possibly leads us to a surer understanding of the enigma which is Droste-Hülshoff:

Oh, my dear Sprickmann, I do not know where I should begin, in order not to strike you as ridiculous, for what I have to tell you is ridiculous, really it is and I cannot deceive myself about that. I have to accuse myself to you of a stupid and strange weakness which really often makes me bitter, but - I beg you again not to laugh - the demon that torments me has a romantic and silly name: it is called 'yearning for distant places'. No, no, Sprickmann, it is honestly not a joke. You know that I am actually not a mad woman. I did not derive my strange and crazy misfortune from books and attics, as everyone would believe, but no one knows, only you know. And it has not been brought to me by external circumstances. It has always been inside me, since I was quite small. Certainly I was only four or five years old, because I had a dream in which I thought I was seven and thought myself a grown-up person. In it I seemed to be walking with my parents, and my siblings and two acquaintances, in a garden which was not at all beautiful but just a vegetable garden with an avenue running straight through the middle which we kept going up. Then it turned into a forest, but the avenue was still there, right through the middle, and we just kept on walking. That was all there was to the dream, and yet for the whole of the following day I was sad and kept weeping because I was not in the avenue and could never come there either. But then I remember how one day when my mother was telling us all about the place where she was born, and the mountains, and our grandparents, whom at that time we did not know, I felt such a feeling of longing that when a few days later we were sitting having a meal and she happened to mention her parents, I burst into such violent sobbing that I had to be taken away. And this was also before I was seven, because when I was seven I got to know my grandparents. I am only telling you all these insignificant things to convince you that this wretched dependence on all the places I have never been to, all the things I do not have, is absolutely inside me and has not been put there by any external matters. This way I shall not seem quite so ridiculous to you, my dear, long-suffering friend. I think a foolishness that the dear Lord has placed upon us is after all always not so bad as one that we have brought on ourselves. However, for several years this condition has increased so much that I can really count it a torment. A single word is enough to put me in a bad mood for the whole day.

This passage is extraordinarily revealing. It shows a young woman, just twenty-two, plagued by introspection and a sense of being different, conscious of a deep inner pain which she can hardly describe but knows to be an inescapable part of her make-up. It also shows how, despite her vulnerability, she is capable of revealing herself to someone she trusts to accept her, although she knows that, to many people, she appears strange and even a figure of fun.

Her choice of Sprickmann as a confidant is typical, too, of the deep friendships she formed throughout her life, not always lasting but powerful at the time and crucial at points in her life that she possibly could barely have faced alone. It also provides a key to an important feature of her writing, both prose and poetry, in which places, times and describable experiences assume a significance far deeper than the superficial.

At the time she wrote this, Annette was approaching two very significant points in her life. The one was the inception of the project which would occupy her for much of her life, the cycle known as *Das Geistliche Jahr*, and the other the turmoil resulting from the confused emotional relationships with two young men which was to prove devastating to her and, some would say, leave her with a lasting sense of guilt and self-reproach. As is the way with the story of her life, the two events coalesced and interacted upon one another in a powerful way.

Thus the next single most striking poem, 'Not', marks what can be seen as the first major turning point in her life and draws together these two events. It is again characterized by an amazing power and maturity in a poet who had not, up to this point, established herself in any real way.

Agony

Why do you talk so much of fear and agony in your blameless doings?
You pious people, strike care down dead, for it certainly
does not wish to remain with you.

Yet while the agony, over which compassion weeps,
is only like the drop on the hand of the drinker, the dark flood,
which no one notices, stands hidden right up to the very edge of the soul.

You pious people profess that you know care,
and yet you have never seen guilt, but they, those others,
can already put a name to life and its terrifying heights.

A noise as though of song and praise rises up,
and the rays of light play around the flowers. The people dwell silently
in the valley, and up above the dark vultures are nesting.

This poem, a succinct expression of the emotional pain which would ravage Droste-Hülshoff for most of her life, bears as its title a German word (*Not*) which defies satisfactory translation into English, or perhaps rather contains in a single syllable so many emotions that could be expressed in a variety of ways. 'Suffering', 'need', 'urgency', 'desolation', 'pain', 'devastation' are all contained in it, and the title chosen here, 'agony'- or it could also be 'anguish'- are all strangely less effective than the stark original .

In four strophes she encompasses the human lot of suffering, but most important is the way she separates two groups of humankind: the 'ordinary' people who live in the valley and the select ones who, like the vultures, live on a higher plain. Though prey to fear and pain and doubt, the 'ordinary' people cannot comprehend the immeasurably greater anguish of others.

The poem makes its first appearance on the final page of the manuscript of the first poems of *Das Geistliche Jahr*, and although it does not strictly belong within that cycle, the juxtaposition is telling. The date is 1820 and Annette has progressed from the younger sister entertaining her social circle with her piano-playing and her 'occasional' poems in celebration of members of her family and of family events, and slight poems often of a humorous nature which prompted any interested relatives to encourage her into comic writing. By now she has also completed the first part of a collection of religious poems which she originally intended to give to her beloved step-grandmother, the second wife of her mother's father and very much the focus of the large extended family in Bökendorf where Annette spent many happy times with young aunts and uncles with whom she consorted as with cousins close to her own age. As the work progressed she became increasingly aware that it was quite unsuited to the original purpose, as she had expressed it in letters at the time. The pious elderly lady had no need of spiritual counsel from her young relative, and Annette herself saw that what she had written would be likely to distress and even shock her. Instead she handed them to her own mother, with a letter of dedication, but the gift was received with ambivalence, if not exactly with rejection. She took the poems back and one cannot be sure whether she intended at that point to return to them at a later date. (See below for section on 'The Spiritual Year').

For the time being she was occupied with matters of a more intimate nature, when she became involved with two young men and precipitated the event which some critics refer to as the *Jugendkatastrophe* and to which some would attribute far-reaching effects on her artistic and personal life. Whether the diagnosis is as clear-cut as that is open to dispute, or at least to discussion, for already there is evidence that Annette bears a burden of self-analysis and the tendency towards self-accusation which will mean that life will not be easy for her.

Exactly what happened is far from clear, but Annette herself admits some months after the events of the summer of 1820 that she had loving feelings for both young men, probably a sign that neither would have been ultimately successful in winning her. August von Arnswaldt was socially a much more likely candidate for marriage to her and for a short time it seemed to her hosts in Bökendorf that that was the way the relationship was heading. However Arnswaldt arrived for a visit with his friend Heinrich Straube, a fellow student at Göttingen, and for him Annette seems to have developed a particular affection, possibly drawn to him by his sharp intellect and his rather shy, awkward manner. What followed appears to have been a tragic muddle, the result of misguided good intentions rather than any deliberate ill-will, and Annette's youth and inexperience doubtless contributed to the situation which she was later to regret so bitterly. When Arnswaldt, apparently prompted by Annette's young uncle August von Haxthausen, approached her, ostensibly to discover the nature of her feelings towards Straube, she seems to have admitted to these but, unguardedly to say the least, to have added that she was drawn also towards Arnswaldt himself. The result was, unsurprisingly, that the two young men felt they were both being badly treated by the same woman and that the best solution was to abandon the awkward triangle of relationships. Annette herself was left feeling humiliated and betrayed by her relatives, who appear to have become embroiled in the situation without malicious intention. Arnswaldt eventually soothed any hurt or indignation he may have felt by marrying Anna von Haxthausen a decade later, but the hapless Straube appears to have nurtured his lost love to the end of his days and retained the lock of her hair which she had given to him during a brief period which probably came closer to a real love affair than anything she experienced in her strangely unfulfilled personal lifetime. It seems reasonable to accept that the poignant poem 'The Yew Hedge' (see below p.116) which she wrote twenty years later was her attempt to recapture the special quality of a youthful love long lost and deeply mourned.

The torment that Annette went through in the weeks following this episode is vividly conveyed in her letter to her aunt Anna von Haxthausen dated December 1820. In it she reveals her profound hurt and humiliation over the whole affair, which, as she sees it, has brought disapproval upon her from the family in Bökendorf: she actually speaks of being 'condemned on all sides'. In trying to explain herself to those who, as she believes, have judged her without knowing the truth of the situation, she reveals the depth of her feelings for Heinrich Straube, speaking of having loved him like a brother, but further, of having believed that he would always be a part of her life. In expressing herself again so unguardedly, she lays herself open to further pain and humiliation. She admits to suffering very deeply and wishing that she could see him again, or at least know that he forgives her.

Anna, again one hopes out of a lack of wisdom rather than any wish to compound the damage already done, chose to send this letter to Straube himself. Unsurprisingly, one may well say, since so many youthful emotions were at work, he did not respond, and history is left to conjecture what he suffered as a result of what looks like a foolish episode and even - dare one say?- a lucky escape for him.

What Annette endured is apparent. Those who believe that

the experience coloured her emotional life for ever and made it impossible for her to achieve a fulfilling relationship with an eligible man may be right, but they fail to take into account what is already plain to see: her inherently introspective nature, her tendency to self-criticism and her ability to assume a burden of guilt way beyond her years. She is simply incapable of letting the matter pass over her, as she tells Anna she has tried to do, and the whole of the letter, with her detailed analysis of the relationships she recalls with both Arnswaldt and Straube suggests that, on the contrary, she is indulging in self-pity and brooding which militate against any gentler emotions and burst out in the bitter cry of 'Agony'. The stark little poem expresses more powerfully even than the letter to Anna the anger and resentment she feels and, divorced from the circumstances which we know to have given rise to it, it expresses her sense of total isolation from the greater part of society in which she lives, or, as she would see it, is condemned to exist.

It is significant that she placed this poem with the twenty-five poems she had written towards the projected 'Spiritual Year', for that cycle was already undergoing a transformation and was by now associated with the wordless response of her mother. 1820 must be seen in the life of Annette von Droste-Hülshoff as a turning-point both personal and artistic, and, in the context of a lifetime punctuated by powerful emotions and crucial circumstances, as the first year that would change her and eventually dictate the direction she was to take.

'Eventually', is important, however, for Annette seems to have descended into a period of withdrawal and possibly deep depression which lasted for well over five years. Such letters as survive – and it is almost inconceivable that someone so committed to correspondence would have given up the activity – are relatively trivial and unrevealing. It is more likely that the faithful Jenny, the elder sister who was so different from her and so protective, destroyed letters from this period which might have betrayed too much of her distraught frame of mind. It seems to accord rather with the whole picture of Droste-Hülshoff's life and her way of working that she took refuge in a long interval of contemplation and self-searching, in order to embark on the next and truly fruitful years of her creative life.

On a personal and domestic level these years brought major changes which must have caused her great distress: her father died in the summer of 1826 and she and her mother and sister moved from Schloss Hülshoff to the relatively modest Rüschhaus. In 1829 her beloved younger brother Ferdinand, the youngest of the family, also died. In the absence of written evidence, one can only surmise the impact on her of the two bereavements, and the domestic upheaval resulting from her elder brother's move to the ancestral home when he succeeded to his father's title. A poignant expression of loss is contained in the wistful reference to Ferdinand, "my dear boy, slim and blond", in the nostalgic poem 'The Bench' which she wrote thirteen years after his death (see below, p. 120), but by this time this is no outpouring of grief, but a characteristically bitter-sweet recollection among many. She must have been lonely in the remote and somewhat gloomy Rüschhaus. Even today, despite the committed upkeep by Droste-Hülshoff devotees and the occasional pilgrimages from those who seek to honour her memory, the modest house gives the impression of being lost in time, and much had changed for the family with the move from the relatively lively society of Münster. More change was to come, however, with the marriage in 1834 of her sister Jenny to Joseph von Lassberg and their move first to Switzerland

and then to the impressive castle of Meersburg, where the Count could pursue his enthusiasm for medieval literature and remain influential in social and political circles.

Although during these years Annette travelled quite frequently within Germany, visiting friend and relatives in the Rhineland and her sister and brother-in-law further afield, she was increasingly immersed in the countryside and culture of her native Westphalia. Temperamentally, that was undoubtedly where she belonged, and some of her most important earlier poems, and indeed many written towards the end of her life, too, bear witness to this powerful sense of her roots. If her life appears to have been even more restricted and the new circumstances of her domestic existence relatively straitened, this may not have made much difference to Droste-Hülshoff, who lived primarily in her mind. Moreover, she had a remarkable capacity for friendship, and throughout her life she formed significant new connections with people, both men and women, irrespective of age difference very often, and maintained them with her prolific letter-writing.

Most important for the years after the events of 1820 was what she did not do. She suspended her work on the novel *Ledwina* which remains an interesting fragment not least for its autobiographical touches, but, as far as her prose writings are concerned, it does not really hint at the brilliance she would achieve much later in *Die Judenbuche*. She did not take up the work on her religious cycle, and may even have intended never to do so. The searing experience of the affair of Arnswaldt and Straube had left her with an overwhelming self-doubt and challenged the belief in a kindly God which may not ever have been as firm as her family would have liked to think it was.

During this time she became involved in the literary circles that were springing up in the relatively cultured climate of Münster. Publication was difficult for a woman of her class, and what did appear, mostly in journals and newspapers, was often anonymous or under a disguised name. The first time a consolidated volume of her work appeared, somewhat tentatively, was as late as 1838, and in this she was aided by her loyal friends and associates, some of them stalwarts of the informal literary circles. There were a few such people who saw her potential, but they were not really equipped to promote her work in the way that, nearing forty years of age, she needed to be known.

CHAPTER TWO

THE 1838 EDITION OF HER WORK

When one looks at this small volume - and it is possible to do just that, thanks to a charming facsimile edition published in 1978 by the Droste-Gesellschaft- it is not difficult to understand why its impact was so slight and contributed relatively little to her reputation.

The explanation probably lies in the selection of material, which gives scant insight into the scope and power of the work she was on the verge of producing. The volume is strangely unbalanced. Well over half of the 220 pages are devoted to the three remarkable epic poems: 'Das Hospiz auf dem großen Sankt Bernhard', 'Des Arztes Vermächtnis' and 'Die Schlacht im Loener Bruch'. There follow a handful of lyric poems, and finally a small selection (eight) from the existing first part of 'The Spiritual Year'.

It is not entirely clear how much Droste-Hülshoff herself contributed to the decisions about which work she should publish at this stage, although she undoubtedly knew how she saw the prospective volume and made her views known to Wilhelm Junkmann and Christoph Bernhard Schlüter, who had undertaken to negotiate with publishers on her behalf. Such dealings lay beyond her experience at this point in her life and it would not have been considered seemly for a woman of her class to engage in the negotiations herself. Also, evidence from that time makes it clear that there were logistical problems and that the fact that she was living away from the town made communication very slow or actually impossible between her and her two friends. Sometimes this determined and opinionated woman had to leave the decision-making to them in order to expedite the publication, and it is also likely that Junkmann ceded to the judgement of the considerably older and more authoritative Schlüter, who, for all his affection for her and his respect for her work, was less poetically attuned than his colleague, particularly when it came to selecting which of the religious poems should be included. Certainly the poems from 'The Spiritual Year' in the 1838 edition do not suggest the often tormented thinking and tortuous language about to emerge as she proceeded, precisely in response to the urging of Schlüter, to continue with the great cycle and bring it to completion. (See below for a discussion of 'The Spiritual Year'.)

The 'nature' poems are fairly conventional and pale in comparison with the highly original ones which were soon to come from her hand and assure her position as a truly great lyric poet. Poems like the two already quoted, 'Unruhe' and 'Not', which express a deep personal passion, do not figure at all, but tended at the time to appear anonymously or under a pseudonym in journals with a very narrow circulation, or to lurk in drawers or within private correspondence. In fact, she herself wished to include precisely these two poems, but they were explicitly excluded, along with a number of others favoured by the poet herself, by the cautious Schlüter on the grounds that they should avoid anything that might be deemed "strange and disturbing" (*fremdartig und störend* , see letter from C.B. Schlüter to Droste-Hülshoff, 2 August 1838). For all his good intentions, Schlüter did no service to his friend, who, at 41 years of age, was still unknown beyond her intimate literary circles.

The four poems addressed to the Säntis, the group of mountains just over the border in Switzerland with which she was beginning to become familiar now that her sister and her husband had set up home in Eppishausen following their marriage in late 1834, describe the effect of the different seasons on the landscape. Although she did not feel comfortable there and expressed her dislike of the place in no uncertain terms in her 'Farewell to Switzerland' after her first lengthy – too lengthy! - stay in 1835-36, she clearly recognized its beauty, so different from the relatively flat, wooded, green countryside of Westphalia, and in this early group of more or less purely descriptive poems she shows her acute powers of observation of places and natural phenomena and her sensitivity to their changing moods.

As time goes on, these will become dominant features of her work, expressed with force and often clothed in remarkable language and imagery.

The Säntis
Spring

The vine is blossoming, its gentle fragrance
fills the dewy place,
and far and near the air wafts
the bright adornment of many coloured flowers.

What fluttering around me, what a humming sound

from birds and bees and butterflies!
How the branch, lately heavy with frost,
stirs its silken pennants!

People still seek out the sunshine
and choose the little dry spots,
for at night-time the departing winter
still creeps back towards the frontier.

Oh, you my stern old man, my mighty one,
my Säntis with your whitened hair,
walled up in blocks of cliff,
shuddering beneath the snow-storm,
laced up in your icy suit of armour:
ah! how you shiver, how cold you are!

Summer

Good linden tree, shake yourself!
A little air, a gentle west-wind!
Or close your branches so tightly
that the leaves press against each other.

No bird chirps, no dog barks.
Only the brightly-coloured flies
hum their way across the slope
and roast themselves in the heat.

Even the trees' dark foliage
seems to have expanded and breathes out dust.
I lie here as if parched
and can hardly chase away the gnats.

Oh, Säntis, Säntis, if only I were lying there,
precisely on your rocky yoke,
where the cold white layers
stretch over you so fresh and vibrant,
many thousands of clear drops playing together!
Blessed Säntis, it is cool where you are.

Autumn

Whenever I lie on a lovely day
and contemplate the noon hour
and lean beneath my tree
amidst the splendour of the grapes,

when the autumn crocus weaves across the valley
its amethyst carpet on which
the last butterfly
trembles as shimmering as the first,

I ponder little on how it fades
away day after day,
and with my eyes half closed can
dream of springtime and of happiness

You hurt my eyes,
you with the snow so recently fallen upon you!
Are you already preparing us for winter?
One already sees it slide from one chasm to another
and soon it will come hurtling down, soon,
O Säntis, from you, you barren grave.

Winter

Out of snowstorm and swirling mist
a clear day breaks at last,
and all the windows open wide,
and each one looks to see what he can see.

Are those solid blocks houses?
Is that flat space a pond?
Indeed, in this uniform
one can hardly recognize the church tower.

And all living things lie pressed down,
as though stifled beneath a shroud.

Yet look, on the far horizon
a living land is coming to meet me.

You stern watchman, release him,
that wind out of the depths of your prison. f)
Where those black cracks are appearing
he must be waiting (as though) in quarantine,
that stranger from Lombardy.
Oh, Säntis, let the springtime wind go free!

f) She actually uses the word *Föhn* to describe the warm, dry southerly wind associated with the Alps.

Likewise, the only other two poems to appear in the 1838 volume under the heading 'Poems of Mixed Content', which actually meant not ballads or religious poems, are descriptive, devoted to the pond on a gentle winter's day and a hard winter's day respectively. The sights and sounds of nature are evoked in a perceptive but unremarkable way and only at the end of the second poem does something more obviously personal surface, with a brief reference to a yearning which will become so evident just a few months and certainly years later, but which, as we have seen, has been there from her early youth.

By the Pond
A mild winter's day

At the end of that forest
where the pond lies in silence
and all along the ranks of pine-trees
a soft murmur ripples,

where in the bright sunshine,
so cold and weary as it is,
nevertheless the wave again and again
flickers against the bank and kisses it.

There I know, too, a narrow gorge
perfect for the artist to paint,
where all the little rays of light
become caught up in the bay:

a dry little corner, protected from the wind
and so abundantly green
that in the entire spot
not a single dried-up twig harms me.

If now I care to lay my thick coat
over the moss
and lean up against the pine tree,
and then spread out twigs and plants

on my lap,
the best that I can find,
who will take it amiss from me
if I pretend that it's a summer's day?

Even if the grasshopper is not making a noise,
the reeds are whispering,
and if the nightingales are silent,
I myself am singing a song.

And if Nature has contributed
only a little to the feast,
the pleasure that one makes oneself
is always the best.

A harsh winter's day

That I see you so dejected,
my beloved, lively watery realm,
that, quite hidden in ice and snow
you look like the clumsy earth,

and that your row of pine trees, glazed over,
is hung with frost and clods of soil,
it is not that which distresses me
if I walk along your edge.

To be sure, decked out in evergreen,
you seemed to me, you friendly element,
like the oases
which the Arab yearns for.

When beside the parched meadow
your mosses were still filled with flowers,
when through silent Nature
your waves resounded nonetheless.

Today I was wanting, too,
to delight in your crystalline flickering,
eavesdrop on every coloured star
and not regret a single summer's day,

if it were not that along the bank
the smooth ski-track on which at midday
many a bold heel makes its progress
is so broad and so well-swept.

So now I think how many a year
I did not see a single ice-track,
and certainly it seems strange and sad to me,
and a thousand images approach.

Then wishes that stayed unfulfilled
I still take in my stride,
but ah! the frost covers so many
who once slid merrily over it.

What is absent is the passion which will dominate in the years ahead, along with any sense of demonic forces at work. Doubtless Schlüter felt that these were safe enough poems to appear in her name, with nothing 'strange or disturbing' to cause too much consternation. In the event they did not provoke much attention at all, although, in the context of her whole *œuvre*, one can discern what was to come.

Indeed, Droste-Hülshoff had a considerable corpus of poems to hand, many written very much earlier, but still unpublished. Many of these she put forward for inclusion in the projected volume, but they were apparently rejected, most likely by the well-meaning but overly cautious Schlüter. There were other, practical limitations on this first volume, too. The publisher selected, who eventually, after some delays and doubts, agreed to take on this project, was frankly not an appropriate choice. Aschendorff was a local firm, established in Münster, but lacking in experience of the kind needed to propel a totally unknown Westphalian woman poet to recognition. Moreover, since there was a sense that time was not on her side, Droste-Hülshoff seems to have acquiesced in decisions that conflicted with her own better judgement and her already pronounced sense of her poetic vocation.

One poem which did not find its way into the 1838 volume although it was included in her own list is the short but immensely moving *Herzlich*, a poem of great passion, characteristically expressed with restraint and commitment:

Heartfelt

All that I say, and every word,
and every press of my hands,
and the tender look in my eyes,
and everything that I have written,
that is no mere breath, and no air,
no movement of the fingers:
that is the flaming blood of my heart
which forces its way out through a thousand gates.

Like the already quoted 'Unruhe' and 'Not', this poem could belong to the mature Droste-Hülshoff in its power and directness. It contains all the honesty of the woman and the poet, and, although the coming years would bring the confidence to expand in thought and expression, the essential and unmistakable Droste-Hülshoff is there in its stark beauty.

For the time being the public was denied an insight into many of her qualities, however, although it must be said that her unflinching view of life and her ability to express herself in powerful, sometimes shocking, language, is evident in the narrative poems which dominate this modest first volume. Reviews at the time reflect the puzzlement and shock of those who received a somewhat ill-conceived and ill-balanced offering from an unknown author. This was not the kind of poetry they were used to, a response which, at one end of the scale, led to accusations of a lack of clarity and even confusion, and of diction that was more prosaic than poetic, and at the other to the acknowledgment of its originality. That this emanated from the hand of a woman, and an aristocratic lady at that, might have signalled the end of a career not yet begun, and it was probably only the unshakable conviction of Droste-Hülshoff herself that prevented her from sinking back into depression and despondency. She appears to have believed, and she was doubtless justified in this belief, that the time was just not right, but that it would come. That, anyway, would seem to be the message of another poem originally proposed by her:

The Right Time

In the cheerful room by candlelight,
when every lip is sparkling,
and, even drunk by the sunshine,
when every finger is breaking off flowers,
and when Nature swims in flames around

> the mouth of the beloved:
> that is not it, the right time,
> that genius has ordained for you.
>
> But when day as well as joy has sunk away,
> then you will know a little place,
> perhaps in the cushions of your sofa,
> perhaps on a garden bench,
> then there will be a sound like a half-understood melody,
> and it will seem as if a shower of half-faded colours
> were flowing round you,
> and then gently, gently, your genius will touch you.

As early as 1835 she had sent this poem to Schlüter, but the theme of her vocation, and of her belief that she would be recognized, but only when the time was right, recurs throughout the work of this woman. She seems to have taken nothing lightly but always with conviction and in response to deep thought.

Happily for her frustrated ambitions at the time and her ultimate reputation, a new influence was pending, once more in the form of a close personal friendship which this time would have far-reaching consequences. (See below for section on Levin Schücking.)

CHAPTER THREE

'THE SPIRITUAL YEAR'

For many critics, 'The Spiritual Year' is the centre of Annette von Droste-Hülshoff's poetic achievement; others regard it as an unsuccessful attempt at a religious cycle. Possibly both are acceptable viewpoints, or perhaps neither extreme is entirely just. What is indisputable is that it occupies a central position in her *œuvre*, and that the story of its conception and composition is a significant guide to an understanding of this complex poet. It is also a fascinating story, for the work was begun by a young girl barely out of her teens, unknown to any public and completed by a frail woman, a mature poet facing imminent death and fully aware of the fact. Added to this is the fact that, even as she apparently laid it down, she was still occupied with it in her mind and probably believed that she would return to it and, as was her habit with all her writing, make further adjustments and changes to it. Moreover, she handed it over to one of her most trusted friends with the firm instruction that it should be published only after her death. That the work mattered immensely to her seems apparent.

In the present volume the discussion of this important part of her whole poetic work is placed centrally, considered at the point in her creative development when she began it, but looking forward to the time eighteen years later when she would resume work on it, write the larger part and bring it to some kind of completion. It thus forms a bridge over a whole lifetime of creativity, and, whatever the assessment of it by individual critics, it cannot be divorced from the study of her whole *œuvre*.

The young Annette had a very close relationship with her step-grandmother, Anna Maria von Haxthausen, the second wife of her maternal grandfather. She spent long holidays in her early years on the von Haxthausen estate near Abbenburg, not far from Paderborn, and the very large family of young aunts and uncles were more like cousins to her and her sister. The first suggestion that she was planning a series of religious poems for her devout grandmother comes in a letter of February 1819 to her friend and mentor Anton Matthias Sprickmann (see above). At this stage, these were fairly conventional, rather derivative poems alongside others of a more secular nature, and she had not arrived at the idea of a consolidated project such as would eventually develop into the first part of *Das Geistliche Jahr*. By the end of that year, however, she had moved to something more formal and presented her grandmother with a small album, no longer extant, devoted exclusively to religious verse. It was on the basis of this that she conceived the idea of a series of poems for her grandmother, each poem devoted to a Sunday in the Church year. As time went on, this concept developed, to include poems for all the major feast days of the Church, in many cases based on the Gospel reading for the day.

As she proceeded with this new concept, however, she came to realize that they would not be at all appropriate for the devout Anna Maria. Already she had come to recognize that, despite her traditional Catholic upbringing, she was assailed by doubts and questions that would trouble and distress her older relative, especially now that she was suffering such anguish as a result of the experience of the summer of 1820. Even as a very young girl, she had been aware of her psychic powers and her interest in matters expressly forbidden by the Church, but now she was contending also with the guilt and self-accusation aroused by her sense of responsibility for the events surrounding her handling, or, as she saw it, her mishandling of the relationship with Heinrich Straube and August von Arnswaldt. That these events had occurred precisely at Bökendorf, the von Haxthausen estate so dear to her from an early age, did not help matters, and she cut herself off from those connections for many years.

Instead, she presented the first twenty-five poems of the cycle to her own mother, but this was hardly a better decision. Therese von Droste-Hülshoff responded with silence, putting them away and not referring to them, even when eventually her daughter removed them. That Annette was aware that she had misfired badly with her gift to her mother emerges in a letter she wrote to her young aunt Anna early in 1821. In it she speaks for the first time of her devastation at what she calls the 'scandal' of that summer, but also of her error in adding further to the distress of her family with poems which were likely to disturb them deeply. She had no right, she says, to inflict such unhappiness on her nearest and dearest. Clearly, in her mind, the two things were linked, and together they added to the guilt and self-reproach which seems to have been innate in her.

It is the letter to her mother that she enclosed with the twenty-five poems which provides the most significant insight into her purpose in writing these poems at this time. They are intended, she says, for those whose love is greater than their faith and who in a single hour ask more questions than seven wise men can answer in seven years. Undoubtedly she allied herself with such people, while knowing that her mother and grandmother did not belong in that category.

When, after the poem for Easter Monday, she abandoned work on the project, there is no indication whether she intended ever to resume it. Her state of mind at the time was not conducive to her continuing with it, and her mother's reaction cannot have encouraged her to do so. How much she thought about the cycle in the following fifteen years and more is not known, but in any case, these were very busy years, and productive in many ways.

It was her dear friend Christoph Bernhard Schlüter who urged her to take up the work again. He must have been one of the very few people who were aware of its existence, even if, as he said on a number of occasions, he did not always understand, still less share, her spiritual doubts and religious attitudes. Above all, he was concerned by the fact that her faith never seemed to bring her complete happiness, as he said after her death, when, in 1851, he fulfilled the role she had entrusted to him of bringing 'The Spiritual Year' before a public. That she had always been so insistent that it should remain unpublished during her lifetime is another pointer to her view of it, and in particular to her awareness of the effect it might have on other people. Whether she would have allowed the letter of dedication to her mother to have been published along with the poems, is also not certain, but, personal though that undoubtedly was at the time, it remains an essential ingredient in the story of the conception of the work and its unusual history. Her later editors and those closely involved in her publications were certainly right in seeing that it must be included.

Viewed as a component of her whole *œuvre*, 'The Spiritual Year' can be seen to have its place in her development over these middle years of her life. It begins with relatively conventional poems which were certainly influenced by poets familiar to her from her home background, some of them going back in thought and diction to the German Baroque, some closer to her own age, and by the teaching of her Church. Yet even these poems, when she was still quite unknown outside her immediate circle and finding her way to the fulfilment of her earnestly perceived vocation, show signs of the originality which stood out from a very early age. They are also quite varied in tone, form and language, and this is certainly the case with the second 'half' of the cycle, where one sees the mature poet in all her power and versatility. In this respect, one is justified, even positively required, to see 'The Spiritual Year' as a part of a whole lifetime's work.

One should not, however, look to the poems as a reflection of an evolving spiritual life. There is no such development in a cycle which is marked by contrasting moods and fluctuations of attitude. Doubt is never far away, but this is not doubt in the existence of God, nor in His benevolence, but in her worthiness to receive that. A questioning tone dominates, and if at times she seems to reach a certain serenity, this can almost immediately be dispelled. These are flashes, but they are no more than that, and it is easy to see why the devoted Schlüter found her enigmatic and sometimes deeply troubling. Her purpose is not to teach: she is too conscious of her own frailty for that. At times one glimpses consolation, but this is not sustained. Yet one can read these 'religious' poems alongside those better described as 'secular' and find that there is joy there, and hope, and consolation, and that the picture of this puzzling woman and her puzzling life is far from one of unmitigated gloom.

In this sense she does speak, as she hoped she would, for all those people, not individuals known to her, who are assailed, as she is, by questioning and doubt, and her achievement is to show that there is precious light within the darkness.

The selection of poems offered here is no more than that. Fewer than a third of the seventy-two poems of 'The Spiritual Year' are included in this volume, which aims to show the balance in her whole lyric *œuvre*. A reader seeking a complete picture of this cycle may wish to refer to the volume *God's Sorely-tested Child*, also published by Memoirs Books and including all the poems of the cycle in English translation.

The poems of 1820

'The Spiritual Year' opens with a poem for New Year's Day, different from many of the others of the cycle in that it does not take as its basis the Gospel reading for the day, or indeed any biblical reference. Instead Droste-Hülshoff uses the first day of the New Year as an occasion to meditate on the past and look forward to the future: this is the beginning of the secular year, not the Church year. She employs the familiar literary device of a dialogue between the human heart and, in this instance, the New Year. This was one of three poems she had written by the end of January 1820, by which time the idea of a cycle was established in her mind, and it already strikes the tone which will prevail throughout the cycle, of doubt and questioning. The Heart is afraid of what the future may hold, and despite the religious message of the poem, and the assurance of the goodness of God and the prospect of joy, the uncertainty that will surface repeatedly throughout 'The Spiritual Year' is there from the beginning.

On New Year's Day

My eyes are closing, my senses are about to leave me.
"Fare well, Old Year, with joy and sorrow!
Heaven will bestow a new one, if it so desires."
Thus does man incline his head towards the goodness of God.
The old blossom falls,
the new one is sprouting, silently,
out of ice and snow, God's plant.

Night is fleeing, sleep from my eyelids:
"Welcome, young day, with your brethren!
Where are you then, beloved New Year?"
There it is in the splendour of the morning light.
The whole earth has embraced it
and gazes earnestly and clearly into its eyes.

"Greetings to you, human heart with all your frailty,
you heart full of power and regret and pain,
I bring you from the Lord a new time of trial."
"Greetings to you, New Year, with all your joys.
Life is so sweet and - ah! - one accepts everything,
even suffering, willingly along with life."

"Oh, human heart, how has your house collapsed!
How can you, heir to those halls,
how can you live in such desolate horror?"
"Oh, New Year, to be sure I am never at home.
A wanderer, I traverse distant spaces.
It may be called my house, yet it is not."

"Oh, human heart, what have you to do

that you cannot remain in your homeland
and keep it in readiness for your Lord?"
"Oh, New Year, you have much to learn.
Do you not know war and pestilence and perils?
And my dearest cares dwell far away."

"Oh, human heart, can you compel everything then?
Must heaven bring you dew and rain?
And does the earth open itself to your word?"
"Ah, no, I can but see and be sad.
Things have remained, alas, as they were,
and continue along the given paths."

"Oh wily heart! You simply do not wish to say it.
The world has set up her tents
And refreshes you in them with her dizzy wine."
"That bitter goblet cannot bring me joy.
Its foam means sin and its liquid means remorse,
and sorrow never leaves me alone either."

"Listen, oh heart, I want to explain it to you.
Do you want to bind the arrow in its flight?
You do not see its target. Does that mean it has none?"
"I know indeed that a day is prepared for us,
and then it will be clear that all has turned out well
and all the thousand goals are nevertheless one."

"Oh heart, you are completely gripped by foolishness.
You know all this, and can you still be afraid?
Oh, wicked servant, faithless to all duty!
Each thing fulfils its role with honour,
goes its way and never allows itself to be disturbed.
Thy likeness does not exist on earth.

You have wickedly banished peace.
Yet the grace of God is endless, like His love.
Oh, come home to your desolate house!
Come back into your dark and barren cell,
and wash it clean with your tears,
and breathe fresh air into it with your sighs

And if you wish, faithfully, to cast your gaze upwards,
then the Lord will send His holy image to you,
to treasure it in faith and trust.
Then some time I may entwine myself upon your garland,
and if the New Year were yet to find you,
may it gaze into a little house of God."

From that relatively simple opening, she moves in the second poem of the cycle to the familiar story of the journey of the Three Kings to visit the Child Jesus. Although she does not refer to the Gospel reading as she will on many occasions afterwards, she evokes all the details of the account of St Matthew and retells it with characteristic colour and vitality, and emphasises the sounds along the way. Characteristic, too, is the way she links the journey of the Magi as they follow the star towards their momentous destination with her own journey, fraught with doubt and peril, towards her personal light.

On the Feast of Epiphany

Three travellers make their way through the night,
with purple bands about their foreheads,
and burnt from the hot winds and the trials of the long journey.
At a distance the host of servants follows
through the rustling green of the palm trees.
Golden jewels gleam
from the flanks of the dromedaries,
as they step forward with a clinking sound,
and sweet fragrances waft through the air.

Darkness, black and dense, conceals
whatever that region contains.
The figures threaten like giants:
travellers, are you not afraid?
Yet even though the meadow of clouds
weaves a thousand veils, loosely and lightly,
a twinkling little star breaks
triumphantly through the fragile grey.

Slowly it swirls through the blueness
and the procession follows its light.

Listen, the servants whisper softly:
is the town not yet ready to appear,
with its temples and its glades,
the town which is the reward for so much effort?
Even if the desert were burning hot,
even if vipers were coiling around us,
or tigers pursuing us,
even if the fiery wind were drying up our sweat,
our eyes are fixed on the gifts
for the King strong and wise.

Without anxiety, without concern,
the three make their way through the night,
like three silent moons around the glow of the sun.
When the avalanche of dust cracks,
when the flowers of the desert stretch out
with their terrible yet beautiful spots,
they gaze in silence at that power
which will surely cover them,
which has fanned the star into life.

Oh, you lofty, holy, threesome!
Born in darkness, hardly a ray has picked you out,
and yet you follow so piously and so faithfully.
And you, my soul, revelling freely
in the waves of grace,
drawn with force towards the light,
you seek anew the darkness.
Oh, how have you deceived yourself!
For you remained tears, and remorse.

And yet, my soul, take courage,
even if you cannot ever fathom
how you can find forgiveness:
God is good above all things.
Even if in the flood of remorse
you have rescued yourself from the crowd,
although it may burn you to the marrow,

seething in secret fire,
He who wooed you with His blood
never abandons you to the throng.

I am not worthy of a ray,
not the smallest light from above.
Lord, I will praise Thee joyfully,
whatever Thy will grants to me.
Be it suffering that consumes me,
should I lose that which is dearest to me,
should I detect no consolation,
should no prayer of mine be heard:
if it can but lead me to Thee,
then, flame and sword, be welcome!

Already the first two poems, in existence when she first began to refer to her project, show a contrasting approach, but contrasts will be repeated many times over in this youthful first attempt at a coherent series of poems. There are, of course, recurrent stylistic features, and ideas recur, but what is so striking about the cycle as a whole is its variety.

Thus the next poem included in this selection, in fact the next chronologically in the religious year and the next one she wrote, 'On the First Sunday after Epiphany', demonstrates another different approach and tone. This time she does attach the Gospel reference, but, as so often, that is just a springboard for the theme she develops from the very first line. St Luke has Mary reproaching her Son for causing His parents anxiety when they could not find Him, and it is the reference to the pain caused to them which Droste-Hülshoff takes up, for she searches in vain for God. The anguish of the young Annette pours out of this poem based on a well-known biblical event, and she frames the account with that very word. So much of 'The Spiritual Year' will tell of her desperate desire to find the God she knows to exist, and this theme is already there in a poem which is full of questions and desperate pleas. A key emotion is found in the poignant cry: "I know that Thou existeth, but I must feel it, too."

The same desperation is present in the poem which follows in this selection. Based on St Matthew's account of Christ's healing, first of the leper, and then of the centurion's servant, 'On the Third Sunday after Epiphany' addresses the issue of faith as a means to healing and salvation. The verbal echoes of the Gospel account are present throughout the poem, but first and foremost this is a passionate personal appeal from the poet herself. Indeed so passionate is it that one can readily believe that her mother was shocked and dismayed when she was faced with what her young daughter had written, and that Annette herself, tormented by her own agony, knew that she should not inflict it on those dear to her.

On the First Sunday after Epiphany
Luke 2, 42-52: Jesus teaches in the temple.

Behold! I have sought Thee in anguish.
My Lord and my God, where shall I find Thee?
Ah, not in my own deserted heart,
where long ago Thy image was extinguished in sin.
Then, from all corners, if I call Thee,
my own echo resounds around me like mockery.

If anyone has ever lost Thy godly image
that belonged to him like his soul,
with that person has the whole world conspired
in order to conceal Thy holy countenance from him.
And where the pious man sees Thee on Mount Tabor,
there in the valley has he built his house.

CHAPTER THREE

Thus to my horror I must come to know
the puzzle that I could never solve,
when in the bright years of my innocence
that which was evil there seemed quite incomprehensible to me:
that a soul in which Thy image has shone
no longer recognizes Thee when it sees Thee.

All around me sounds the clear singing of the birds:
"Listen: the little birds are singing His praise!"
And I wish to bend towards a flower and say
"His gentle eye looks out from every flower."
I have sought Thee in Nature,
and worldly knowledge was the only fruit.

And I must gaze into the passage of fate,
as a good heart often in this life
in vain steps towards Thee out of its forward march,
until, despairing, it has yielded to sin.
Then all love seems to me like mockery,
and I perceive no mercy, and no God.

And the knots plait themselves so wondrously together
that Thou appearest in light to the faithful gaze.
Then the evil one has stretched out his hand
and builds a bridge of fog to doubt,
and my intellect, which only trusts itself,
believes for sure that it is made of gold.

I know that Thou existeth, but I must feel it, too,
and feel that a cold and heavy hand presses me,
that one day there must be a dark end to these games,
that every deed must pluck its fruit.
I feel that I am offered up to vengeance.
I perceive Thee, yet not joyfully.

Where can I find Thee, in hope and loving?
For that sombre power that I have discerned
is but the shadow that has remained to me
of Thy image, when I had lost it.
Oh God, Thou art so gentle and so radiant.
I seek Thee in anguish: do not conceal Thyself!

On the Third Sunday after Epiphany
Matthew 8, 1-13: Of the leper and the centurion

Go forth, and may it befall you as you have believed!
Yes, whosoever believes, to him will occur good fortune.
But what to him whom life has robbed
of its holiness in hidden pangs?

Lord, speak one word, and Thy servant will be restored to health.
Lord, speak that word: I can but wish for it.
The heart can joyfully bestow upon you love,
but faith reveals itself only as grace.

How does it come about that when I cried to you in the evening
and when in the morning I went forth to find you,
Thou didst allow me to sink into half-heartedness
and the sin of despair, deeply and ever deeper?

Did not my cry in my greatest anguish
rise up to you out of the depths?
And did it not seem as if I were crying out to the cliffs,
when all the while my eyes were red with tears?

Oh Lord, forgive that which is spoken out of anguish,
for I have sensed Thee often and sweetly.
Indeed, I was at one with Thee for hours on end,
and in my torment I did not remember this.

And now it seems to me as if I, all alone,
were banished from Thy vast banquet of grace,
the beggar shut out before the gates.
Yet, oh God, the guilt is surely mine!

Did I not feel in my humility, worthless as I am,
that I have received Thy word in my spirit,
that my sighs have reached Thy ears,
that my soul recognizes Thee and reveres Thee?

My Lord, think not of my sins!
How often, on the path that I have chosen for myself,

have I cried out, God, in the darkness, for Thy mercy,
as for a right and for an obligation!

Ah, if only I had not neglected those gifts,
if only I had not trodden them underfoot, and despised them!
Then I would not be standing so terribly deranged,
as though the light now flown had been a dream.

How often, even before the deed came to pass
which as a thought had flown around me greedily,
did Thy name pass silently past me in gentle admonition,
Thy image on Golgotha.

And if now, recklessly, I have turned aside,
committed that sin which I have clearly acknowledged,
how hast Thou then in remorseful longing
not often burnt within my soul!

Alas, I have committed many grievous sins,
and still more errors, slight to mention,
yet great in the depth of destruction they can sow,
deaf for the sound of the wailing conscience.

Now at last all light has passed away from me,
and often Thy voice has completely died away.
Yet do not cast me – Thou seest that I am still able to desire –
among the dead, for I am alive.

My Jesus, see, I am wounded unto death
and in my broken state I cannot be well again.
My Jesus, think of Thine own bitter wounds
and speak one word; then Thy servant will be cured.

Going forward just a little in the cycle, one comes upon a poem very different in manner but expressing the same torment and ravaged sense of guilt. The feast of Candlemas gives her the opportunity for a tender picture of the Virgin Mary carrying the Child Jesus, with Joseph by her side, overwhelmed by the great task that has been placed upon him. However, the poem falls into two unequal halves, for she quickly moves to the theme of her own situation, obsessed with guilt and seeking aid, not, as one might have thought, from the Virgin Mary, but from the Child Himself. This unconventional standpoint would very likely have shocked her orthodox Catholic relatives, but she explains in her analytical way that the very humanity of the Mother of Christ accounts for her reluctance to turn to her as the traditional intermediary, so overwhelmed is she by the knowledge that this woman is immaculate in a way that accentuates her own sinfulness. The delicate description of the Holy Family with which the poem begins and ends is in sharp contrast to the starkness of her personal pain, and as one becomes more and more familiar with Annette von Droste-Hülshoff's poetry, both religious and secular, one recognizes that this is typical of it, and typical of her deep-rooted unease.

On the Feast of the Purification of the Virgin

Mary passes through the little streets,
in her arms her Son, the dear One,
holds him tightly, holds him gently,
and she gazes down at Him.
How the cherubs sang of Him,
how the shepherds worshipped Him
and the grey-haired Wise Men paid homage:
all that she allows to pass her by in silence.

But at her side Joseph is
quite caught up in care.
Testing, he asks all the stones
if her foot treads too firmly.
He does not know what he will experience,
but wondrous things

have secretly announced themselves to him
out of the eyes of the little Child.
Oh Mary, Mother of Christ,
I will not dare to approach you,
for you are too radiant for me.
My soul grows fearful in your presence.
You almost terrify me
in the immaculate purity
which you triumphantly preserved
when you walked as I do now.

I will much rather go before your little Child,
weeping and dejected.
He is my Lord and my Judge indeed,
whereas you are not so far away from me.
I must pay the price of a foolish deed,
if I am not to disintegrate in fear,
since, after all, has He not conquered,
is He not the hero of eternity?

Dearest Lord, Thou hast created
my poor sick soul,
like that many-faceted lure
that guides us on broad roads,
and Thou knowest that just as before others
fresh breath within my soul
touches me with its glow
so also before others does every earthly joy.

Thou hast bestowed upon me
side by side with abundant powers
the splendid task of ruling over wealthy estates,
and a lofty, rich castle.
And now it lies in ruins,
terrible in its barren immensity,
like a monster turned to bone,
like a dead giant of the ocean.

And when, after many days,
devoid of faith but full of love,

I anxiously tested its walls,
behold, they stood firm!
Oh, my Lord, if Thou wilt hear me,
and open up the treasures of Thy grace,
behold, I will faithfully build
the wretched remnants of my life.

And even though my house must stand,
a barren, threatening ruin,
alas, only there can that which was destroyed
so completely without hope reconstruct itself
and I can build just a little room,
adorned with silent deeds, where, Lord, I can entertain
Thee as my guest, when Thou comest to me.

Mary steps out of the halls,
in her arms her Son, the dear One,
holds Him firmly, holds him gently,
and her eyes rest upon Him.
Ah, she has borne this joy
for nine blissful months.
That which those pious ones announced,
she carried for a long time in her radiant spirit.

But Joseph no longer walks with silent steps
by her side,
for the dear, dear little Child
is now the Lord of the whole world.
Yet, as the sun climbs higher,
he slips softly behind her
and pulls her cloak
so that her veil drops down.

The poems for the season of Lent clearly provide Droste-Hülshoff with scope to explore her own feelings of guilt, and she does so with extraordinary diversity and even what may be described as ingenuity, to the extent that the link between the Gospel reading or the familiar biblical episode and her own experience can sometimes appear quite tenuous. These first twenty-five poems are astounding in terms of her originality and even her confidence in handling her ideas.

When, for Shrove Tuesday, she takes just a small part of the reading for the day and concentrates on the appeal by the blind man that Christ should restore his sight, she makes this the focus of the whole, essentially personal poem, every strophe of which ends with the plea: "Lord, grant that I may see!". For Ash Wednesday, she takes not a biblical reference, but the symbol of the Cross made in ash upon the forehead but this she then widens out for an attack on the corruption of the world and for bitter self-accusation. It is in this poem too that she introduces one of her recurrent themes, when she laments the conflict within her of mind and heart, the fettering power of intellect which she will come to see as acting against the pure faith she craves. One can never anticipate where the power of her mind, her sheer inventiveness, can lead her, but, even at this early stage of her creative development, it is evident that she is capable of much more and that she is not tied to models or precursors.

Again and again one encounters evidence, not only of her spiritual doubts and her agonizing sense of guilt, but also her crippling sense at times of being misunderstood, or at the very least incompletely understood. There are ample signs in these poems of the isolation she felt, probably throughout her life. This expresses itself consistently in her more secular poems, but in this cycle, too, one has no difficulty in identifying the alienation she must have felt, even at times from the God whose love she most earnestly desired.

The twenty-five poems of the first 'half' of 'The Spiritual Year' culminate in the group beginning at Maundy Thursday and ending with Easter Monday. It was at this point that she laid aside her work on the cycle and did not resume it for many years, raising the question of her motivation for seemingly abandoning it. Yet these poems are very fine, as the following examples surely demonstrate:

On Maundy Thursday

O wondrous night, I greet you!
Lord Jesus washes their feet.
The air is quite still,
and one can hear the sound of breathing,
and the drops falling
from His holy hand.

When Jesus leans forward,
whole islands bow to this greeting
into the deep sea.
If He has descended so low,
then I must lie for ever
before the feet of my neighbour.

Lord, if as though deranged
my soul is outraged
at all base deeds,
so that I am ready rather
to surrender my life in torment
for Thy glory,

then grant that I may not lament
if Thou hast banished
all shame into my days.
Let my wounds burn
now that Thou hast found me so firm
in such a harsh state.

Oh God, I cannot disguise
how fearful I am in face of those henchmen
whom Thou perhaps hast sent
in sickness or in grief
to deprive me of my senses,

to kill my reason.
It often seems to me
as if Thy stern trial
were about to begin,
as if a cloud were falling like dusk
about the radiance of my spirit,
yet unknown to the masses.

Yet, just as the pains
that enflame my brain are vanishing,
so also does the mist flee,
and, with secret glow,
I feel myself clothed anew
in fresh, strong air.

My Jesus, if I may choose,
I will rather torment myself
with every shame and suffering
than that the splendour of humanity
be taken from me like this,
albeit to my advantage.

Yet if it is so poisoned
that it produces annihilation
when it flows around my heart,
then let me lose it,
that richly endowed spirit,
in order to lead my soul home.

If, then, Thou hast ordained
that I be poured out,
remain a dead stream of water
for the whole of this life,
then shall I go trembling
towards Thy test.

On Good Friday

Weep, my eyes, weep,
only rather run over with tears.
Ah, the day will avail you nothing,
and the sun will scorn you.
His eyes are closed,
the sweet radiance of His eyes.
Weep, weep, without restraint:
you can never weep enough.

When the sun perceived this,
it drew a mourning veil
across its clear eye,
and its tears fall silently.
And do I still hope to suck joy
from the world, the bright, lovely world?
Weep, weep my eyes, or rather run over with tears.

Be silent, singing and all the sounds
that delight the heart!
"Crucify him, Crucify him!" roars the crowd,
and the Pharisees laugh.
My Jesus, in the midst of all Thy anguish,
their guilt grieves Thee above all others.
Alas, how did Thy heart feel,
when so many had to fall?

And the poor little birds
are so frightened
that they would rather weep
if their little eyes were not dry.
They sit sadly in the branches,
and no sound rings out anywhere around.
My heart, the poor little birds are silent,
and you must force out your pain.

Away with golden goblets,
sweet wine from a noble stem!
Alas, the hot flame of thirst

still burns Him in His agony,
so that He must cry out aloud in pain,
and heaven and earth must grow pale
as the executioner's lads dare
to reach up to Him with vinegar and gall.
Soft pillows, silken cushions,
can I still long for you,
when my Lord, torn in shreds like this,
must hang upon the hard Cross?
Ah, how have you afflicted Him,
thorn and nail, rod and spear!
Yet, to be sure, the book of guilt lies open,
waiting for His holy blood to close it.

In the earth all the dead
start up as though in horror,
as it begins to grow wet
with the sacred red blood.
They cannot rest any more, those dead ones,
where His precious red blood has flowed.
The ground which has enjoyed such precious drink
is much too sacred.

He who is Lord in all things
must conquer His own strength
in order that He may struggle with death
and succumb to it.
He must drink the chalice to the last drop.
Oh, man, can you endure it?
His sweet eyes close,
and His heart ceases to beat.

Now that the heart of Jesus is breaking,
the earth breaks in its very depths,
the sea breaks on all its surfaces,
hell breaks in its abysses,
and the hard hearts of the cliffs
break with a loud crash.
Do they break in joy or pain?
Is it the breaking of salvation, or of downfall?

And for whom then has this fight been fought
in these anguished hours,
and the sacred Body been pierced
with the blessed wounds?
Heart, my heart, can you not leap
with the cliffs and the earth
in order only that I be bound anew
to Him in bloody struggle?

Hast Thou given so much, Lord,
for my poor soul?
Is its eternal, everlasting life
so precious to you, for all its guilt and flaws?
In that case, alas, let it not be found
if that would be to sin still more.
Let it not ever see Thy holy wounds with horror.

On Easter Sunday

Rejoice, oh world, you have Him back again!
His heaven could not restrain Him.
Oh, rejoice, rejoice, sing songs!
Why are you growing dark, my blessed sight?

It is too much, one can but weep.
Joy stands there like grief.
Who can unite himself with such joy,
when he has seen so much sadness?

I have known unending salvation
through a mystery full of pain,
such as no human mind can hold,
no human heart can feel.

My Lord has risen from the Grave,
and greets all His people there.
And we are free from death and bonds,
and cleansed of the decay of sin.

He has rent His own Body,
to wash us with His Blood.
Who can know this secret
and not melt in the glow of love?

I am supposed to rejoice on this day
with Thy whole Christendom,
and it seems to me that I may dare to do so
when the Unnamed brings me joy.

The blessedness of eternity
has struggled with the agonies of death.
Horror has oppressed eternal perfection
like sinners.

My God, what could move Thee
to this boundless grace?
I cannot stir my thoughts
to contemplate our unmeasured guilt.

Alas, are all the souls of human beings -
priceless commodity though they indeed may be -
are they of so much value, that God must torment Himself
and die in fear and fire?

And are not all the souls of men
in His presence but the breath from lips
and stained with shame and error,
like dreary, dark smoke?

My spirit, do not seek to explain
that which is inexplicable.
The stone of a fall awaits the blind man
when he misses the paths of God.

My Jesus has found them precious
in love and justice.
What more do I wish to know?
His will remains eternally.

Thus may I believe and trust
the splendour of my soul;
thus may I look upwards to heaven
in the image of my God.

I should rejoice on this day;
I do rejoice, my Jesus Christ.
And if I have tears in my eyes,
Thou knowest they are tears of joy.

There is so much evidence here of the maturing poet, even though we know that these poems were all written within a few months of one another. The account of the Crucifixion and the Resurrection is so powerful that one can discern the hand which wrote the great 'Gethsemane' over twenty years later, or, at about the same time, other beautiful, majestic poems of her closing years (see below). One has to ask why, at this stage, she decided to go no further with the project, and if she had any intention of ever taking it up again.

In the absence of an answer from Droste-Hülshoff herself, one is left with several possibilities, or perhaps a combination of them. It seems implausible that the negative reaction of her mother, hurtful though it must have been, and very thought-provoking, would have deterred someone of her determination and conviction. She appears, in these poems for the Easter season, to have reached a certain command of her material. The poem for Easter Day betrays a new serenity, yet one senses that this may not last. It is possible that she perceived both of these attainments and felt that she should go no further at that point for fear of losing what she had gained. She was still reeling from the grief and guilt of the Straube affair, and, although there is little in the way of correspondence to support such a view, she may have felt inadequate physically and emotionally to go further. Equally, from what we know of her commitment to her writing, she may have wished to explore other directions in her work, and certainly the coming decade saw her working on *Die Judenbuche* and, extensively, on her ballad poetry. One cannot underestimate the personal and domestic changes that she would encounter: the death of her father brought deep personal grief, along with the life-changing move to the Rüschhaus from the ancestral castle where she had spent her childhood and early adulthood, and she was much afflicted by the death of her younger brother. Not so long after that, the marriage of her sister Jenny deprived her of another close companion. Through all this she was, by all accounts, in very poor health.

It must be accepted that, without the friendship of Christoph Bernhard Schlüter, she might never have felt the urge to return to the project which had once mattered so much to her and on which, once she had resumed it in 1839, she worked with great enthusiasm and commitment. She brought it to a temporary conclusion at the beginning of 1840 but never entirely relinquished her work on it, through the months of her relationship with Levin Schücking and the fevered activity which produced some of her finest poetry, until, persuaded by the ever-supportive Schlüter, she declared it 'finished' in July 1846 and placed it in his hands. Even then, according to Schlüter, she asked him to return it to her so that she could make some changes, and that, he says, was shortly before her death in May 1848. What changes she was able to make when her health and her strength were declining rapidly is not clear. What is clear is that this cycle mattered very deeply to her and that, to a greater or lesser extent, it occupied the whole of her adult life.

One must, then, read 'The Spiritual Year' of Annette von Droste-Hülshoff in the context of a lifetime of spiritual and poetic growth, and certainly it must be seen in relation to her other poetry. In this volume it is presented in necessarily truncated form, although with the suggestion that those interested should seek access to it, if necessary in translation.

The poems of 1839

Only a small proportion of the poems of the second 'half' can be offered here, but they show a poet with a new command of her art, with great power over the language she uses and the thought she seeks to present. They gain in significance when read side by side with the secular poems she was writing at this time (see below). In the poem for Whit Sunday, she creates an atmosphere of anticipation which resembles the drama of her great ballads and she evokes sight and sound in a way that becomes very familiar in her mature poems, though it has been one of her principal skills from her earliest days. There is passion in many of these poems of the second part of 'The Spiritual Year' and this can hardly be a surprise, given that this woman was about to embark on the greatest period of her creative development, when she would show herself capable of expressing her deepest emotions in a powerful and controlled manner. Her language is remarkable for its force and clarity, her imagery often strikingly original (see, for example, 'On the Fourth Sunday after Whitsun').

Perhaps the history of the emergence of 'The Spiritual Year' contributes to its fascination. She seems to have been committed to it to the point of obsession, and how could that not be the case, given that it expresses something very deep within her? One does not look to it for resolution or comfort, for this was a woman who seemed to find neither of these things accessible to her. The fluctuations in her thinking are sometimes hard to bear: a consistent position is impossible to discern, and yet one can never doubt that the desire is there. At no point does she deny the existence of God, nor the significance of God, and faith, in her life. What she doubts is her ability to receive that blessing which she suspects is available to her. When, in the final poem of the cycle, 'On the Last Day of the Year', she thinks she sees the star of love, she seems to be putting into words a hope, a craving, which is there throughout her life. If, in place of the faith which sometimes lets her down, God will accept love from her, as she puts it in the poem for Whit Sunday, then she can offer that. The conflict of which she speaks with great regret, between knowledge and faith ("My knowledge had to kill my faith", see below in the poem for the Third Sunday after Easter) appears to be insoluble for this woman who demanded so much, especially of herself.

On the First Sunday after Easter

And if Thou hast given Thy peace
to all who crave Thy salvation,
then I shall also raise my voice:
here I am, Father, give me my portion, too.
Why should I, a child shut out,
pining alone, weep for my inheritance?
Why should Thy sun not shine
where there are good seeds in the ground?

Often I believe that all right to prayer
has been taken from me, when it is so sad and lukewarm.
Only patient waiting can avail me,
and a fixed gaze up towards the blue of the sky.
Yet, Lord, thou who hast befriended the publican,

do not permit me to drown in night;
Thy voice calls indeed to the lost lamb,
and Thou hast come into the world for the sake of the sinner.

I know full well how things stand within my soul,
how bereft of faith, how defiant and confused,
so that, alas, much must remain concealed.
I feel how it buzzes through my nerves,
and feebly I follow its wretched track.
My helper, Thou knowest well
that which I cannot fathom and knowest well how to find it.
Thou art the physician; I am but the patient.

And if Thou hast gazed deeply into my sins,
as no human eye can see,
then Thou hast seen how in the deepest chasms
many a dark and heavy illusion slumbers still.
Yet I know, too, that no tear slips away
that Thy faithful hand has not weighed up,
and that no sigh has escaped this breast
that has not reached Thy merciful ear.

Thou who canst pass through closed doors,
behold: my breast is a closed gate.
I am too weak to move the bolts
and yet Thou seest how tremulously I stand before it.
Break in, break in! Ah, enter with Thy might!
Lend me the strength that Thou hast taken from me.
Ah, let me see the archway of Thy peace!
And may Thy sun shine into my night!

I shall not move 'til I have seen a ray of light,
even if it be faint as the glimmer of a worm.
And I will not go from this threshold
'til I have heard the breath from Thy voice.
And so, my Father, speak; speak also to me
with that voice that called the name of Mary
when weeping she turned away and did not recognize Thee.
Oh, say "My child, peace be with you".

On the Third Sunday after Easter

I cannot see Thee.
Where art Thou, then, my treasure, my breath of life?
Canst Thou not blow, so that my ear can hear it?
Why dost Thou seem like mist, why dost Thou flutter around
like smoke, when my eye turns towards Thy signs?
My light in the desert,
my Aaron's rod which could gently bring forth leaves,
you do not do it.
Thus I must atone for my own guilt, and my own foolishness.

The day is hot,
the sun blazes forth from the wall of my cell.
A trusting little bird flutters in and out,
its glistening eye asks me unflinchingly:
"Does the Lord not look out of these windows?"
What are you asking?
I must needs lower my head and blush.
Oh, bitter shame!
My knowledge had to kill my faith.

The cloud climbs up,
and slowly a sulphurous cloak
has covered the azure structure.
The breezes waft so warm and full of sighs,
and groans of fear stir in the branches.
The herd coughs.
What does the dumb animal sense? Is it the warmth of your body?
I stand with my head bowed.
My Lord, touch me, so that I may feel Thee!

A clap of thunder!
Horror has seized hold of the stricken forest.
I see my bird cowering in its nest, how branch rubs
groaning and cracking against branch, how streak after streak
of lightning jerks through the lanes of sulphur.
I follow it with my gaze.
Is it not Thy light, mighty Being?
Why then, alas,
why does nothing come to me but what I have read?

The darkness yields,
and, like soft weeping, the dew
falls from the clouds; whispering far and near.
The sun lowers its golden staff of mercy,
and suddenly the arc of peace stands there.
But what is this? Does my eye become moist?
Is not the rain a product of the mist?
I feel so light.
How is it? Can then the rubbing of the stalk touch me?

On mountain peaks
a prophet stood and looked for Thee, as I do.
Then did a storm break the branch of the giant pine,
and fire consume its way through the tree-tops.
Yet the visitor from the wilderness stood unshaken.
But then there came a breeze
like the breath of grace, and trembling and defeated
the prophet sank to his knees
and wept aloud, and he had found Thee.

So has Thy breath proclaimed to me
that which was hidden in the storm
and did not solve itself in the lightning?
Then I will also wait: my coffin is already growing.
The rain is falling on my place of slumber.
Then will the misty schemes of empty wisdom
vanish like smoke,
and I shall also see,
and no-one will take away my joy from me.

On the Fifth Sunday after Easter

I may pray in His name,
this He has told me Himself.
The handmaiden may step before her Creator
with His temple of grace.
Oh, sweet right given unto me!
Oh, trust which sprouts forth from Him.
How do I know today of no trembling
when His sunshine flows about me!

Thus, my Creator, in the name of Jesus
do I step before Thy countenance.
Where the blind stand, and the lame,
there is my place and my judgement.
And if I am one of the lowliest
who kneel beneath His shield,
Thy over-abundant hand is filled
for all, for everyone.

Trusting, I will approach Thee,
and even if my lips were to speak foolishness,
I will receive nothing but mercy.
Thou shalt give to me that which is wholesome.
Even if my thoughts are feeble and misguided,
I shall bring them to Thee trustingly,
and Thou shalt decide the boundaries Thyself,
and faithfully receive that which is best in me.

I ask not for earthly happiness,
only now and then for a ray of light,
that Thy hands become visible,
that I can sense Thy love,
only in the troubles of life
for resignation's merciful greeting:
then Thou shalt already know best
how much I can endure and must endure.

Nor will I ask Thee for fame
for which my shoulders are much too weak.
Let my consciousness be awake
only in the midst of human voices, so that,
however opinions may move around and run their course,
nevertheless there is One who never errs,
and every word which knows Him not
will grieve me a thousand times over.

Health, precious earthly fiefdom,
alas, I have lacked thee painfully.
Yet I can only beg for this:
that my soul should remain undisturbed,

that the feeble mist may not press upon
my whirling thoughts;
that through the barriers of the most frightening fog
I may always discern Thy day.

I am not short of the love of friends:
everyone is good to the one who suffers.
If my impulses grow stronger or grow fewer,
I place all this in Thy care.
Oh, protect me from that gentleness
which is much too silent in the face of my faults.
Hold Thou the mirror before my face
when the right hand of a friend is hesitant.

I should like to ask for much more,
but it is better that I kneel in silence here.
He who suffered for me on the Cross,
my gentle advocate, is standing by my side.
I wander always in darkness.
It was always He who cast the rays of light.
He who knows everything, should He not know
what his poor handmaid needs?

On Whit Sunday

The day was still. The sun stood so clear
against the unsullied vaulting.
The air, as though parched in the fire of the Orient,
let its wings drop dully.
Look, a little crowd of people, men, old men too,
and women kneeling. No words resound.
They are praying softly.

Where is the Comforter, the faithful sanctuary,
whom as Thou hast gone away,
Thou hast promised to Thy people?
They do not despair: Thy word stands firm,
and yet this time must surely seem frightening and bleak.
The hours are creeping past. Already they have been waiting
for forty days and nights in silent weeping, watching for Thee.

CHAPTER THREE

Where is He? Where? Hour upon hour,
one minute follows another.
Where can He be? And if the lips are silent,
the soul is asking it and quietly bleeding.
The whirlwind stirs up dust, the tiger groans
and lumbers spluttering through the billowing sand.
The snake thirsts.

Then, hear, a gentle murmuring sound arises. It becomes
louder and louder, until it sounds like the roaring of a tempest.
The blades of grass stand unbowed.
The palm tree, stiff, astonished, seems to be listening.
What is that trembling through the pious crowd?
What is causing them to exchange fearful, glowing glances?
Look up! Behold!

It is He, it's He! The flame leaps up
above each head. What wondrous circling,
welling up and jerking through the veins!
The future breaks. The sluice gates open,
and the Word streams forth unhampered,
now the cry of the herald
and now as a gentle, pleading whisper.

Oh, light, oh Comforter! art Thou proclaimed
only to that time, only to that crowd?
Not to us, not everywhere,
where a single soul finds itself sleepless and devoid of comfort.
I thirst in the heavy night.
Oh shine, before my eyes grow completely blind.
They weep and are awake.

If it is faith alone that Thou hast promised,
Then I am dead.
Oh, faith, I have need of it,
like the coursing of living blood!
But I do not have it
Ah, if in place of faith Thou wilt not accept love,
and the tear-laden tribute of yearning,
then I do not know how I may still have hope.

The staff is broken, the measure is full
in judgement of me.

My Saviour, who loves as no one loves,
dost Thou feel no compassion
when someone made in Thy image
kneels, dying of fear, so sick and devastated,
on cold stone and pleads with Thee?
Is Thy divine breath only faith, then?
Hast Thou not also
with Thine own blood
sown love deep in our breast?
Oh, please be gentle!

Thou hast pronounced a harsh and heavy word:
that "he who does not believe is judged".
In that case I am broken totally.
Yet He who gave His Son, the only begotten One,
for sinners and for pious ones alike,
will not leave me so deprived.
I, poorest of the lost ones, look to Him
for but one word of hope:
He is so rich,
my light of Grace.

Thou gentle One, who so graciously
Thyself hast sealed the baptism of desire
with the honour of a sacrament,
I do not doubt
that Thou hast surely also blessed
the longing for faith, the sanctity of yearning.
Otherwise Thou wouldst in truth not be
so great in kindness and so full of faithfulness,
if Thou wouldst break a little branch
out of which the flower is bursting and has promised fruit.

Whatever wrong I may have committed
through the errors of my reason,
I have surely atoned for it for many a day and many weeks.
So be Thou close to me!

I will hope and yearn and endure
according to the strength which I know I have bent
by my own guilt and cannot set to rights again.
Then, faithful One,
Thou wilt indeed grant faith
which brings forth aid.

On the Fourth Sunday after Whitsun

Thus from the light of Thy holy Book
a ray has fallen into my night,
into the mould-grey shaft of my heart.
Thou gavest it, Lord, Thou hast brought it Thyself to me,
that which is the jewel of my hope eternally.

It is too much, too much: I can hardly take hold of it.
Around my totally sunken soul, alas,
as barren and ashen as the Sea of Gomorrah,
around that shall be joy in Thy heights.
It is too much, woe unto me! It is a dream.

Can out of tears, like the arm of the polyp,
the lost essence grow again?
Does remorse restore my strength to me?
Is it enough when passion lies eaten up
as though by a swarm of insects?

Is it enough, before Thy grace and love,
if the hand stretches out yearning and beseeching
over the burned-out building,
the hand which banished all evils,
the hand on which, alas, the burning sign remained?

And yet Thou hast sent forth a holy word,
binding us with the powerful duty of grace
to believe against our own judgement
that which bursts groaning out of the chambers of the heart
and itself recognizes its guilt.

To believe, ah, how sweet and ah, how heavy!
Alas, I may not gaze upon my sins,
shall not suffocate trust in their mud,
like a wild beast in the horror of the swamp,
like a bird upon the Dead Sea.

Lord: who can boldly master that which Thou hast spoken?
Art Thou more merciful than human thought can measure?
Then art Thou, Lord, the Saviour and the Christ,
and I, who am only a dim shadow,
what can I do but kneel, believing?

On the Sixth Sunday after Whitsun

I have fished the whole night
for a pearl in the depths of my heart
and caught nothing.
Who has so confounded my being
that desire stands up against desire at all times
in my breast like doves up against snakes?

That I should like to follow Thee –ah!-
that is really true,
and I can say it to myself without deceit.
What is creeping behind me then in ghostly fashion
and, as though by the wings holding back the flight
which should bear me to Thee - ah!- to Thee?

Lord, leave me: I am a poor
and all too sinful being. Release me,
ah, leave me lying here!
Do I know what warms my breast?
Is it the glow of yearning, or does mere suffering
make the pulses fly so hot and tremblingly?

When sin defeats itself,
when out of the need for salvation grows yearning,
who will praise it?
Hast Thou not after all placed the judge

in our blood which froths up against sin,
so that it may release itself from the barren sludge?

This swirling known to everyone
when any breath of life still rises up,
will it avail me?
Yes: when the fire of the sun is extinguished,
Egypt has bowed before Thee,
and its sin was not taken from it.

And if perhaps Thou hast not sharpened
the thorn of conscience for me as for others,
then I will atone for it
if the right thrust does not penetrate
which gives freedom to the warm, pure sea,
from which flow the genuine tears of remorse.

Oh, only a real pearl
from the stone-covered fount of my eyes:
that would be a blessing.
Thou master of all nature,
break in, Thou rescuer, release the bright streams!
Without Thee, I can truly never move.

Thou who hast said: "Fear not",
let me trust in Thy hand
and not grow weary.
Yes, over Thy word, my light of hope,
I will throw my net. Ah, will then the pearl
at last rise on to the land and bring me peace?

On the Eleventh Sunday after Whitsun

My Jesus wept for His city,
and ah! certainly He also wept for me.
Did He not then already know how wretched and feeble,
how helpless, my soul appears today?
Of all that the Holy Bible imparts,
nothing has moved me so deeply, so poignantly.

Ah, if only I might catch His precious tears
in a chalice, in a cloth, just as He wished to leave for Veronica
the sacred traces of His bloody countenance!
She was the most highly blessed of the Lord,
yet the poorest beggar also likes to dream.

I should gladly place in such a chalice
whatever little treasures I possess,
and it would become rich and heavy with my gold,
and my precious stones should sparkle.
Oh, Lord, do not be vexed by my foolishness:
Thy goodness makes me today into a child.

"Alas, if only you knew what salvation there is for you!"
Yes, if I knew, it would certainly be to my advantage.
Yet Thou, Thou knowest it indeed, my Jesus Christ,
and only from Thee can the message come to me.
So, speak to me, Thou my heart's treasure.
I stand here and hearken to Thy word.

To be sure, I must rather search in Thy Holy Book
for the signs of Thy love
than where Thy zeal speaks, and, alas, Thy curse.
I bend like a blade of grass if I hear Thee curse.
I lie like a withered leaf upon the earth,
not shaken off in health but weary unto death.

I am an arid piece of ground, which the burning of chalk,
the scorching of ash can do nothing to help.
I follow the wind like parched sand;
thus will I suck Thy heavenly drops
and in that drink Thou wilt perhaps give to me
that which will suffice for my erring consciousness.

Put into my heart that which I must do,
whether to stand grieving or to step forward in hope.
Mercy is not the price of strength
but can float down also to the sick one.
Thou who art the Creator of the very weakest,
my Jesus Christ, hast for him too a means of salvation.

Thus, when the cloud once more enfolds me
and when my arms grow weak almost in desperation,
then will I remember that He has loved
and raise my eyelids through the shadows.
Ah, my soul, do not be so hard as stone:
you know for sure that He has wept for you.

On the Nineteenth Sunday after Whitsun

I do not know, God,
if I love Thee.
I often think that it is only Thee
whom this breast embraces
full of mercy
and like a redeeming torch
in the radiance of all other love
and dawning longing.

When the spirit soars freely
towards the noblest thing,
that which encircles it as a thought
yet living, invisible,
yet not without its essence,
distant yet everywhere,
whose traces speak out of a human eye
and out of the blessing of a tear,

then am I truly consoled
and prayer arises
so confidently from my lips
as if in strange love, or in Thine –
who has ever fathomed it? –
were offered
everything that remained worthy of longing
and proclaims Thy breath.

Yet then at another time
I feel myself consecrated to the dark earth,
like hair to the head,
so robbed of power,

when in a friend the failings,
weaknesses, pressed to my heart,
delight me like a charm,
that no one could steal from me.

So would it only be a sign from God
that I have recognized,
and not that sinful Nature
was holding out her hand,
when I can tolerate
the virtue of my loved ones with reverence,
yet my heart would surely beat
more purely and more coldly?

As the cheek of Damocles grew pale
beneath the sword,
or like one who, on the bank of the river,
looks at his reflection, smiles and drinks,
while the treacherous sand is slipping gently away
and his foothold is sinking:
woe! a cold cloud
is passing over me.

Oh, Saviour, Saviour, who suffered also
for the fools,
come to me, before the wave
slides over my head!
Stretch out Thy strong hand
and I will go on battling against the waves.
To be sure, Thou hast dragged many a man
out of the deep mud and on to the land.

If I have once extricated myself
completely from the mud,
my yearning for Thy image
will at last be real.
Then I can love strongly and wholesomely,
devoid of all shame and subterfuge,
from the very depths of my heart
and my whole soul.

On All Saints' Day

Blessed are the poor in spirit,
who at the feet of their nearest One
are happy to warm themselves by His light
and give Him the greeting of a servant,
take pity on the misdeeds of a stranger,
rejoice at the happiness of a stranger.
Yes, at the feet of their nearest One, the poor are blessed,

Blessed are the meek,
in whom anger turns to smiling
and the seed of gentleness sprouts no less
from thorn and sharp spiny prickles, f)
whose last word is a gentle breath of love
amidst the death rattle,
when the jerking turns to smiling.
Blessed are the meek.

Blessed are those who mourn
and eat their bread with tears,
lament only their own sin
and do not think of that of strangers,
beat their own breasts
and cast their eyes down at the guilt of strangers.
Those who eat their bread with tears,
blessed are those who mourn.

Blessed is he who is seized by thirst
for the right, for the good,
brave even on decaying ships,
bravely steering towards the waves,
should bleed to death
beneath the shore and the reefs.
For the right, for the good,
blessed those whom thirst has seized.

The merciful are blessed
who look only at the wound,
not extorting coldly and selectively,

as harm could arise,
softly and protectively,
gradually letting the balm sink in.
Those who look only at the wound, the merciful are blessed.

Ecstatically pure hearts,
the senses of spotless virgins,
to whom jesting is childish pleasure,
to whom loving is the breath of heaven,
who lit their radiant beginnings
like candles on the altar.
The senses of spotless virgins, ecstatically pure hearts!

And the pious guardians of peace are blessed,
commanding the barriers,
and the champions of unity
holding up the white banner,
gently and resolutely towards the opponent,
like the sword splitting the feather cushions.
Blessed those who command the barriers,
blessed are the guardians of peace.

Those who endure persecution for Thy sake,
Almighty Commander,
Thy hosts are blessed when they avoid everything
to preserve Thy banner for themselves.
May it never be parted from them,
neither in pleasure nor in peril.
Blessed, blessed Thy hosts who endure persecution!

Thus I must call blessed all those
to whom my deeds are foreign,
must, while my wounds are burning,
remain the herald of alien happiness.
Will nothing separate me from Thee then,
wild, arid, decaying deeds?
Must I crush myself?
Will no one call me blessed?

(f). This translation is really a paraphrase: the English term is 'restharrow': 'Hauhechel' is the plant Ononis spinosa.

On All Souls' Day

The hour is coming when the dead walk,
when long decayed eyes see.
Oh hour, hour, the greatest of all hours:
you are with me and will not let me go;
I am with you bound in duty.
I breathe for you; my wounds bleed for you.

You are terrible, and yet valuable.
Yes: my whole soul turns
towards you in life's fear and erring,
my firm refuge, my fortress,
to which unbending hope flees,
whenever fear and brooding roam like ghosts.

If I did not know that indeed
in the darkness of those places
you lay slumbering, hidden like an embryo,
then I should like to conceal my face in terror
from the light of the sun
and vanish like a pool of rain at dawn.

It is not lack of recognition that drives me towards you.
The sternest voice is gentle to me,
takes my shillings and gives millions in return.
No, where injustice has ever befallen me,
I felt at ease, and felt your soft breath
wafting through the aeons of time.

Yet love and honour urge me forward
to you as my last port,
where the inside of my grave
will appear clearly before me.
Then on the true scales my guilt and my shame
will rise up like a tower
and my fighting and my weeping will approach trembling.

I should vanish completely before you,

bereft of consolation, like a shadow.
Yet through no fault of mine
it is not like that.
My gaze stares as if motionless towards you,
as to the greatest happiness,
and I can barely, barely endure the waiting.

Yet when once hope starts,
the hand which it has placed
into the legendary depths of this bosom
will not tear from the ground like a weed
the shoot which grew up with no will of its own,
and not out of arrogance.

When the time comes,
when the vanity which the world has set out drops down,
talent and fortune, about the gaunt skeleton,
the beggar will be standing there: look at him!
Then it is time; then the lips of the poor man may,
trembling, beg for mercy.

Then a cheap and tawdry trifle will not make me blush with shame;
then the right hand will have brought me down and impoverished me,
as I deserved.
Then, from that time on, an eye full of the light of love
will not pierce me like the thrust of a dagger:
I am brought low and am redeemed.

On Christmas Day

Through all the streets the tumult comes rolling along,
mules, camels, drivers: what sound of ringing bells,
as though the seed of Jacob were wanting once again
to move into the plain, and the sky of Judaea
lets its shining streams of sparks scatter a sapphire light
over the seething mass.

Women are walking veiled through the alleyways,
old crones slip wearily from their loaded beasts.

CHAPTER THREE

Everywhere shouting and pushing,
as though at the head of Jehu's chariot.
Is Jezebel once more allowing her face to rise up
out of the airy gateway of those pillars?

It is Rome, the voluptuous priestess of the gods,
the most radiant and the cruellest of the strumpets,
who is counting her slaves at this time.
With a chisel, still dripping with blood,
she engraves on tablets, heaping number upon number,
the names of the suitors whom her sword has freed.

Oh, Israel, what has become of your pride?
Have you not rubbed your hands until they bleed,
and your tears, were they seething blood?
No, when your multitudes swirl towards the market-place,
selling, bartering, haggling beneath the halls of the temple,
their courage has perished with their God.

The pillar of fire became a miserable will-o-the-wisp,
the green rod of Aaron the executioner's axe,
and the dead word lies hideously petrified,
a mummy in the Holy Book,
in which the Pharisee searches after the curse,
thundering it out over friend and stranger.

Thus, Israel, you are ripe and ready for cutting,
just as the thistle ripens in the midst of the seeds,
and as you stand there in your fierce hatred
opposite your painted, empty lover,
the two of you are equal before the rightful throne of justice,
she wet with blood and you with spittle.

Oh, melt, heaven, melt the righteous one!
You clouds, send Him as rain, the one true Messiah,
for whom Judaea does not wait,
the holy One, the gentle and the just One,
the King of Peace among the warring knaves,
come to warm that which has frozen stiff.

The night is silent. Hidden in his tent
the scholar peers anxiously
to see when the mighty tyrant of Judah will appear.
Then he lifts the curtain, staring long at the star
which glides across the face of the firmament,
like a tear of joy that heaven weeps.

And far from that tent, above a stable,
as if it were falling on to the low roof,.
it pours its light in a thousand radiuses:
a meteor! that is what the scholar was thinking
as he turned slowly back to his book.
Ah, do you know whom that lowly roof encloses?

In a manger lies a slumbering new-born child.
The mother kneels, as though lost in a dream,
wife yet virgin.
An earnest, simple man, deeply shaken,
pulls their bed close to them. His right hand trembles
as he draws her veil close around her cloak.

And at the door stand humble people,
Hard-working shepherds, yet today the first to arrive.
And in the air there is a sweet and gentle singing,
lost sounds from the song of the angels:
"Glory to the Highest One, and peace to all men
who are of good will!"

On the Last Day of the Year

The year is coming to an end;
the thread unwinds itself with a whirr.
Just one short hour remaining, the final one today,
and that which once was living time
trickles like powder into its grave.
I wait in silence.

It's dead of night.
Is there perhaps an eye still open?

In these walls, Time, your passing
shudders to a close. I am afraid,
but the last hour must be lived through
awake and solitary.

Everything that I have done or thought
must be seen,
everything that arose from my head and my heart.
That stands now like an earnest guard
at the gate of heaven. Oh, half a victory,
oh, sombre fate!

How the wind tears
at the window frame!
Yes, the year is going to crumble against the shutters,
not breathe itself out like a shadow
beneath the clear and starry sky.
You child of sin!

Was not every day a hollow,
secret murmur left behind
in your barren breast,
where slowly stone broke upon stone,
when it pushed the cold breath
from the icy pole?

My little lamp is going out,
and eagerly the wick
sucks the last drop of oil.
Has my life also turned to smoke like that?
Is the hollow of the grave opening up to me,
black and silent?

Indeed my life is breaking in that circle
which the course of this year describes.
I have long known that.
And yet this heart has glowed
with the pressure of vain passions.
On my forehead simmers

the sweat of deepest fear,
and on my hand. What?
Is a star not dawning damply over there,
through the clouds?
Could it perhaps be the star of love,
showing its anger towards you with its bleak light,
that you are so afraid?

Hark! What a humming sound is that?
And there again? The melody of dying!
The bell moves its bronze mouth.
Oh Lord, I fall upon my knees!
Have mercy on my final hour!
The year is over!

CHAPTER FOUR

LEVIN SCHÜCKING AND THE FLOWERING OF DROSTE-HÜLSHOFF'S POETIC GENIUS

The fifteen-year-old schoolboy who visited Annette von Droste-Hülshoff in the Rüschhaus and stood rather stupidly (*etwas blöde)* in front of her, as he put it in his memoirs so many years later, was almost certainly intimidated by what was clearly a striking presence, those piercing blue eyes so often remarked upon and the sharp intellect which she could not disguise even as she tried to put the young boy at his ease with her natural hospitality and by showing him her array of disparate treasures. Interestingly, since this was presumably his observation at the time and not just written with the benefit of hindsight, he describes her as 'fragile and suffering in appearance' (*leidend aussehend*). Perhaps he already sensed the vulnerability which he would see throughout their acquaintance, and even perhaps a rapport between them which would determine a surprising and remarkable friendship.

At that stage of his life he was soon to embark on his further studies and was probably dependent on others to further the acquaintance and even for transport. He visited her, he recalled, only once or twice more before a major event in his own life drove him to respond to her summons. This was the first great anguish of his young life, he writes as a middle-aged man, when his mother had just died, leaving him, in the now almost permanent absence of his father, in the care of his grandparents. Annette greeted him with tears in her eyes as she spoke of her grief at the death of her friend, which she had heard of by chance and rather belatedly from reading the announcement in a newspaper, and expressed her profound regret that she had left a letter from her unanswered. She urged Levin to visit her often, and later, he remembers, she told him that she had the feeling that his mother had bequeathed him to her. This sounds very like her: a warm, kindly woman who would have been moved by the plight of a bereaved young man, but also almost certainly felt a posthumous obligation towards someone who was not the very close friend she might have hoped she could be.

This ambiguity is evident in the poem she wrote ten years after the death of Katharina Schücking, by which time she and Levin were close friends. It is not that of which the poem speaks, however, but of her encounters with Katharina herself, and of the qualities she has come to see in the older woman:

Katharina Schücking

You never suspected, never knew
how great my love was for you.
Your clear eyes never read the
runes in my breast,
when you stretched out your hand to me in friendly fashion
and we wandered through the woods together.
You never knew that I saw it as a pledge from the gods,
as a precious jewel.

You did not see how, intoxicated by the first kiss from the young muse,
I knelt, a passionate child,

in the garden where the stream runs
and sank weeping into the grasses,
how, trembling, I turned the key of the door
when I was about to see you for the first time,
Westphalia's poetess, and how at that moment
a blessed thrill shuddered through my turbulent heart.

I was very young and full of love,
eager emotion the very breath of life to me.
Ah, much that once quivered through my veins like a flame
has turned to dust, like ash.
My vision became clear and my understanding strong:
many things had to come down from their throne
and that which I once called the marrowbone of life
I now felt to be my own with new-found pride.

Thus I avoided looking again into your dark eyes
as a devoted pupil.
I did not wish to stand before my mistress
proudly and with my head covered,
and I was sick, too, my senses completely muddled,
and did not wish to pronounce a name with longing.
Yet this did not change your love
and you found your way to me after many years of separation.

And when you stood before me, firm and resolute,
and looked deep into the chasms of my soul,
I truly recognized my weakness
and what I had thought seemed to me like a weighty sin.
The sight of you, you strong one forged in the fire of purification,
rose up again like a phoenix from the ashes,
and deep in my heart I understood
that you were ten times greater than your poems.

You did not see, you modest one, that at that time
I was drinking from your gaze my own recovery,
that at that time the sounds you uttered
sank into my soul like naphtha.
Your every word, transparent as crystal
and potent as the purest of wines,

> seemed to cry out to me "Come on, you tangled mass of moods,
> get up! Stand on your feet, you weak little thing!"
>
> Now you are gone, and of God's purest creature
> only a green hill remains to us,
> around which the savage winter storms rage,
> and the thoughts of those who love you.
> And I hear that they have laid a wreath of laurels
> in the dark mosses of your grave,
> but I, Kathinka, trembling with emotion,
> offer you ivy and the most thorny rose.

Droste-Hülshoff had met Katharina Busch, a young relative of her friend and mentor A.M. Sprickmann, in 1813, at a time when the older girl was beginning to be known locally as a writer of unremarkable verses and enjoying some small acclaim, in the absence of much competition, as 'Westphalia's poetess'. Her fame was short-lived and, despite the admiration Annette may have felt at the time, she later recognized that this was the product of her teenage years, and that, as the poem puts it, Katharina was more significant as a person than as a poet. In fact, they did not meet again until 1829, by which time Katharina was unhappy in her marriage and the mother of the teenage Levin, living at a distance from her original home and in Münster only on a visit. Her poetic aspirations had frankly come to nothing, including even her hopes of inaugurating a literary circle. Two years later she died. There is nothing to suggest that the friendship between her and Droste-Hülshoff was a strong one, although the latter was capable of deep and enduring relationships with both men and women, and distance and the passage of time seemed to make no difference to them.

It is interesting that Jenny, Annette's older sister, was

unimpressed by Katharina and clearly did not see what the fuss was about. Even taking into account the superiority of the older sister, it seems likely that Katharina was an unremarkable young woman whom Annette quickly outgrew but who, at the time, represented the model for the aspiring poet in her.

What the poem does show is the generosity of Droste-Hülshoff in her relationships, and her always present tendency to accuse herself and to analyse herself and others with great perception. It belongs, too, with a type of poem at which she excels, which examines human responses with the passing of the years, and through the barrier of death.

The link between Levin and Droste-Hülshoff was Katharina: that much is clear, and for a time at least she appears to have adopted a maternal role in his life, even using the disconcerting word *Mütterchen* ('little mother') to describe herself in her letters to him. His devotion to his real mother is expressed in a letter to the woman he was about to marry when he wrote to her in 1842: "If there was ever a saint, it was she". How Louise von Gall responded to this is unrecorded, but there is reason to believe that between her and Droste-Hülshoff relations were, unsurprisingly, never warm.

By late 1837 Levin Schücking had completed his law studies and was a new addition to the group which gathered in Münster and increasingly endeavoured to promote Droste-Hülshoff's work. An ambitious young man, he was beginning to be recognized as a critic, and, although she was initially unimpressed by some of his affectations, she saw a sharpness of intellect and judgement which soon established him as a favoured companion on the long walks she enjoyed in the countryside around Münster, during which, despite the difference in age, they could exchange views in a way she seems never to have known to this extent with her trusted friends of some years' standing. Wilhelm Junkmann and Christoph Bernhard Schlüter were to remain in her life until its end, and Schücking would join with them in ensuring that her work received recognition both in her lifetime and after her death, but the three men all contributed something different. It seems evident that Schücking, with his youth and less deferential approach, contributed a challenge not forthcoming from anyone else.

Schücking was a journalist and writer. He was not a poet, yet he possessed critical powers which she valued and respected, even when, as often happened, she did not share his views. The nature of their relationship is hard to define, and history may have been presumptuous in attempting to do so. It is too easy to assume that he cultivated her friendship as a means to an end: he was certainly ambitious, and time would show that he had a ruthless streak, but the cynical assumption that he devoted hours and weeks to her company in the hope of personal benefit is unrealistic and in any case overlooks the evidence that she was a woman of considerable personal charm, lively, kind and an intelligent and entertaining companion. She, for her part, must have found him a breath of fresh air and relished his pungent statements. If, as some believe, this was more than a friendship, then that is hardly surprising, for this is a woman who had a huge capacity for warmth and love, and, to the end of her short life, she seems to have craved the close relationship with one person – and even with one God - which eluded her.

For two short periods in two very different parts of the country, in Rüschhaus and on the long walks in the Park and the neighbourhood in 1839-40, and during that brief winter of 1841-2 in Meersburg, recalled by both as a time of especial closeness and something at times approaching perfect happiness, she found herself truly herself and free in a way she had never done earlier and never did again. This freedom released something within her, and, whatever one chooses to call the emotion she felt, it allowed her to release the poetry within her and express it in language of rare beauty and intensity.

It was Schücking who saw that her true genre was lyric poetry, and it was in response to a wager from him that she wrote at such speed in the extraordinarily productive years during and after the Meersburg winter, before illness and frailty overtook her and she declined towards her death. Schücking did not make her into a poet of stature, but he ensured that she made herself into one, as she had always been. If this is testimony to mutual love, then, conventional or not, perhaps that is what it may be called, but the label is immaterial, for she fulfilled her creative potential, and he, in writing so movingly of her in his *Lebensbild* and seeing to it that her work should endure long after her death, paid homage to their pairing and erased any lingering doubts about his motivation.

The Levin Poems

Six years elapsed following the moving encounter of the recently-bereaved seventeen-year-old and Annette von Droste-Hülshoff. Again the *Lebensbild* of the middle-aged Levin provides a vivid picture of the renewal of their acquaintance and its development into the much warmer relationship which was to have such significance for them both, and for her growth as a poet. It seems from what he writes that in those six years he did not take up her invitation to visit, and indeed both of them were fully occupied, he with his university studies in Law, and she with the preparation of the 1838 edition in which he had no part and the resumption of her work on 'The Spiritual Year'. She was collecting the material for the brilliant *Novelle* on which her future most obvious fame would rest, but, as was her way, she worked slowly and with interruptions, and in fact *Die Judenbuche* did not appear until 1842. There were other ideas in her fertile mind, too, and she was undecided which direction her work should take. Both of them record in their separate and characteristic ways how decisive this extraordinary new friendship was: he in urging her to concentrate on the lyric which he maintained was her true strength, and she in responding to his appreciation of her work which was refreshingly realistic and honestly expressed. Between them there was warmth and respect and increasingly a genuine enjoyment of one another's company. That did not, however, mean that they always agreed with one another, and there is evidence in the poems that she wrote about their relationship, or actually dedicated to him, that there were times of harsh disagreement and conflict. It was never going to be a smooth association, and indeed how could it be, given the difference in age and background, and the clash of two very distinct, and distinctive, temperaments?

The first period of closeness between them in the period between late 1839 and September 1841 is vividly described by Levin many years later, and he describes with tenderness and insight the life that she was leading at that time. She was essentially alone in the Rüschhaus, following her sister's marriage and permanent move to Switzerland, then to Meersburg, where their mother often joined Jenny and her family for lengthy periods. He does not suggest that she was lonely, welcoming visits from friends when they were able to make the journey into what was a fairly isolated region, while he himself made frequent visits and observes that, despite obviously poor health, she was lively and seemingly content. It was a time of great creative activity for her. Her meticulous work on *Die Judenbuche* was progressing towards eventual publication in 1842. She completed the second part of 'The Spiritual Year' in 1840 and laid it aside, giving no explicit indication of whether she planned to resume it at a later date.

Their conversations were lively and thoughtful, based on the literary matters which they had in common, but also on their common interest in the countryside of Westphalia which surrounded them and, increasingly, in its history, its customs and its folklore. Her awareness of her own psychic powers intrigued him, and she felt free to relate some of her supernatural experiences to him. In these conversations and the regular walks during which she took in the nature of the landscape and registered its details lies the substance of some of her great ballad poems ('Der Fundator', 'Der Tod des Erzbischofs Engelbert von Köln', 'Vorgeschichte: Second Sight'), and the group of poems entitled *Heidebilder*, ('Poems of the Heathland'). During these two years she maintained her prolific correspondence, with many friends and acquaintances, notably Christoph Bernhard Schlüter, but above all with her mother and her sister, whom she was to visit for two prolonged periods in Meersburg, where she would die. The Rüschhaus years saw the beginning of a very close friendship with Schücking, and she recalled them with great warmth when she wrote to him two years later, describing it as 'the most poetic time', while the months in Meersburg were 'the cosiest and most tender in both our lives ' (Letter dated 10 October 1842)

The frequent visits of Schücking to the Rüschhaus could hardly have passed unnoticed, and they prompted some suggestive gossip from Luise von Bornstedt, a writer of sorts who had not been received with open arms by the literary circle of Münster. It remains impossible to tell what Levin's own view of the relationship was. He was busy with his career as a critic, in which he was attaining considerable repute; his review of her 1838 volume is widely regarded as particularly perceptive. As a poet in his own right he was much less successful, but Droste-Hülshoff was impressed by his critical judgement, and certainly he was to make a name for himself as a respected literary commentator, not least, of course, because, through his achievements in editing her work and seeing it to publication, his name is always linked with hers. From the beginning, though never without the cautiousness that she exercised with regard to her own work, she listened to his advice and sometimes heeded it. Presumably this was the case when, as he emphasises, he urged her to concentrate on the lyric which he firmly believed was her true genre, though she would certainly never have pursued this course if she had not known that he was absolutely right.

With characteristic candour, she observes at one point that it always surprises her that he is so much less a poet than a critic. There can have been no doubt in her mind that Levin was to be more and more significant to her creative development when, coinciding with her own journey to Meersburg and the Lassberg family and in collusion with her sister Jenny, she engineered a summons to him from her brother-in-law, who suddenly needed a librarian for his prized collections, particularly of medieval manuscripts. There seems to be a certain amount of irony when, twenty years later, he recounts how he received this prestigious invitation for which, on the face of it, he may not have been outstandingly qualified, but he was an ambitious young man and it was doubtless seen as typical of Annette von Droste-Hülshoff to seek to help a worthy cause. There is, again, tenderness in his description in his *Lebensbild* of his arrival at the great slumbering Castle of Meersburg, on the shore of Lake Constance, where he was to spend the winter of 1841-42, but the true picture of the ensuing months is gained from the group of five poems unambiguously devoted to the friendship between the middle-aged and increasingly frail Droste-Hülshoff and the vibrant young assistant librarian as they slipped away separately in the afternoons and surreptitiously joined up for their long walks and companionable talks.

The five poems span the period between the late autumn in Meersburg in 1841 and the last time they met, in May 1844. The differing moods convey the sense of the kaleidoscope which was their brief but so powerful relationship. These were two people of strong personality in a situation which may have seemed unlikely but which changed the shape of her poetic creation. That the emotion was intense is clear, sometimes sheer bliss, but also friction and misunderstanding, and all overlaid with sadness and nostalgia.

The dating of the first poem is not difficult. Clearly the place is Meersburg, and the time must be late autumn: the grapes are ripe, and Levin arrived that year in October for his months as librarian to Joseph von Lassberg, joining Annette who had come down from Rüschhaus in September. The second and third poems must also belong to that winter, reflecting the period of closeness between them in that brief period, before Levin left and later became engaged to Louise von Gall, whom he married in 1843.

The fourth was probably composed soon after the arrival of the couple in early May 1844. Strangely, it reads as though it is a continuation of an earlier difference of opinion between Droste-Hülshoff and Schücking, although they had not actually met since his departure two years earlier. Correspondence between them in that interval contains evidence that she had not been reluctant to express her opinion of an intended union which she considered ill-advised, although she seems to have done her best to receive his bride with her customary hospitality when they came for their first and only visit. The fourth strophe points out the changes that have taken place in both their lives: his circumstances have changed and he can hardly be surprised if she has taken new directions. The final poem is clearly a farewell to him, and may have been written very close to their departure on 30 May. She gave it to him along with a group of some other very important poems which were published later that year or, in some cases, in the *Letzte Gaben* of 1860.

The Inn on the Lake (To Levin Schücking)
Autumn 1841

Is it not a cheerful place, my young friend,
the little house that clings to the steep slope,
where the innkeeper comes up to us in his
comic way, and the landscape stretches out so
magnificently, where the little root man **f1)**
with his mischievous manner, winding his way like an eel
and almost curling himself into a ball, delights us in teasing contrast
against the backdrop of the proud Alps?
Sit down! "Grapes!" and nimbly the bustling little man appears,

wagging his pigtail.
Oh, look how the wounded berry
weeps tears of blood at the approach of the first frost!
Fresh! Put your hand into the crystal bowl! The juicy rubies
gleam and draw us towards them - fresh!
Already I can sense from the rich table of the autumn
the winter approaching in its silent socks.

These are hieroglyphs to you, you young thing,
and by your dear side I will joyfully drink up
the last goodness of my declining years.
Look that way, look over there, both near and far,
and see how the cliff rises up at our side
as if we could grasp it with our hands,
and how the water foams at our feet as if
we could cross it in a single leap.

Can you hear the alphorn across the blue lake?
The air is so clear it seems to me I can see the herdsman
wending his way home from the fragrant heights.
Did it not seem as though the cowbells were chirping?
Look, where the gorge pushes its way into the rock
It seems to me I see the bold hunter creeping along
and if a chamois were clinging on to the face of the mountain
my eyes would surely see it.

Drink up! The Alps are hours away.
Only the castle, our familiar walls, is close,
where dreams of times long past are lurking,
strange tales and fierce adventures,
It seems to me a good idea to brood in heavy, grey rooms
upon the remains of dark deeds, but you, Levin,
you gaze out of the gloomy building like a swallow
from its nest in the wall.

See, down there, on the lake in the setting sun,
how the scaup f2) slips up and down.
At one time it sinks down like the plumb on the net,
then bobs up again with the waves.
A strange game: just like life itself!

And we two look down at it eagerly.
You smile and whisper: "She always comes up again",
But I, I am thinking, "She always goes back down."

Just one more look at this blessed land,
the hills, the meadows, the abundant rushing of the waves,
and then homewards, where, from the edge of the battlements,
friendly eyes are watching our path.
Let's go! Here comes the little innkeeper tripping along,
waving goodbye with his pigtail and gabbling away:
"Peaceful night! Don't get up too early!"
That's the night-time blessing of the cheery Swabians.

f.1) The reference is to a little gnome-like creature made from a mandrake root and, in popular legend, magically brought to life.
f.2) The scaup - a species of diving duck, Aythya marila.

To Levin Schücking, (Oh, do not ask.....)
(Winter 1841-42)

Oh, do not ask what moves me so profoundly,
when I see your youthful blood surging so joyfully, or
why, when I lean against your handsome brow,
heavy drops fall from my lashes.

Once I dreamt that I was a foolish child,
working diligently away at the edge of the table.
How overwhelming are the words which have become
hieroglyphs again to me!

And then, when I woke up, I was weeping hot tears,
so that I felt clear and sober,
felt that I was so uninhibited and so precocious,
so unafraid of scolding or the rod.

Then, when I gaze into your gentle face,
in which a thousand fresh buds are bursting into life,
it seems to me as if Nature had held up my image
in front of me in a magic mirror.

And all my hopes, the fire in my soul,
the twilight radiance of the sun of my love,
that which has yet to vanish and that which has already vanished,
for all that I must weep in you.

To a friend (No word, and even if it were......)
(Winter 1841-42)

No word, and even if it were as sharp as the blade of a sword,
shall separate that which is united in a thousand threads,
no thought so powerful that it might force its way
like poison into the goblet of pure wine.
Life is so short, and happiness so rare,
such a precious jewel, to be, rather than to seem to be.

If fate has set us up, as in a careless joke,
upon two alien frozen poles,
then know that there, at the peak of separation,
the magnet reigns, there, king above all things.
It does not ask if cliff and current endanger it,
but runs like a ray of light through the heart of the earth.

Look into my eyes: are they not your eyes?
Is even my anger not like yours?
You smile and your smile is mine,
rich in the same pleasure and the same thoughts.
That which other lips joke about in friendly fashion,
we feel it in our hearts more sacredly.

Pollux and Castor, alternately glowing and turning pale,
the light of the one simply taken from the other,
and yet the sign of the most pious devotion.
Give me your hand, then, my Dioskur **f)**
and on the top of the helmet let the sweet myth be renewed,
in which the twin flame shone.

f) In Greek mythology, Castor and Pollux were twin brothers, known as the Dioscuri (or, in Latin, Gemini or Castores). Their mother was Leda, but Castor was the son of Tyndaerus, King of Sparta, while the father of Pollux was the god Zeus.

To a friend (For the second time.....)
(May 1844)

For the second time a word is wanting
to push its way between our hearts.
A boy is trying to blast
the hoard of ore guarded by rocks.
Look into my eyes: are yours not fixed
upon the window's edge?
Has then my face become so unfamiliar to you,
my voice so alien?

Look kindly into my eyes.
Even if Nature petulantly created them
in a harsh shape, I must answer
their call with an alien voice.
The bird sings as Nature commands,
the dragonfly describes coloured circles,
and until today no one has stirred it out of anger
into a butterfly.

Silently, at the edge of my years,
Fate has let the spindle slip.
I intended only to stretch out my hand
to take up old threads.
Only I found yours rich,
found it tangled together with many new movements.
Can you be surprised if at the same time
I achieved new things?

That much in me is abrupt and stiff,
Ah, who could know that as well as I do!
Yet, for the benefit of my soul,
I was given a second, gentler conscience,
and that has toned down my arrogance
which had forced itself upon me like a monster,
and has often struggled with that demon,
has glowed, as remorse does battle.

But you, that blood sunk deep into my heart,
could you think that I was wanting in this way
to harm my own being, my own crown?
Oh, my words flowed out thoughtlessly and vividly,
In the belief that they would please you,
that this mouth was not shaped for any breath
that could harm you.

Do you doubt the sympathy of one
so totally akin to you?
Then I can only say that you could not have
climbed up to the glacier of true devotion,
or you would know that on the heights
base weeds huddle together,
and that we see the phoenix there
where our beloved cedars stand in flames.

Look this way: I stretch out towards you
not just one hand but both of them,
to lead you back to the forgotten track,
to loving and to blessing.
Only honour Him who fanned
the light of life at my cradle.
Accept me as God made me, and
do not attribute unfamiliar looks to me.

Fare well!
(30 May 1844, on parting from Levin and his bride)

Fare well: it cannot be otherwise.
Spread out your fluttering sail
and leave me alone in my castle,
in this desolate house filled with ghosts.
Fare well, and take my heart with you,
and my last ray of sunshine.
Let him go away, only quickly go away,
for after all he must go away some time.

Leave me at the edge of my lake,
rocking with the movement of the waves,
alone with my spell,
the spirit of the Alps, and my own self.

Abandoned, yet not alone,
shocked but not shattered,
as long as the blessed light
shines upon me with the eyes of love,

as long as the fresh forest
rustles its songs from every leaf,
and an elf listens kindly to me
from every cliff and every crevice,

as long as my arm reaches out free
and all-embracing towards the air,
and the cry of every wild vulture
awakes the wild muse in me.

The final poem of this group is characteristic of her courageous personality. She surely senses that they will not meet again, and indeed they did not do so, although his involvement with her publications, in particular the appearance of the second, much more significant edition of her work later that year, meant that they remained in touch by letter. The correspondence between them clearly changes, as it was bound to do, although she remained courteous and frequently included Louise in it.

When he published his novel *Die Ritterbürtigen* ('The Gentility') in 1846, she was deeply hurt by his satirical references to the customs of her class and to easily identifiable figures from her family circle and even a barely disguised portrait of herself: this she saw as an act of betrayal by the man she had treated as an adopted son and someone to whom she had offered so much hospitality. When she turned in her outrage and distress to Christoph Schlüter, her dearest friend over so many years, she did not, of course, speak of the nature of their relationship but expressed in forthright terms her indignation that anyone could do something so blatantly improper in order to further his professional position (letter of April 1846). She concedes that Schücking may not even be aware of the damage he has done, and adds that, when he had last contacted her, it was to inform her with some delight that he was able to enclose a fee he had negotiated for her. This little touch tells us a great deal about both of these unlikely friends. Schücking may well deserve the condemnation of some people as an over-ambitious, selfish man with little regard for finer feelings. Her refusal, in this long letter to Schlüter, to give way to undiluted self-pity and resentment, but to pass on to happier topics speaks for her essentially generous nature and, even more, of her extraordinary resilience. That she remained deeply wounded was inevitable, and she was glad when, a few months later, she did not need to visit him in Cologne when she was passing through because he was not there at the time. Again, from this very small piece of information, we can glean much about this puzzling woman and the way she viewed people, the vicissitudes of life, and the complexity of human relationships.

As for Levin Schücking himself, our view of him is probably somewhat softened by the knowledge that he devoted so much of his life to the furtherance of her reputation. The 1844 edition of her works is a huge improvement on that of 1838 and when in 1860 he published the 'Last Gifts', he saw to it that she was at last known to a German public which for most of her life had been unaware of her existence. In addition, we owe to him, through his introduction to her works and the picture he gives in his autobiographical writings, a privileged account of her personality and her creative methods. Possibly he was the one person who could have supplied this information.

If we return now to that last poem, her farewell to him, we can place it, too, in a broader context. The letters she wrote to him after that blissful winter of 1841-42 leave no doubt that, rightly or wrongly, she attributed to him the surge in her creativity. "My talent rises and falls with your presence" she tells him. If only she could have a few minutes in his company every day, she would be able to write even more, she writes. She longed to be with him again, and when she returned to Westphalia after his departure, she fell into a deep depression and suffered terrible physical afflictions.

If, in the fullness of time, this courageous woman found the strength to stand alone as she bade him goodbye for the last time, this cannot surprise us. The wild muse of which she speaks is not Levin himself, but the force within her which he released. The last poems, written well after she had accepted the finality of their parting, speak a new language and reach heights barely anticipated before.

CHAPTER FIVE

A SELECTION OF THE POEMS OF ANNETTE VON DROSTE-HÜLSHOFF IN ENGLISH TRANSLATION

Annette von Droste-Hülshoff was drawn to writing from an early age, and some of her early poems show power and originality, but it is almost certainly true that the most formative influence on her creative activity was her friendship with Levin Schücking, as she maintained in her letter to him after he had left Meersburg: "whatever I become, I become because of you and for your sake" (Letter dated 5 May 1842). When he had come back into her life as an adult, in 1837, she was busy with a range of projects but lacked a sense of direction. She had the support of loyal friends, in particular Christoph Schlüter and Wilhelm Junkmann, but she lacked the experience to ensure that her work became known at a time when German literature was occupying an increasingly important position in Europe, and they too, for all their goodwill towards her, were insufficiently informed, too unworldly perhaps, to offer her sound guidance in this respect.

Moreover, she herself was hampered by the inhibitions she felt throughout her life. Her conviction that poetry was for her a sacred calling was counterbalanced by the sense, so often expressed, that she did not belong to the age and the environment into which she had been thrust, and that recognition would not come to her during her lifetime. The circumstances known of her, and the tendency of much of her writing, suggest that she may have been conscious of the relatively short span of time granted to her.

The relationship with Levin, however one views it, gave to her an exuberance and a sense of purpose which she needed at the time. She respected his judgement even if she did not greatly admire his own literary efforts, and one also senses that she enjoyed the equality of their unlikely association, which seems to have lacked the somewhat deferential attitude of her other close friendships. They enjoyed one another's company from the early days in the Rüschhaus, which he visited with increasing frequency after he joined the close circle in Münster in 1837, to their easy exchanges in Meersburg in the winter of 1841-1842. Cynics would have it that his thoughts were primarily on his own advancement, but this view is not borne out by the warmth with which, after her death, he writes of those months, by which time, admittedly, his name has become firmly linked with hers, to the benefit of them both. In one way, she did not need to be made into a poet, but she did need, it seems clear, to have her creative powers set free through the release of the emotion pent up within her since her earliest years. With that release came the flood of ideas which came to her at great speed, as she describes, and the ability to express them in some extraordinary language, and again, as she relates, at great speed.

Her manuscripts, with many crossings-out and often with alternative versions, bear witness to the way she worked and to the impact of inspiration almost out of control. Yet this is the same woman as the one who was assailed by doubts and prone to dark depression. Levin seemed able to raise her out of these moods and prompt her to activity and confidence. Most important, he recognized that her true domain was the lyric and urged her to pursue it, which she did almost exclusively for the remainder of her life. Thus her last eight years are marked by two peaks of activity, the winter of 1841-1842, which saw the two of them side by side in Meersburg, and the spring and late summer of 1844, when, following the marriage of Levin and Louise, and the acceptance that the love she believed she had for him must give way to her commitment to her poetic muse, she hurled herself into a consoling frenzy which produced some of her finest poems. It is as though what she identified as love was able, in the end, to express itself in the passion which was central to her being.

For a time, at least until the publication of *Die Ritterbürtigen* led to a bitter break between them, Levin Schücking remained in correspondence with her and facilitated the more representative and much more successful edition of her poetry published in 1844 by the renowned house of Cotta. The poems selected for translation in this volume belong largely to that period towards the end of her life, although some of them were written too late to be included in the 1844 edition and, apart from occasional appearances in periodicals and journals, had to await the posthumous collection by Schücking of 1860, entitled *Letzte Gaben* ('Last Gifts') and the complete edition of Droste-Hülshoff's work, again by Levin Schücking, of 1878/9. It is extraordinarily difficult to group her poems thematically, although she herself, and subsequent editions, did place some of them in groups (the *Heidebilder* – 'Images of the Heathland', for example, or the poems described as *Fels, Wald und See* – 'Cliff, Forest and Lake'). This difficulty stems from the fact that her themes overlap and merge into one another, so that it is characteristic of her that the poems defy rigid categorization, an aspect that adds to their fascination.

Some of her most interesting and challenging poems belong to collections that she described as 'Poems of Mixed Content', rather an interesting description in itself and one which points to the complexity of thought within individual poems and the range of her work. It is, of course, possible to follow a broadly chronological order, but this is not entirely satisfactory, since she very often held back poems for many months and even years, and their eventual appearance, or their publication, sometimes occurred long after the original impetus to their writing.

This is particularly the case with poems relating to her Westphalian homeland, many of which were actually written far off in Meersburg, when her present mood evoked memories of long before. What emerges clearly from collecting some of her most successful, or most obviously representative, lyric poems together in the way attempted here is both their striking range and, at the same time, the recurrence of themes. The aim is to introduce non-German speakers to a sadly inaccessible writer with the intention of demonstrating her extraordinary qualities, although, even as one articulates this aim, one is aware of the presumption of the enterprise. Anyone attempting to translate literature from one language into another must be aware that the result is likely to be less than adequate, and this is probably more the case with poetry than with any other form. The best one can hope is that the outcome is somewhat better than nothing.

Droste-Hülshoff's language is difficult, even to a native German speaker. She was writing two hundred years ago and seems to have had a facility for picking up dialect forms, of her homeland but also of her adopted home in the very south of Germany. Without being conventionally 'poetic', her diction is very distinctive and often highly evocative. Her imagery often takes one aback with its originality and even sometimes its sheer daring. The sound of her poems is powerful and often very beautiful. She produces remarkable cadences which one can only hope to emulate, but to do so without attempting to imitate either rhyme or metre. Already the presumption is coming closer to hubris, and yet the purpose is a sincere one and a valid one.

There is some important critical writing on Annette von Droste-Hülshoff, though inevitably much of it is in German. The bibliography, necessarily select and highlighting work in English, directs to further reading those who perhaps find in this volume the impetus to further investigation and more thought. The introductions to the individual poems are just that: brief pointers to further thinking and perhaps deeper understanding of a challenging writer to whom it was not granted, as she well knew, to be understood in her tragically short life but who now, with the perspective of the years, must rank highly in German and European literature. Not only that; she speaks to the human being who finds in her an experience which is recognizable. It seems appropriate to begin the selection of her poems with three which date from about the same time, before she had attempted publication, but which together show very different aspects of this puzzling and unrestful personality.

Farewell to Switzerland

On a green slope stands a pilgrim,
his gaze like a waking dream.
He makes his way along the broad path
and pushes through the area round the gorge.
Then he climbs up the rocky track
and speaks on the edge of the clouds:

You noble, gifted land,
with your valley so richly endowed,
your diamond heights,
across which soft perfumes waft,
and your deep emerald lakes,
what a torment you are to me!

You have never done me any harm,
nor is my gratitude to you small.
Yes, everything that you have bestowed,
I have carried the burden of your gifts
like a poor guest
and smiled as well

And no matter what else I am going to do
the wheel refuses to go on.
I look back and think back,
and turn my gaze backwards without wanting to.
Since the happiness of my youth fled from me
the spoke has been at a standstill, too.

Ah, your sounds have not awoken
a heart fast asleep;
and I laid a cold hand
into the fire of many a loyal right hand,
and tied only a playful ribbon
by way of a short-lived jest.

For through the fall of the rapids
there came the whispering over and over again:

"Where are you, my nightingale?
My row of poplars on the green embankment?
When will the yellow lotus **f)** show itself to me,
a ball of gentle waves?"

So farewell then for a long time,
you unloved land,
with the echo of your thunderclaps,
your stern wall of rocks,
the land where I found no nightingale,
and found no love.

f) The reference is probably to the bright yellow flowers which grow wild in water in Westphalia.

This relatively slight but rather telling poem was originally identified only by its first line. It was written at the end of her stay in Eppishausen, in the Thurgau, where, with her mother, Droste-Hülshoff spent a whole year in 1835-36 in the home of her only sister and her family. It is apparent that her host, the erudite and greatly esteemed Joseph von Lassberg, went out of his way to entertain his sister-in-law, and Annette was always close to her sister Jenny and the recently arrived twin girls, for whom, to the end of her life, she had the greatest affection. She appreciated the spectacular landscape and enjoyed, in moderation, the readings of medieval German literature which were a regular feature of their social evenings, but a long letter to her dear friend Schlüter, makes it clear that she did not share the Count's passion and desperately missed the company of much more like-minded friends at home in Münster.

The 'heaps of manuscripts' which filled the house and which were rapidly establishing Lassberg as a formidable expert in a subject that was becoming central to the early development of

Germanic scholarship, did not impress her, and she felt alone, even in the midst of a loving family. Above all, she was deeply homesick for her beloved Westphalia and felt frankly alien in Switzerland. She expressed herself in no uncertain terms, both in this poem, which, happily, remained unpublished until well after her death, and in the letter to Schlüter: "After all, the beloved face of a friend is worth much more than a thousand mountains, and if all the snow on them were silver-dust and every block of ice a hundredweight of crystal, I shall not be sorry to see again the brown heathland around Münster, and the good city of Münster, and still less [sorry to see] my Schlüter...", she wrote in November 1835, when ahead of her stretched almost a year of restricted and largely unproductive existence. It says much for the devotion of Jenny that the visit continued for so long, although she can have been in no doubt about her sister's unhappiness, and later, inviting her to join them in their new home in Meersburg, just across the border, she expressed her hope that this would be a more congenial experience.

A poem already mentioned in another context (see above, p.28) can appropriately be inserted again here:

The Right Time

In the cheerful room by candlelight,
when every lip is sparkling,
and, even drunk by the sunshine,
when every finger is breaking off flowers,
and when Nature swims in flames around
the mouth of the beloved:
that is not it, the right time,
that genius has ordained for you.

But when day as well as joy has sunk away,
then you will know a little place,

> perhaps in the cushions of your sofa,
> perhaps on a garden bench,
> then there will be a sound like a half-understood melody,
> and it will seem as if a shower of half-faded colours
> were flowing round you,
> and then gently, gently, your genius will touch you.

This is an important little poem, which Droste-Hülshoff actually included in the 1835 letter to Christoph Bernhard Schlüter and in which she voiced her extreme discomfort in Eppishausen. It shows a very different mood, and probably at least in part explains the distinctly disgruntled tone of the previous poem. She had become used to her own company and was increasingly aware of her poetic gift and the need she had to fulfil her vocation, but she must have felt hampered by the domestic life of the Lassberg family, devoted though she was to its members. In contrast, she shows here the compulsion she feels to write, but, by implication, that this can be achieved only when the time is right.

There is plenty of evidence that she could be a sociable companion and an amiable hostess, but this early poem tells also of the cost to her in terms of what increasingly she would see as a sacred duty laid upon her. Ordinary social intercourse must have militated against the opportunity to seize the precious moment, 'the right time' for inspiration to come to her. Other, later poems go further and speak of the suffering which comes with her vocation, for which, as she puts it, the poet pays quite simply with his very soul (see below p.226). She dismisses the two strophes as inconsequential when she writes to Schlüter, describing them as 'blameless'. However, she underestimates, as she is inclined to do at this point of a career barely begun, that the motivating force of her life is, and will remain, the awareness of the creative power within her, demonstrated so clearly and yet so early in 'Restlessness' and already with the additional ingredient of suffering, in 'Agony'.

The third poem chosen to demonstrate the range of her themes and her manner at this relatively early stage is very different from the other two. 'The Sick Eagle' treats in an allegorical manner the theme of status and calling. On the face of it, it is a slightly humorous account of the conversation between the bull, contentedly chewing the cud in the meadow, and the wounded eagle contemplating his miserable lot and the failure of his aspirations. However, the date was 1838, and Droste-Hülshoff was fully aware both of her passionate desire to write and the restrictions she was encountering as a woman and particularly as a woman of aristocratic background. This was one of the poems she put forward for her first slim volume, although in the event it was one of the many suggestions rejected. It is, however, probably a sign of the significance she attached to it that she set it to music, something she was not often moved to do. Like the eagle, she ultimately does not doubt the validity of her calling, and, though her wings may be clipped, she would always prefer to settle for a higher ambition and a superior standing. The very idea that an eagle should be satisfied with the humble alternative of the domestic existence of a hen, with all that that entails, is repugnant to the proud bird. His hopes have been destroyed, it seems, by his many rivals, but at least he had those hopes.

Members of Droste-Hülshoff's immediate circle were at one point adamant that she should make use of her talent for comedy, and although this view was almost certainly based on the impression she chose to convey to her nearest and dearest and disguised her actually deeply serious nature, there is a lighter veneer to this fable which expresses a very serious issue which must have preoccupied her as she contemplated the direction she should take and the possibilities open to her, or rather, not open to her.

The Sick Eagle

By the withered tree, in the lush green of the meadow,
a bull was contentedly chewing the cud.
On the lower branch sat a wounded eagle,
a sick eagle with broken wings,

"Fly up, my bird, into the blue sky.
I'll watch you from my fragrant herbs."
"Alas, alas, the sun is calling in vain
to the sick eagle with his broken wings."

"Oh bird, you used to be so proud and daring
and wanted never to be chained."
"Alas, too many above me,
and all of them eagles, broke my wings."

"Then flutter to your nest, away from that branch,
your moaning is spoiling my grassy patch."
"Alas, alas, I shall never have a nest again,
Banished eagle with the broken wings."

"Oh bird, if only you were a hen,
you would have a little nest inside the oven."
"Alas, I'd much rather be an eagle,
much rather an eagle with broken wings."

One of the most famous of Droste-Hülshoff's poems is the one which follows here. Written some time later, in that extraordinarily productive winter when she and Schücking enjoyed some precious months of closeness in Meersburg, it speaks, too, of her aspirations and her sense of being restricted by circumstances. Yet the exuberance of the poem is quite different from the resignation of 'The Sick Eagle', and the passion with which she describes the waves below as she stands on the tower suggests that, probably for the first and only time in her life, she sees the fulfilment of her hopes in this joyful period of unrestrained emotion.

On the Tower

I stand on the tower, high up on the balcony,
with the shrieking starling circling above me,
and like a maenad **f)** I let
the storms ruffle my flowing hair.
Oh, wild companion, oh, crazy lad,
I should like to grip you tightly,
and, sinew against sinew, two steps from the edge,
wrestle for life or death.

And down below on the shore
I see tall waves tumbling, like mastiffs playing,
yapping and hissing,
and tossing shiny snowflakes about.
Oh, I should like to jump in with no more ado,
right into the raging mob,
and chase the walrus, the merry prey,
through the coral forest.

And in the distance I see a pennant waving,
bold as a banner,
see the boat turning this way and that
from my airy watchtower.
Oh, I should like to sit in the battling ship,
seize the rudder
and like a sea-gull move hissing
over the foaming reef.
If I were a huntsman in the open field,
or even a bit of a soldier.

> If I were simply just a man,
> heaven would advise me.
> As it is I must sit so refined and sweet,
> like a good little girl,
> and can only secretly loosen my hair
> and let it flutter in the wind.

> **f)** In Greek mythology the maenads are female followers of Dionysus and traditionally associated with uncontrolled frenzy, induced by drink or ecstatic dancing.

The final strophe makes it clear that the constraints which bind her relate to her being a woman, forced by that very fact to suppress the passion which overwhelms her as she contemplates the raging waters below and longs to become a part of them. The physical struggle she envisages is with the elements themselves, and for once she expresses this physical urge which for most of her life she concealed, learning to acquiesce, as she put it in the poem 'Restlessness' of her teenage years (see above p.3). There is little of acquiescence here, as she describes the struggle on the cliff-top with her 'wild companion', 'her crazy lad' – the storm itself – or imagines herself jumping into the foam. The boat in the distance lures her as she watches from the tower which, as we know, actually did confine her.

Years later, in his *Lebenserinnerungen*, Levin Schücking was to describe the room in which she spent her days, a round room in the tower of the castle, apart from the family, where she could be alone, "like a solitary tower swallow, thinking, dreaming and not doing very much" and she herself wrote to Louise Schücking from her later visit to Meersburg of being confined like "a bird in its egg with much less desire to emerge from it" (Letter 4 March 1844). Yet from that confined space and the insuperable restrictions she knew to exist around her came some of her most serene and most nearly carefree poetry, in months which saw her attaining a personal peak and the beginning of her artistic fulfilment.

That is by no means to say that the poems which emerged at this point from the famous wager between her and Levin all have the relative lightness of touch which marks 'On the Tower' or the gentle warmth of 'The Inn on the Lake' (see above). Already in that second poem, the mellow pleasure in the autumn afternoon is tempered with a sense of nostalgia and the awareness of the chasm which threatens to open up between the two friends, while 'On the Tower' leaves no doubt that the reckless imaginings of the speaker cannot be fulfilled. This prevailing sadness, at times bleakness, pervades many other poems of this period, a number of which must have had their source in her solitary months in the brooding countryside of her beloved Westphalia, before she came down to join her family in the more obviously lovely surroundings of Lake Constance. Again one notes the impact of Levin Schücking and his capacity to prompt her to put into words thoughts that must have been crowding into her mind for a long time already. Thus a poem very typical of those she produced during the frenzy of writing in the 'Meersburg winter' of 1841-1842, 'Farewell to Youth', is again characterised by her ambivalent view of her subject, and the ambivalence of her treatment of it.

Farewell to Youth

Just as the trembling exile
stands on the borders of his homeland,
he turns his face back,
his eyes turn back gleaming,
winds which pass gently across,
birds envied in the air,
shuddering before the little piece of land,
which separates one country from another,

how the graves of his dead ones,
his living ones, the dear ones,
all stand on the horizon,
and, weeping, he must greet them.
All the little trinkets of love,
unrecognized and unperceived,
all burn him like sins,
and like ever-open wounds.

Thus, too, on the threshold of his youth,
a heart stands, full of proud dreams
and looks into their paradises,
and the barren chambers of the future,
his aspirations, withered away,
his hopes buried,
all stand on the horizon
and wish to give way to tears.

And the years which slowly, cunningly,
strung themselves together from the minutes,
all break out in his heart,
all now bleed like wounds,
with his poor, meagre possessions,
plundered from the rich shaft,
devoid of courage, a broken wanderer,
he steps into the foreign land.

And yet the summer's sheaf
is not smaller than the blossoms,

and only in the damp earth
can the new seed protect itself.
The river must pass over rocks and barren plains,
before it can broaden itself out,
and the right hand of God blesses
the day after tomorrow just as it blesses today.

The opening of the poem suggests the Romantic idea of the wanderer at the crossroads, surveying the open countryside which is his future, but this idea soon gives way, in the second strophe, to a starker thought as he contemplates the losses which lie behind him, and the memory of which will remain ahead for him. This thought prompts the immensely moving second half of the second strophe, which speaks of 'all the little trinkets of love, unrecognized and unperceived', a formulation which echoes in another poem of the same period, 'In the Moss' where, in a heightened state of nocturnal musing, she sees herself as an old woman, arranging 'dusty tokens of love in the ancestral chest', and summons up a vision of herself weeping 'lifeless tears' for loved ones long departed.

Thus, on the threshold of his youth, this exile trembles with the awareness of that which was to be and has not been, the hopes and dreams which have come to nothing and the inexorable passing of time. Only the final strophe brings an alleviation of this barren landscape, with a somewhat surprising lifting of the mood into an optimism not often found in Droste-Hülshoff, but occasionally glimpsed in 'The Spiritual Year'. For it seems to be faith which wins through as the poem closes, and the rarely evident confidence in a divine order of things, in which all will be ultimately well.

Much of her poetry during this period is characterised by nostalgia, and very often this shows itself as a preoccupation with loved ones often now long dead. Margaret Mare, in her very sound, largely factual book, comments on the affinity Droste-Hülshoff seems to have had with the departed, seeking comfort from them, and counsel. This preoccupation, which amounts almost to an obsession, gives many of her poems a deep, brooding sadness, but, just as 'Farewell to Youth' is lightened by the confidence in ultimate serenity, so the often heart-rending grief of other poems can be counteracted by the security which she derives from the memory of past love and loyalty, for she was a woman of very deep affection and enduring commitment.

This is evident not only in the many letters she wrote to close friends and relatives but in the poems she specifically dedicated to individual people. It also marks many of the very moving poems she wrote at this time of her life, when she was enjoying an important new phase through her friendship with Levin Schücking, but also, in some respects more significantly, gaining in her awareness of her poetic destiny. Thus her writing at this stage finds her pondering on those loved ones who belong so crucially to important phases of her past life, and the tone is not so much of regret and loss, as of an understanding of what they meant to her.

Two poems in particular demonstrate this quality, 'The Yew Hedge' and 'The Bench'. They must have been written within weeks of one another, while she was staying in Meersburg but deep in thought of events and times intimately related to her life in the place of her birth and in earlier years. Past and present merge in both of them, but they are, surprisingly perhaps, not tainted by thoughts of old age and decline, still less of her own death, though this frail woman, now well into her middle-age was more than capable of expressing such thoughts at other times.

The Yew Hedge

I love to stand before you,
you with your surface black and rough,
you jagged visor before the face of my beloved.
I like to stand before you,
as though before a cloth painted with one first coat
and see sliding over it
the pale coronation procession,

when it was my crown,
given by hands that now are cold,
when people sang to me in melodies
now old,
a curtain across a sacred place,
the gate of paradise to me,
all flowers behind it
and in front of it all thorns.

For on the other side, I know it,
is the green garden bench,
where I drank the beginnings of life
with glowing lips,
when my hair fell about me in waves,
still golden in the light of the sun,
and when my cry still rang out,
the sound of a horn, through the valley.

The fragile spray of ivy,
which love tended there,
six steps and I know,
I know then, that it's gone.
And so I will venture only
as far as your dark cloth
and wipe out eighteen years
from the book of my life.

At that time you were already
staring out, as dark and faithful as today.
You, the throne of our love,
and many a time our watchman.
They say that sleep, a harmful sleep,
comes out of your needles like smoke,
but ah! I was never more awake
than when I was surrounded by your breath.

But now I am tired
and I should like to slip down beside you
like a leaf,
thrown by the nearest tree.
You draw me to you like a harbour
when all storms are silenced.
Ah, I should like to sleep, sleep,
until my time is passed.

This moving poem belongs to the large group which emerged during her first stay in Meersburg in the winter of 1841-42, but it is likely that the idea for it, or indeed perhaps an early version, was in existence before she left the Rüschhaus. What is known is that in the early summer of 1837, while staying with her relatives in Abbenburg, she had visited Bökendorf, the scene of her meeting with Heinrich Straube and all that that entailed. It had taken seventeen years for her to return to Bökendorf, where she had suffered such grief and humiliation, and this poem says much about the love she believed she had felt for Straube. It implies a great deal, too, about the memories this return after such a long period of self-imposed absence must have stirred in her. Like so many of her poems, particularly of this period of her life, it exists on several levels, with the yew hedge the link between that distant experience and her thinking about it at the time of writing, but also the recollection of her return to stand before the hedge twenty years later. The whole effect is deeply poignant, and the poem is a fine example of her capacity to express emotion with heart-rending honesty.

The letter she wrote to her cousin Anna von Haxthausen soon after the events of that, to her, devastating summer had left no doubt of the impact upon her, which meant that the rift between her and her Haxthausen relatives had taken a long time to heal, and one can only imagine what it had taken for her to return to the actual place eighteen years later. The poem stresses the intensity of the love she experienced at that time, with the third strophe emphasising the youthfulness she recalls in the references to the 'beginnings of life', her 'glowing lips' and her fair hair glinting in the sun. Of this love, her description of which leaves no doubt that it was a reality, the yew hedge was the guardian, this formidable wall of dark, rough growth, unchanged as she stood before it on that visit. That is the constant in the passage of the years, protecting the lovers then from prying eyes and still the custodian of their secret. Yet beyond that hedge she will not venture, knowing that all else has changed, that hands are cold and melodies long past.

The message of the poem is, again, resignation; not the negative acceptance of what cannot be changed, as in 'On the Tower', but a gentler emotion, epitomised in the sleep which is now dispensed by the needles of the tree. This, it would seem, is her deliberate attempt to put the past behind her, to wipe out the pain of eighteen years and surrender to the weariness which overwhelms her. It is sleep rather than death which she appears to be embracing, though that too will come.

The images which close this poem are gentle ones, of the leaf swept from the tree, the boat drawn to its harbour, and they balance the starker one with which it opens, as the hedge seems to resemble a knight in armour, upright and protective, and, above all, unmoving and unmoved.

A similar mood of calm acceptance pervades 'The Bench' which belongs in theme and mood with 'The Yew Hedge'. Written at about the same time, it too speaks of a bench and a tree, but there is evidence to suggest that she is thinking of another time and a different love. Although she is writing this in Meersburg, probably after Levin's departure in May 1842, she is deep in thought of the countryside around the Rüschhaus, where they had spent some very contented times. It is typical of her to merge distinct times and distinct places, and this is what she does here, as well as in a letter to him dated 27 May 1842, when she reminds him of how she used to sit and wait for him, on a bench among some oak trees, with her telescope in her hand, watching as he approached.

This is what she describes in 'The Bench', but it is not only Levin Schücking she is watching for. Two other figures from her past can be identified. The pious old man in his simple garment is her dear friend Kaspar Wilmsen, chaplain at Hülshoff, who had died in February of the previous year and whose passing she had lamented in an emotional letter to her sister Jenny. This kind of allegiance was characteristic of the loyal Annette, who formed close bonds with a wide range of people and showed in her letters what an active part she played in all their lives.

A much earlier loss is recorded here, too, for the 'dear boy, slim and blond' of the fourth strophe is her younger brother Ferdinand, a great favourite of hers, a sickly young man who died before he was thirty. These two characters, the aged clergyman and the young boy, do not need to be depicted in greater detail: the total commitment to his vocation of the former as he struggles on his missions, and the carefree progress of the doomed youth are enough to identify them and the place in her heart and her memory. She is capable of great delicacy in such vignettes, and great perception in her understanding of her fellow beings.

However, these friends are dead, and the time is long since past. Once more, as in 'The Yew Hedge', she sees herself poised between past and future, suspended in a present that looks both ways. Yet the phantom of the last two strophes belongs, as we know, to the present, and though she situates herself in this little spot in Westphalia, one can assume that she watched and waited for him, too, in their favourite haunts above the Lake.

Although both these poems, very beautiful in their own ways, have a lingering sadness, they do not have the stark, harrowing sense of loss of which she was capable and which so often reveals itself in deep sorrow. Yet this was another mood which she projected in the poems of this amazing period of her creative life and which is exemplified in a number of poems in this selection.

The Bench

I know a bench in the park.
It is not the most shady one,
but elder trees, slim and spare,
cast scant lines across it.
There I sit on many a summer's day
and let the sun warm me.
Round about me is no sound of splashing water,
but in my heart a spring spurts up.

This is the place where
one can survey the paths in all directions,

the dusty track, the green path,
and over there the clearing among the oak trees.
Ah, many, many precious ways
have flown beneath the wheel!
All that delights and troubles me
comes only from that place.

You pious old man in your simple garment,
faithful friend for twenty years.
to whom no journeys were too difficult or too long,
if it meant observing the sacred office.
How often did I see you raise the heavy barrier
with unskilled hands,
and see your little cap as it gradually
climbed along the bank of the stream?

And you, my dear boy, slim and blond,
so dear to me in the depths of my heart,
with your shotgun and your brown dog,
with your clear eyes and cheerful tongue,
how often did I hear you whistling as you approached,
when you were speaking to your hound?
My dear brother, if only it were really you,
why should my heart not be beating?

And many a thing that time has blown away,
and many that time has left to grow cold,
pass like the procession of Banquo's kings
and trot out of the gaps in the forest.
And no matter what still remains to me,
or what blossoms anew in the garden of my life,
I must await the happy band of friends
from over on the other side.

And so I sit for hours as though transfixed,
half in yesterday, half in today,
my trusty telescope in my hand,
and let it pass gently across the distance.
There is a wild bush by the stream:
Ah, it has deceived me shamefully,

for if the wind catches it I believe
that someone dear is coming towards me.

He knows how to walk with every step,
to adapt his every gesture,
and so too he can stand on the slope,
a precious phantom and a loved deceit.
But I hope that for ever and ever,
as long as I have life,
I can warm myself here in the sun,
a patient martyr to my devotion.

Annette von Droste-Hülshoff's introspective nature is evident almost wherever one looks in her work, but rarely more so than in the poem which follows, again dating from that winter of 1841-42. The theme of 'The Reflection' is clear from the title on, particularly in the German word *Spiegelbild*, for here she is looking intently at herself in a mirror and assessing what she sees with the self-critical, self-accusing stance so typical of her. It is significant that a close analysis of this poem by Clemens Heselhaus, one of the foremost experts on Droste-Hülshoff, is included as one of the three devoted to her in Benno von Wiese's comprehensive account of German Lyric Poetry (1959), while, a generation later, Wilhelm Gössmann focuses on it in his pursuit of an understanding of this enigmatic poet, *Annette von Droste-Hülshoff. Ich und Spiegelbild*, 1985. Both of these eminent critics, each with an acute insight into her nature and a rare understanding of her poetry, recognize that this poem, which sees her looking deep into her own image in the mirror and accepting it without distortion or disguise, is a vital key to her as a person and as an artist, and to the intermingling of the two.

At its most basic, the theme may be seen as the Romantic motif of the double, the *Doppelgänger*, but, of course, she handles it in her own way and in the process says something very different with it and something which goes to the heart of the enigma which she represented to those close to her, and to herself. No-one was more aware of the contradictions within her than Droste-Hülshoff herself, and she expresses this on a number of occasions, suggesting that she was not always comfortable with herself and that this unease may have been the source of some of her unhappiness. When she admitted, in her poem addressed to Levin Schücking (see p. 95 above), that there was much in her which was 'abrupt and stiff', she swiftly sought to redress this acknowledgement with her next statement, which speaks of her 'second, gentler conscience'. So it is with this poem, and in the course of it she moves from awe and even fear at the image she contemplates to the realization that, were she to meet this image, this 'Phantom', face to face, her response would be to weep.

This final line would seem to be the answer to the question implied at the end of the second strophe when she says she does not know if she would love or hate this image, this other self of hers. The poem is full of contradictions and antitheses, like the woman herself, one senses. The two people who knew her best, Schlüter and Schücking, both expressed this in their own ways: Schlüter, who loved and respected her very deeply, and to whom she remained devoted to the end of her life, in his simple but totally sincere admission that she was an enigma to him and his sadness that her faith did not seem to bring her real and lasting happiness, and Schücking in his extraordinarily apt summary of the nature of her poetry, which combined the two distinct sides of her personality, 'lyric strength...the depth of a truly feminine sensibility... the softness in the depths of her heart and her poetic soul' (a paraphrase rather than a translation of what he says in German) and 'simultaneously the coolly critical approach and the brooding scepticism and urge for knowledge.'

We lack convincing information about how her mother and her sister saw their much-loved relative, but it is likely that the one accepted her without pretending to understand her and the other regarded her with sheer love and loyalty. When she herself looks into the mirror, she sees what others see and consistently remarks upon the striking eyes and the deep forehead. The contrasts are there: warm blood turned to ice, dark hair turned light. This is a face that she knows but does not truly recognize, and the explanation comes: a double light is playing round it, confusing the onlooker, who is almost repelled by the haughty look, the cold gaze. The images she uses are those of subservience and sovereignty; the attitude is of meekness in the face of scorn and aggression. Like Moses venturing on to holy ground, she approaches shoeless. It is strange, yet with the suffering there is pleasure, and there is no escaping the awareness that they are related: two sides, as she knows, of the same being.

This is indeed a powerful poem, and an important one, written at a most significant time in her life when she was almost overwhelmed with new emotions, some of them unfamiliar to her: the stirring of her poetic gifts and the realization that they were becoming very real and tangible, and the dawning recognition of the special emotions she was feeling for Levin Schücking. These two things cannot be separated, and they come together in this remarkable poem.

It is worth noting that the title she gave to it was originally '<u>My</u> Reflection', and the change is important. This is a conversation with a separate being: the address throughout is 'you'. Interesting also is the calm that characterises this address, though the content is overwhelming. There is a steady recognition of the facts she presents, and, although there are striking images, they are not the sometimes grandiose ones of which she is capable, but almost simply stated, in keeping with the restraint she maintains throughout this moving experience.

The Reflection

When you gaze at me out of the crystal
with the misty balls of your eyes,
like fading comets,
with features in which strangely
two souls creep round each other like spies,
then indeed I whisper:
Phantom, you are not like me.

You have simply escaped the protection of dreams,
to turn my warm blood to ice
and make my dark locks pale,
and yet, you slowly dawning face,
in which, strangely, a double light is playing,
if you were to step forward, I do not know
if I would love or hate you.

I would glance meekly towards the sovereign throne of your brow,
where your thoughts offer their fealty, like vassals,
but, shy guest that I am,
I would move my stool far, far away
from the cold, glazed look in your eyes,
full of dead light, almost broken, ghostly.

And that which plays about your mouth,
so gentle, soft and helpless, like a child,
that I would like to conceal in loyal protection
and, again, if it plays scornfully,
as though aimed by a taut bow,

if it whirls quietly through your features,
then I would like to flee as if from henchmen.

It is certain that you are not I,
but an alien being whom I approach
like Moses, shoeless,
full of powers I know not of,
full of strange suffering and strange pleasure.
May God have mercy on me if your soul
rests slumbering in my breast.

And yet I feel myself as if related,
held spellbound by your shuddering,
and love must unite with fear.
Yes, Phantom, if you were to step out of the
ball of crystal and on to the ground,
then I would tremble gently and it seems to me
that I would weep for you.

In many of the poems written during this important and productive winter in Meersburg in 1841-42, and in the months she spent back in the Rüschhaus the following year, Droste- Hülshoff is very much present, reflecting on a deeply personal issue. Very often that issue is death. It has already been seen that her relationship with the departed is a close one, giving her comfort and counsel. Nowhere is this more apparent than in the next poem chosen for inclusion here, a poem so important that it could not be omitted from any selection of her lyric poetry. It belongs with poems which critics usually call *Totengedichte* ('Poems of the Dead' not 'Poems of Death'), but interestingly, when she came to select and arrange poems for the 1844 edition, she placed it with just two others in the introduction and this decision provides an important clue to its context. It follows 'My Calling', and from that one can reasonably conclude that the journey on which she is about to embark, this 'sombre venture' as she describes it, is her poetic vocation.

Her reputation was beginning to be established, and, with the appearance of the 1844 edition, under the direction this time of Levin Schücking and with the eminent house of Cotta to give it credence, she was at last on her way to the public recognition she had hoped for. That this, in the event, would be limited during her lifetime is irrelevant. That the third poem in this small group is the one addressed to Katharina Schücking (see above) surely suggests that she wished to pay tribute to the person who, more than anyone else, was responsible for this consolidation of her place in the literature of that time.

The poems eventually recognized as dedicated to Levin himself appeared in this edition, but in the body of the work, and often under a disguise. Meanwhile, this poem is very much of that time and very characteristic of her, as she seeks the blessing of her dear departed at their graves. This woman, who lived so much in her past, acknowledges what these loved ones have given to her. Silent they may be now, but their voices still sustain her. When she speaks of Nature in discord, she is referring, surely, not to a cosmic turmoil, but to her own turbulent existence, and the part these faithful ones, their hands cold, their eyes now lifeless, have played in bringing her to this point.

My Dead Ones

When someone sets out on a sombre journey,
in need of blessing and fair wind,
he gazes longingly into the distance,
in search of the warmth of a loving eye,
the fervent press of a hand,
a word to accompany him on his way.

I am embarking on a sombre venture,
and so I come to you,
my severe and silent dead ones.

I have woken up upon your tomb.
Your voice has summoned me
from water, fire, earth and air.

When Nature was in discord
and through the turmoil of the clouds
there broke a spark from those thousand suns,
did you not from the conflict of the elements
speak of eternity
and the fountain of eternal light?

I crept along the slope, sick and tired,
and you brought towards me with whispered warnings
the limp leaf;
you smiled at me from the encircling wave
and from the frozen ice of the green patches
opened wide the flowers.

That which must course through my veins,
did I not see it burst into flames and then burn itself out,
not turn cold on your shrine?
From your eyes you breathed out the radiance,
you, my judges, who alone
hold the balance in your faithful hands.

The press of your hand is cold,
the fire from your eyes has been extinguished,
and the sound you uttered is the breath of desolation,
yet no other right hand presses so loyally,
no eye has had this look,
no word is uttered like this vapour from the grave.

I grasp the staff of your Cross
and incline my head towards the grasses,
the silent grasses of your graves f).
Loved most of all, first greeted,
let truth, flowing purely as the ether,
well up in my soul.

f) The grasses may not speak, but popular belief had it that their breath communicates with the living. That is the truth which they will give to her and which she, in turn, will pass on through her words.

The link with her beloved homeland remains, though not specifically identified, in the next poem from this time, 'In the Moss'. It is a beautiful, evocative poem which anticipates some of the even more striking ones of her last years, the brilliant 'Moon-Rise', for example (see below, p.272). She is there throughout, as the observer, musing on the emotions prompted by what she says is a specific experience, lying alone in the forest as night approaches and absorbing with all her senses both the setting and what it means to her. Time is important here, the time of day, but also her position in time more generally, as she contemplates 'the passage of the years' and even the prospect of her own death.

However, this is a gentler poem than some of those already considered, without the stark sense of loss so dominant in them, and the absence of consolation. Indeed, there is a richness here, particularly in the first two strophes which evoke the atmosphere of the occasion through her senses, of sight and sound and fragrance. Droste-Hülshoff's famous powers of observation and her closeness to nature are apparent and employed with extraordinary effect and quite without pedantry. The language and imagery she uses are effective because they are so simple, although she was capable at other times of convoluted and sustained imagery, and language of bewildering obscurity. When she describes the stars as 'soft messengers of the twilight' coming to the 'sun-weary land', she achieves so much with what looks like effortless simplicity. The silence is palpable, broken only by the sound of the caterpillar as it gnaws away, and the beating of her own heart, stirred as it is to memories of past experiences, and then to visions of the future. Once more she bridges time as she does with such skill so often.

When present time gives way to thoughts of the future, these come with another dimension, for she sees herself, old and frail, busying herself with mementos of loved ones long since departed and contemplating the very personal reminders they have left behind to be treasured by her. In this state, real or imagined, she comes before the names on the tomb and appeals to her loved ones in prayer rather as she does in 'My Dead Ones'. The purpose is different here, however: she does not seek support on a destined journey, for she is deep in a reverie which lies beyond that. When the cry of the quail breaks into this state of deep thought, it cuts across that moment but it cannot dispel her thoughts. In the second strophe, characteristically, she had likened the distant light, now described as a star, to a huge glow-worm, before understanding that it must, rationally, be the light from the lamp in the home she has walked away from that evening. However, that now undergoes a further transformation, in the context of what she has just experienced, and the poem ends with an implied question. Given the merging throughout of past and present, and both with the future, that reassuring light could just as easily be the light which will one day be placed upon her grave.

In the Moss

Once lately when the night had sent forth
soft messengers of the twilight to the sun-weary land,
I was lying alone in the mossy forest.
The dark branches were nodding so tenderly,
the plants were whispering at my cheek.
Unseen, the wild rose of the heathland sent out its fragrance.

And through the lime-tree I could see
a faint light that the tree seemed to be carrying in its branches
like a mighty glow-worm.
It looked as indistinct as a vision,
and yet I knew it was the light of my home,
burning in my own room.

CHAPTER FIVE

Such silence all around that among the leaves
I could hear the caterpillar gnawing away, and little flakes of leaves
gently whirled about and landed on me like green dust.
I lay there and thought – ah! - of so many things.
I could hear my own heart beating,
and it almost seemed to me as if I had already fallen asleep.

Thoughts surfaced, one upon another:
the games of children, the swift passage of the years,
faces which had long been strange to me.
Forgotten sounds buzzed round my ears,
and finally present-time stepped forward,
and there the wave was standing, as on the edge of the shore.

Then, like a spring which runs away in the gorge,
and comes gushing back up from the ground,
I stood there suddenly, in the land of the future.
I saw myself, small and completely bent,
my eyes weak, carefully tidying up
dusty tokens of love in the ancestral chest.

I could distinctly see the pictures of my loved ones,
in costumes that were now old-fashioned,
and I saw myself releasing from their faded wrappings
little locks of hair, decayed and almost turned to dust,
and saw a lifeless tear
run slowly down my furrowed cheek.

And then again, in the graveyard upon the monument
on which stood names familiar to my love,
I lay praying, on my bended knees,
and – listen! – a quail was singing and a cool breeze passed over me,
and finally I saw myself, like smoke
gently drawn into the pores of the earth.

I got up suddenly and shook myself,
like one who has just escaped near-death,
and swayed along the dark hedgerows,
still not knowing whether the star on the ridge
was really the lamp beside my bed,
or the everlasting light upon my coffin.

Very different in intention, but another example of Droste-Hülshoff's imaginative powers, is the next poem, in which she fuses seascape and landscape to extraordinary effect. Once more, in 'The Steppe', she chooses a time of day to which she must have been particularly sensitive, the mysterious twilight time when day and night are precariously in balance and the light can play tricks on the eyes. No answers are given, or perhaps even invited, in this brief poem, of which the first two of three strophes end in a question. This time the illusion is optical but fed by the imagination of the poet who addresses herself to an unknown companion, or to her reader, and invites him or her to follow her in the strange transformations she proposes.

Her acute observation is there, of course: the rivulets of rain in the sand, the yellowing foam on the waves, the single pine-tree, but this can all be changed to suit her vision of it, and then changed back again. Although the third strophe does not end in a question, the questions are there. Is this land or sea? are those shepherds' carts or cannons? what is this about lighted fuses? Is that in fact a pine-tree, or a ship? and who is the only human figure in the picture, and is he there at all?

Of course, the answers are unimportant, for this is, as much as anything, an exercise in illusion, and a demonstration of the human mind's capacity to entertain illusion, something that Droste-Hülshoff does in many ways on many occasions. Above all, as it stands, it is an interesting addition to the fascinating range of this unique poet.

The Steppe

Did you ever stand upon the shore
when day and night are balancing one another,
and see the channels of rain
slowly approaching out of lime and sand,
numerous little streams for smugglers,
and then, as far as eye can see,
the waves of the sea,
coloured with yellow lather?

Here is the dune, and down below
the sea. There are shepherds' carts
resembling cannons, their ignited fuses
sliding along the ground.
Is it intended for the corsair
in his fluttering kaftan
whom I can make out in the yellow ocean?

He seems to be tying the rope.
The dune is hiding his ship,
yet the mast can be seen towering up,
a withered giant of a pine-tree.
From the distaff of the mast-head
the ropes (hang) taut as branches,
and the crow's nest, rough and dark,
(looks) like a harrier's nest

'The Steppe', which must have had its origins in the barren heathland of her native Westphalia, may have received its final form in the very different landscape of Meersburg, and the same is true of the following poem, which could hardly be more different in form and content but which shows yet another aspect of her active imagination and her skill in putting this into words. Given the overall title 'The Pond', this is a long poem, divided into sections, each attributed to a distinct feature of the pond. In it she shows her acute powers of observation and, combined with them, the sharp, sometimes almost humorous, quality of her imagination. This time the poet is not directly involved, save as an observer, as she describes the pond, the reeds at its edge and the overhanging linden tree, whose branches protect the water weeds beneath it. However, she leaves the speaking to the reeds, the tree and the water weeds, as each describes its relationship with the pond.

Thus far, this is pure description, marked by Droste-Hülshoff's sharp observation of natural things and her awareness of the interrelationships among them. That each in turn speaks for itself underlines the personification that has been present since the opening strophe, when the pond itself is lying peacefully like – a very characteristic image – 'a virtuous conscience'. Each natural growth has its own personality and responds differently to the pond which is the focus. From their vantage point the reeds can observe the movement above the pond: the dragonfly and the bird flying over it, but also the movement of the linden tree which will be the next speaker and the shadow of the bird reflected in the water of the pond, 'like a fish slithering by'. The pond itself is motionless, until something touches it, like the twig falling from the beak of the linnet as it makes it way to its nest. In the first two strophes it is 'peace' and 'sleep' which dominate, but when the linden tree makes its speech, there is a different mood, for its function is to shelter the pond and protect it, from the birds and the insects, but also from the sun.

So many impressions are piling up, gently but surely, and by now we are aware of two silent individuals, the poet watching and whispering, as we know from the first strophe, of what he sees, and the sleeping shepherd. Even a caterpillar plays a rather passive part.

By now, however, there is a further element, for the sun is shining harshly in what appears to be the middle of the day. The heat which the children will use as their pretext to leave and go home at the end of the poem is already causing discomfort to the tree.

And so we move to the water-weeds, who know that they are the object of envy, protected from the heat in the crystal water which reflects the stars and the sun above the pond. So intimate is the link between the weeds in the water and the sky above that Droste-Hülshoff can speak of blood relationships, and of the weeds as boring their way into the heart of the pond 'like a loving woman'. They in their turn protect the creatures of the pond, the loach and the carp, and the 'noble water fairy', identified as the lovely trifolium flower, with its brief, majestic life, gives its trust only to the water weeds.

Thus, with an amazing accumulation of detail, Droste-Hülshoff builds up this picture of mutual dependence and perfect accord. But then the tone of the poem changes suddenly, with the intrusion of the children by the side of the pond, commenting, but in a different, childish way, on the features already mentioned. However, their excitement is short-lived, for something else lurks in the pond: potential danger in the form of the Water-Man of popular superstition. Just as the Heath-Man inspires fear in her poem of that name, so does this creature, his face concealed among those water-weeds which hitherto represented no threat, cause them to abandon their bravado – they were all set to wade into the water and poke about with a stick, and they were not scared of frogs and pikes - and go home.

The Pond

It lies so silent in the morning light,
so peacefully: like a virtuous conscience.
When west winds kiss the mirror of its surface,
the flower of the shore does not feel it.
Dragonflies tremble above it,
little sticks of blue and gold and dark red,
and on the reflection of the sun
the water-spider performs its dance.
A wreath of irises grows upon the bank
and listens to the lullaby of the reeds.
A gentle whispering sound rises and falls,
as though it were saying: peace, peace, peace.

The Reeds

"Be quiet, it is sleeping: quiet, quiet!
Dragonfly, move your wings gently,
so that the gold web does not make its humming sound,
and you green plants on the bank, keep on your guard,
and do not let a pebble drop.
It is sleeping on its downy cloud
and above it the ancient tree makes its leaves
whisper as they swirl about.
High above, where the sun is shining,
a bird flaps its wings
and its shadow passes through the mirror of the pond
like a fish slithering by.
Silent, silent, it has stirred:
a falling branch that a linnet was just bringing to its nest
has brushed it.
Sh, sh! spread out your green cloth, branch:
Sh, sh! now it is fast asleep."

The Linden tree

"I spread out my leafy roof over it,
as far as I can stretch it from the bank.

Look how far my arms reach out
to shoo away from it with my fans the insects
which tremble in the air and in a hundred colours.
I breathe the best fragrance of my breath on it,
and onto its resting-place I drop
the loveliest of all my blossoms.
And against my trunk leans a bench
where from the bank gazes a poet
whom I hear whispering amazing songs
of me and you and the dragonfly, so softly
as not to awaken the pious shepherd.
Otherwise in truth the caterpillar
which I flung out of the leafy hedge
would have frightened him.
How harshly the sun is shining! The day is becoming heavy.
Oh, if only, if only I could stretch out my roots
right into the middle of the deep crystalline basin,
like the water-weeds which, greenish asbestos,
peer so comfortably out of the watery nest,
as though scornful of me, standing here alone on the edge of the bank,
parched with thirst in the burning sun.

The Water-weeds

"Envy us, envy us! Let your branches hang down,
not because we drink liquid crystal
and the stars of heaven twinkle
and the sun has become caught up in our nest:
no, it holds us all clasped to its breast,
the blood relation of the pond,
and we bore our delicate weeds
into its heart, like a loving woman,
force our way like veins through its body,
dawn like the thoughts of waking dreams.
Anyone who knows us calls us sweet and loyal,
and the loach and the mother carp
hide their brood in our protection.
Waves can caress in our veil.
The noble water-fairy trusts only us,

the beautiful one, more lovely than the rose.
Open up your bells, Trifolium :
your day is short, but its course is regal!"

Children on the bank

"Just look! Can you not see the cloud of flowers
over there in the deepest hollow in the pond?
Oh, that is beautiful! If only I had a stick!
Chalices, white as lard with dark red spots,
the coiffeur of each bell so fine,
like our little wax angels in the cabinet.
What do you think? Shall I cut a hazel twig
and wade down a little way into the pond?
Pah! Frogs and pikes cannot scare me –
Only… can the water-man perhaps be
lurking there in the long weeds?
I'm going, I'm going…..I'm not going.
It seems to me that I saw a face at the bottom.
Come on, let's go home! The sun is burning!"

The next two poems chosen for inclusion here belong to those months of 1841-42, and they belong together in their evocation of Lake Constance and, beside it, the old castle. Artistically, they also belong with the preceding poem, in their detailed description of place and atmosphere. Yet, whereas 'The Pond' has its source in her life in Westphalia, as a child and a young woman, and more recently, in the time she spent in the Rüschhaus before making the journey to Meersburg, these two are clearly linked to her more recent observation of the beauty of the Lake, where, as we know, she spent a great deal of time watching and thinking. What emerges from these periods of contemplation is her own thoughts about the nature of the Lake and its past. This is very much her own response to its atmosphere, not the expression of the superstition that ultimately hangs over the pond, and indeed colours much of her poetry about the Westphalian landscape in which she was so firmly rooted.

Unsurprisingly, given what we know about her state of mind at this time and the mood of so many of the poems which emerged during these months, both of them express thoughts of the past: the Lake itself and the old castle are custodians of a history which in both cases she expresses with great poignancy and tenderness. In both cases, the speaker is the observer, in the first contemplating the expanse of the Lake as it stretches out in the mist, and in the second seeming to walk around in the castle, summoning up images of people long since dead who went about their business there. In both there is the thought, so familiar in Droste-Hülshoff, of a future in which she will herself be a part of the past, joining in the history of the Lake and the castle. On both occasions, however, thoughts of her death come without any sense of loss and with no suggestion of regret.

Both poems convey an awareness of a continuity in which she has a place. In each case she conjures up the stillness of the place. In the first strophe of 'On Lake Constance', the dominant impression is of silence and weariness. It is what is not there which seems to be important, what is not happening: no lamp is burning and there is no sound of a grasshopper. The waters of the Lake move slowly and gently, but they do move, for they are the constant in this changed time. Even the two images she uses in these first two strophes contribute to this sense of unreality against the background of what is unchanging. The shore seems to groan, but like a horse which is not there and whose rider is in any case asleep.

The rumbling of the waters of the Lake resembles the grumbling sound one might imagine one might hear from a storm in its dreams. These are not obvious comparisons, but they are extraordinarily effective and perfectly comprehensible.

And so the poem goes on, as she places herself more firmly in it as the observer, linking herself physically to the Lake with the reference to her hair, damp and heavy from the spray. It is restless, despite the initial impression of calm, and the mention of the boat setting off from the shore also implies continuing activity, and even the presence of human life in what has seemed to be emptiness. Thus she moves to the human beings who once inhabited the place, extremes of society, rich and poor, weak and strong, but all in any case now assigned to the memory which the Lake itself contains.

Side by side with those who once were there is the fleeting thought of someone who is there still: we know that Annette's sister Jenny did indeed pursue her pastime of drawing in the depths of the castle which had become her home. As she goes on in the penultimate strophe to identify more closely the people who once were there, she selects individuals who at one time had a future: the child, the young bride, the singer and the pilgrim have all played their roles. Only then does she come to herself, knowing as she does that she too will become a part of the memory held so tightly by the Lake, the pious old water sprite who takes in the past and preserves it for ever. Absent is the regret and something close to bitterness that she expresses sometimes as she contemplates her own death.

What she describes in the poem, and in 'The Old Castle' which follows here, is a much more mature resignation, and a sense of her own place in a wider context. 'The Old Castle' has a more tangible sense of her presence there: after all she tells us at once that this is where she lives and where the past is a part of her daily life, in the form of the armour chests and iron shields which are her furniture, and the family portraits which are her companions. However, Droste-Hülshoff's lively imagination, which allowed her to transform a landscape into a seascape in 'The Steppe', or to have small boys terrified by the face they think they see at the bottom of a calm pond (see above), lead her here to examine her surroundings more objectively and then to ask about them. What lies in the depths of this ancient castle? Can she penetrate its secrets? Is that noise she hears on the rampart the sound of young boys or the screeching of an owl? Is she alive or dead?

This time she leaves such questions hanging in the air and does not pursue them. However, the very fact that they have been asked contributes to the subtle mystery of this poem and the atmosphere she seeks to evoke. If at the end, she allows herself a rare moment of what, in Heinrich Heine, would be called *Stimmungsbrechung* – a sudden intrusion into the mood of a poem of another, contrasting mood – then this is another example of her power as a mature poet to vary her impact and demonstrate another side of her work which is far less monotone than an initial acquaintance might seem to suggest. Already she has introduced the faintest suggestion of self-mockery, when she described herself as walking across the terrace 'like a ghost upon a rune-stone' and this is the mood on which the poem ends, with herself 'like a giant surrounded by decay'.

Unlike her scholarly brother-in-law, Joseph von Lassberg, and her dear friend Levin Schücking, who shared the leanings of the German romantic writers towards all things medieval, Annette von Droste-Hülshoff had little time for what she calls 'the romanticism of the castle' and fears to break her neck or her limbs if she allows herself to investigate too closely. She can soon have too much of such matters, despite her sensitivity to the past and the value she attaches to her place in the continuum.

On Lake Constance

A smoky haze has spread itself with gentle movements
across the weary expanse of land;
the tired, tired air on the shore groans
like a horse which bears its sleeping rider.
No little lamp is burning in the fisherman's hut,
no grasshopper is shrilling in the deserted tower.
The pulse-beat swells but slowly with a rolling motion
in the trembling element.

I hear it swirling on the moist sand,
swirling away beneath my feet.
The pebbles crackle, the sand roars
and stone upon stone crumbles on the shore.
The foam turns to nothing on the soles of my feet;
a mournful voice sounds in the hollow earth,
muted, with half-closed mouth,
like the dream of a grumbling storm.

I bend forward to listen on the tower:
the spray spurts up.
Ah, my hair is damp and heavy!
What are you doing, then, you restless lake?
Can blessed sleep not come to you?
But no: you are asleep, I see it clearly.
Your grey eyelashes cover your eyes.
The boat is setting off at the edge of the lake.

Have you known so much, experienced so much
that it must come back to you in a dream
and that your blazing nerve must tremble,
if a human foot approaches you on the shore?

Gone, gone! those who were once so full of health,
so rich and powerful, or so poor and weak,
and only their fleeting reflection
is lying now, floating away, in your depths.

The knight who used to trot out of the castle
from the mountainside in the early morning
- now the ash-tree bows from the grey portal,
my lady is drawing in the dungeon -
the poor little old woman who used to bleach
her shroud along the shore,
the sick man who coughed his last,
walk at your edge,

the playful child who used to hurl
his snail shells in jest,
the radiant bride who, smiling,
gave to you each petal from her posy,
the singer who with drunken eyes
went splashing about in your waters with his tunes,
the pilgrim who rested on the stone:
all of them, gone like smoke!

Are you so pious, you old water sprite:
do you only clasp tightly to you, never let go?
Has loyalty fled from the mountain
into your holy womb?
Oh, look at me! I vanish like foam
when the thistle springs up from the grave:
then my long shattered image will surely one day
burst up through your dream.

The Old Castle

I dwell in the castle in the mountain,
beneath me the blue lake;
by night I hear the goblins,
by day the eagles in the heights.
The grey ancestral portraits
are my room-mates,
armour chests and iron shields

my sofa and my wardrobe.
If I walk across the terrace,
like a ghost upon a rune-stone,
and see beneath me in the moonlight
the pale old town,
and if there's a lot of whistling on the rampart
- is it a tawny owl or little boys? -
it is often not clear to me
if I am alive or buried.

Opposite me the great hall yawns,
with its grey gate, long and hollow,
inside which a heavy footstep
booms slowly with a strange echoing sound.
I carry with me the tool to move the bolts: **f)**
ah, I open up and let the lamp
shine on the loose ramp, green with age,
of the spiral staircase,

which lures me like an omen
into the unfamiliar depths.
Is there a spring down there? or a prison?
No living being knows,
for the steps are crumbling
and a stone dropped down finds no way through.
Yet when I called down
it kept on thundering like a hurricane.

Yes, if the romanticism of this castle
does not very soon pall for me,
I shall break my limbs and my neck
without the hope of mercy in the ruins,
for, however defiantly the dune
may rise up on the flat shore,
I feel like a giant
surrounded by decay.

f) There must be a technical term for this appliance, but I have failed to find it. Expert advice would be most welcome. MET.

The poems which follow in this selection could hardly be more different in their content and their mood from those just considered, but they have something in common. Throughout her life Droste-Hülshoff felt deeply attached to the region where she was born and spent most of her youth. When she was not there she was homesick and at the end, when she was frail and sick and knew that she had not long to live, she yearned to return there, a wish that was probably denied her, given her debilitated condition and the long journey. At the same time, she undoubtedly appreciated the beauty of the countryside around Meersburg and enjoyed the walks, increasingly restricted, at the edge of the Lake and the hours she spent simply gazing at it and relishing its peacefulness and its changing moods. It is also more than likely that the climate suited her very much better, and she had the company of her sister and the beloved twin nieces. All these factors undoubtedly account for the relative serenity of much of her late poetry. Against that, however, she was drawn, deep in her roots, to the spirit of Westphalia, and she almost certainly felt closer, temperamentally, to its dark, brooding landscape.

What is also certain is that she shared with her kinsfolk of that region the superstitious nature that shows itself in most of her work, both poetry and prose. Fairly early on, before she had settled to her ultimately chosen genre of the lyric, she had embarked on a project on the history and customs of Westphalia, in collaboration with the writer Ferdinand Freiligrath and encouraged to some extent by Levin Schücking. This path was not to be particularly fruitful for her, though it was another of the directions she pursued for a time.

Much more successful were the ballads she wrote at about this time, several of them with a regional or historical background and many influenced by her fascination with spiritual and psychic matters. There is evidence in her letters as early as her teenage years, and reports also of conversations she had with acquaintances, mostly outside her family of course, that she knew she had that second sight for which the people of her homeland, particularly in rural regions, were famed. Although this was not something she could share with her pious Catholic relatives, this did not prevent her from allowing it to enter her writing, particularly once she had established herself in literary circles.

Some of her ballads – 'Der Fundator' (The Founder), 'Das Fräulein von Rodenschild' and 'Vorgeschichte. Second Sight' - are important examples of long narrative poems in which the supernatural dictates the content and the tone, and they belong to the same significant time, 1841-42, as the very powerful shorter poems which follow here, even though these cannot strictly speaking be classed as ballads. The generic description is less important in this instance than the very fact that Droste-Hülshoff excelled at a kind of poetry which depends on the telling of a story and evoking atmosphere, and this is what she does in the poems which follow, all of which have their source in the regional setting and folklore of the countryside around her home. Certain elements recur: a refrain sometimes, the build-up of tension and even of threat, and the dependence on deeply-held beliefs and superstition. 'The Boy on the Moor' is one of her better known poems, and it demonstrates another aspect of her skill in creating an atmosphere, this time quite unlike the serene setting of the Pond, or the mysterious character of the Lake. This time she is not present, either as observer or narrator, and yet it is a story, or a part of a story which is told here. While there is a narrator present, the emotions are entirely those of the boy as he walks across the moor, absorbing all the sights and sounds of a terrifying experience which escalates as he makes his way through this threatening terrain at a particularly frightening time of day when the mists are swirling about him and transforming what is presumably a familiar journey, at the end of a school-day towards his home. His fear of being alone out there is increased not only by the semi-darkness and the distorting mist, but by what he has heard about the dangers which lurk there. Everything takes on a new and terrifying quality, not just the things he sees, the hedges and the reeds, which he must have passed many times, but the sounds which conspire to frighten him and remind him of the stories he has heard of ghostly figures who people the moor and which he can convince himself are pursuing him. He knows that these are characters from the past, doomed to roam the moor as punishment for their sins and their weaknesses, and for the duration of his terrible walk, which becomes a desperate run, he believes that he will perish there, join them in their awful fate.

When suddenly the mood changes, he senses that he is safe. The ground is firm again, no longer threatening to swallow him up, and above all he glimpses the familiar light which he knows shines from his home. This is not the only time that Droste-Hülshoff seizes on the protective light shining from the window of a home which represents security (see above, p.132), but still the boy is suffering the effects of this experience. As he glances back, the memory of what he has been through is with him. He is, specifically, on the 'threshold' and one can ponder what she means to imply by this. He can, and doubtless will, go forward and embrace the safety of his familiar home, but he cannot resist looking back, for something has changed for ever, and the final line repeats the first. In general it is frightening to be out on the moor at dusk, but for him the experience was a reality: it was frightening, and he is unlikely to forget it.

We may assume that Droste-Hülshoff had heard accounts of such experiences from her earliest days, and that her vivid imagination will have conjured up the horror of it. The phenomenon of the mist on the heathland round her home will have been something she grew up with, and the personification of this threat with the 'heath-man' must have been a feature of local stories and superstitions with which she was very familiar. With her genius for evoking atmosphere she succeeds in conveying movement: the twirling and the swirling of the mist which she will surely have observed, even if only from the safety of her home, and her capacity to evoke sounds and sometimes even to make up words to convey them contributes greatly to the effect throughout, although this is an instance where one is conscious of the inadequacy of a translation to convey these different sounds. However, one can hear that, in just seven lines, there is 'hissing and singing', 'crackling', whistling' and 'rustling' and even what sounds like, but presumably cannot be, the snorting of a mad cow.

The visual impact of the occasion is powerfully described, too, when the strands of mist hook on to the bushes as the child races past the reeds which he knows so well but which now represent such a threat. Other familiar features are distorted too, and, to add to the terror, they take on semi-human shapes and movements, as the tree-stumps 'stare out from the bank' and the pine-tree 'nods eerily'. The effect of the whole poem is increased by its rhythm, again difficult to do justice to in a prose translation, but nevertheless one can sense the increasing panic as the boy runs on.

He is, after all, only a child, we are reminded, and there is the touching gesture of his clutching his school-book, as though his life depended on it, which is surely what he himself does feel. The relief as he lets out a deep breath at the end is palpable, but the fear remains with him.

The Boy on the Moor

Oh, it's frightening walking across the moor
when the mist of the heath is swirling around,
when the vapours are twirling like phantoms
and hooking their tendrils on to the bushes;
when a little spring spurts up at every step
and there's hissing and singing from every crevice.
Oh, it's frightening walking across the moor
when the clumps of reed crackle in the breeze!

The trembling child is clutching his school-book
and running as though someone were chasing him.
The wind is whistling hollowly across the plain –
What's that rustling sound over there by the hedge?
It's the spooky ditcher-lad who squanders his master's
best peat with his drinking.
Hah, hah! the snorting sounds like a mad cow!
The little boy cowers down in terror.

Tree-stumps stare out from the bank;
the pine tree nods eerily.
The boy is running, his ears alert,
through giant reeds like spears.
And what trickling and crackling inside!
That is the wretched spinner woman,
that is the banished spinning Lenor,
who's turning the bobbin in the reeds.

Keep going, keep going! Just keep running!
Onwards, as if someone were trying to catch him!

There's bubbling up in front of his feet,
there's a whistling sound under his soles,
like a ghostly melody.
That's the faithless violin player,
that's the thieving fiddler Knauf
who stole the wedding money.

Then the moor cracks, and a sigh goes up
from the gaping hollow.
Alas, alas, then damned Margret cries out:
"Ah, ah! My poor soul!"
The boy leaps like a wounded deer,
and if there were not guardian angels close about him
a grave-digger would discover his little white bones
late one night in the smouldering marshland.

Then suddenly the ground becomes firm,
and over there, near the willow-tree,
the lamp is flickering so cosily.
The boy is standing on the threshold:
he lets out a deep breath, and still looks back
timidly towards the moor.
Yes, it was terrible in the reeds.
Oh, it was frightening on the heath.

The same kind of atmosphere pervades 'The Heath-Man', and this is full of the detailed effects of sight and sound and movement at which she is brilliant. This time, however, there is not a lone figure, a vulnerable child, out in the terrifying landscape, and the thrust of the narrative is not a desperate, panic-stricken race against time and dark forces. The 'heath-man' is a real threat, however, and the arrangement of the strophes accentuates the almost carefree playing of the boys against the alternating strophes which contain the warning of the unidentified narrator. This certainly does change and become more urgent as the poem progresses, and if the boys appear almost indifferent to what is going on all around them, the listener/reader can be in no doubt that they are in constant and increasing danger.

This dual impression is skilfully achieved by the different rhythm of the alternating strophes, particularly accentuated by the repetition of the address ('children' or 'you children') followed by the imperative, which becomes more and more urgent in response to their seeming indifference. Similarly, the final line of the narrator's advice, though broadly recurrent, changes from the factual ('the heath-man is coming') to the descriptive ('the heath-man is swirling up'/'brewing') and then to the threatening reality ('the heath-man is burning'). By the time the inexorable approach of the 'heath-man' has been accomplished, the children are safe, having without emphasis apparently heeded the advice they were being given throughout.

The mood changes completely for the final three strophes. A calm replaces the fear and the threat, and the dramatic change in the landscape is what is stressed. What remains, however, despite the restoration of some kind of order and the children, at least temporarily, out of danger, is the sense that this has been a huge event, a transforming experience, a cosmic happening which is the forerunner of ill to come. Against this, the only protection is the prayer on which the poem ends.

The Heath-Man

"Children, don't go too far into the swamp.
The sun is going down. Already the bee is buzzing
more wearily as she flies, slowed down by sleep.
A pale cloth is floating on the ground.
The heath-man is coming!"
The boys go on playing in the field,

tugging up grasses, hurling stones.
They splash about in the gutter of the pond,
catching the moths on the marsh and
are delighted when the water-spider
with its long legs flees into the rushes.

"You children, don't lie down in the grass!
Look, just where the bee was perching,
how white smoke is filling the open flower.
The hare is staring timidly out of the bushes.
The heath-man is swirling up!"

The hair-grass can now hardly raise its heavy head
above the mist. The beetle shuffles its way
into its hollow, and the sleepy moth
struggles upwards, fleeing from the dampness
that forms beneath its wings.

"You children, stay at home!
Do not run out into the swamp!
Look how the thorn is already turning grey.
The thrush groans from out of its nest.
The heath-man is brewing."

You can see the shepherd's pipe glinting,
and in front of him the herd floating along,
like Proteus driving his flocks of seals
home in the grey ocean.
On the roof the swallows are twittering as they gather,
and the cock is crowing gloomily.

"You children, stay close to the yard!
Look how the damp streak of fog
is already reaching up to the latch on the gate.
A false light is swimming down on the ground.
The heath-man is climbing up!"

Now only the tips of the pine trees still
stretch their green heads above the mist,
like clumps of juniper across the snow.
A soft bubbling sound starts up on the moor,

a humming, high-pitched yet faint,
a hissing noise forces its way out of the valley.

"Come, you children, come in quickly!
The will-o-the-wisp is lighting its lamp.
The toad is swelling up, the snake in the marsh.
It's scary now to be outside.
The heath-man is on his way!"

Now the last needle is slipping down,
the pine-tree is disappearing in the smoke.
Slowly emerging patterns of fog are rising up from the moor,
advancing with giant strides.
A wayward light suddenly appears among the reeds.
The choir of toads starts up on the bank.

And all of a sudden a faint glow
seems to penetrate the giant's limbs.
There is a seething, colouring of the waves:
the North, the North is set alight.
Arrows of fire, fiery spears are hurled,
the horizon a stream of lava!

"God have mercy on us! What flaring up, what threats!
What smouldering on the edge of the dunes!
You children, put your hands together.
This is bringing plague and hard times to us.
The heath-man is burning."

Both the following poems, again from the group entitled 'Images of the Heath' *(Heidebilder)*, are very visual, but in both cases this quality is more static, evoking the impression of a painting, truly an image. Yet in both cases Droste-Hülshoff introduces figures of human beings, and there is movement, too, from the creatures which inhabit thc landscape and which she observes so closely and with the keen eye of the naturalist. In 'The Shepherds' Fire', she begins with the description of the darkness that pervades the heath, yet this is interrupted by the glimmer of light from the fire, and after that the emphasis is on the changing quality of the light, the patches of concentrated light, but then the sparks, as they spray and sprinkle over the ground – a rare occasion where the English translation offers an alliteration actually not there in the original but typical of the kind of effect at which she excels. Side by side with the fluctuations of light from the fire are the sounds, the clinking and cracking noises, and the sound of the flying sparks, and the focus is the group of shepherd boys, crouching round the fire and warming their hands. A few moments of activity interrupt the relative calm, as one of their number fetches some juniper branches to feed the fire. This provokes a cry of jubilation from his companions and a new noise of crackling branches and spluttering needles. The light has changed, too, with the rise and fall of the burning wood giving way to the smouldering of the peat which now suffuses the faces of the youngsters and turns them into sub-human creatures. The whole poem is a brilliant example of her ability to convey transformation, but very subtle this time, in response to the fluctuations of light and the introduction of new sounds.

There is also subdued drama, as one character emerges to lead into the finale which changes the tempo and the mood. The single detail of his shoeless state, so insignificant it seems, identifies him, as he points out something new happening in the distance. Another fire is burning somewhere, and the poem ends with the awareness that what these lads are engaged in is repeated somewhere else, and, in all probability, as Droste-Hülshoff knows very well since she is so familiar with the customs of her homeland, again and again across the heathland which is the characteristic terrain. The singing of the 'old song of the heathland', almost certainly her own composition, echoes as the poem closes and moves it from description to narrative and then to something rather more akin to ballad.

The Shepherds' Fire

Dark, dark on the moor,
night across the heathland,
only the trickling pipe
beside the mill is awake,
and great drops are creeping along
the spoke of the wheel.

A toad crouches in the swamp;
a hedgehog cowers in the grass;
in the decaying tree-stump
a natterjack starts up in its sleep, f)
and on the sandy slope
the snake curls itself up more tightly.

What is that glimmering there, beyond the gorse,
forming patches of light?
Now there are sparks spraying about,
sprinkling over the ground as they die away.
And then again, everything goes dark.
I can hear the clinking of steel,
a crackling noise, and the sounds of sparks flying,
and then the flames are darting up.

The shepherd boys are squatting
in a circle. They stretch out their hands,
and I can see the fire
licking at the lumps of peat.
Then one strong lad breaks away
from the huddle in the undergrowth,
and, as he trots off, drags
a tangled bundle of juniper after him.

He tips it on to the fire –
hah! how the lads yell
and flick these sparkling fireworks with their fingers.
How their pointed caps
flap cheerily about their ears,
and how the needles splutter,
and the branches crackle!

The flame subsides, and they
crouch back down in the circle,
and again bits of peat fly about
and the fire is smouldering gently.
A bright red glow lights up their faces
and their tousled hair,
and the little creatures of the heath
look just like demons.

That one there, the one with no shoes on,
why is he stretching out his arm at the darkness
like a rod?
What is that muttering in the circle?
They are peering out of their gorse hut
like young vultures.
Ha! There's another shepherds' fire
right in the middle of the dyke!

You can just see it rising up
and spreading its light about,
the jumbled jig of sparks
dancing across the juniper.
The lads are whispering softly
and clearing their throats,
and the old song of the heathland
ebbs away through the hair-grass.

"Hallo, hallo!
Halloee!
Come to our heath
where I'm grazing my sheep!
Come, oh come on! into our dyke.
There are plenty of flowers there.
Hallo! Halloee!"

The boys fall silent, listen across the forest,
and slowly through the gorse it comes:

(Anti-strophe)

"Hallo, halloee!
I'm sitting on the hill.
My little sheep are all asleep.
Come, oh come, into our camp!
There's grass as high as gorse growing here
Hallo, halloee!
Halloee!"

f) I must admit to taking some zoological licence here. There are two words in modern German usage for 'toad', and Droste-Hülshoff undoubtedly used both of them: 'Unke' and 'Kröte', as she does here. However, with her considerable knowledge of the region and of all such matters, she almost certainly distinguished between the two and used them in reference to different species of toad. Not knowing which word might refer to which species, I have used the specific term 'natterjack' in the second instance, having established that this creature still inhabits her region and probably did then. It may not be strictly speaking correct, but it seems the best solution in the circumstances.

Similarly evocative of place and time and mood is 'The House on the Heath', a gentle poem which begins with a description of a place at one of her favourite times of day, early evening, with all that that implies. The focus is the simple thatched cottage in the neat little garden, but the fact that it is listening suggests in the very first line that it is strangely alert and anticipates the ending of the poem with the question which makes it clear that this is no ordinary habitation but the place intended for the birth of Christ. As the poem proceeds, the details accumulate to set the scene: the calf at the window produces sounds which break the silence implied in the first strophe. The neat little garden seems to be dominated by the *Sonnenwende*, a word popularly used in German to denote a number of tall plants which turn their heads towards the sun, but here it can hardly be a sunflower but is likely to be the winter heliotrope, with its drooping flowers. A 'child' is kneeling in the little garden and weeding, but – another hint - the flower she picks is the lily, traditionally the symbol of the Virgin Mary. Then other components enter the scene: the shepherds with their 'Ave Maria', and the distant noise of the carpenter at work. By the time the evening star rises and appears to bow above the little house, the transformation is complete, and the whole scene has been changed into a painting by some medieval monk. This is not the anguished work of the Droste-Hülshoff of 'The Spiritual Year' but the simplest expression of a belief central to her faith. As such it surprises, but only as so much of her lyric surprises, with her capacity to express a mood powerfully yet delicately, and to prompt the imagination of the reader as it utilises her own.

The House on the Heath

How does the thatched hut listen,
with evening light darting about it,
like a bird cowering in its nest,
from the midst of the dark pine trees.

At the window the heifer with the white star-shaped patches
stretches her head,
blows into the evening air and snorts
and bangs against the wooden framework.

To the side, a little garden, hedged with thorns,
in a neat patch of ground,
where the heliotrope stands erect
and droops its bell-like head.

And inside a silent child is kneeling,
seeming to weed the ground.
Now she is plucking a tender lily
and meandering along the flower-beds.

On the horizon are shepherds
stretching out in the heather
and waking the dreaming air
with the melody of 'Ave Maria'.

And now and then from the barn
comes the sound of hammer blows,
the noise of a plane; the shavings drop down,
and slowly the saw is rasping.

Then the evening star gradually
rises from among the branches of the pine-trees
and precisely above the roof of the hut
it seems gently to be bowing.

It is a picture, silent and fervent,
such as Old Masters created it,
skilled monks, diligently
pressing it upon a gold background.

The carpenter, the shepherds
with their pious song,
the Virgin with the lily branch,
and all around the peace of God.

The wondrous radiance of the star
from fragile fields of clouds ....
is perhaps here today in this stable
the little Christ Child born?

There could hardly be a greater contrast between this delicate little poem and the one chosen to follow it here, but this is indicative of the extraordinary variety in these poems which she produced at such speed in that winter of 1841-42 in Meersburg, prompted, as she believed, by the confidence that Levin Schücking inspired in her with his own confidence in her poetic genius. 'The Hunt' is an extraordinary poem, in its length and its evocation of the excitement of the hunt. Droste-Hülshoff is not taking issue with the morality or otherwise of the pursuit of an animal by human beings. Lover of nature and keen observer of all creatures though she was, this seems not to have been her concern at all. The hunt will have been a part of her experience of rural life, and, though one may assume that she did not actually participate, the male members of her family did, and she will have been acquainted with its rituals, and possibly, as the poem appears to suggest, enthusiastic about them. In the famous poem 'On the Tower', she speaks of her desire to be a 'huntsman in the field', clearly on a par with the life of a soldier and epitomizing for her the freedom of a man which is denied to her. Such enthusiasm may be implicit in her choice of subject here, but no more than that. To exclude this poem on grounds of length or personal preference would be to fail in the attempt to present a selection of her mature poems in their range and originality.

Within the *Heidebilder* , the hunt is as much a part of her portrayal of the rural setting and the characteristics of her native Westphalia as the marl-pit or the megalithic stone (see below). When she came to arrange this group of poems, she placed this one second, following 'The Boy on the Heath'. Subsequent editors have taken a different view, but the order is not very important, particularly as she was constantly changing her mind about it. The poem is essentially descriptive, from the serene beginning when the first eight lines set the scene for what is to follow, to the detailed account of the hunt itself and the jubilation of the human victors. She really does not invite comment on the rights or wrongs of the pursuit of a fox by the mounted human beings who have set their minds on its destruction. Nor does she pass such comment, beyond her use of the word 'rascal' to describe the fox in the quasi-folksong which ends the poem: to her countrymen, the fox will doubtless have been seen as a pest better disposed of than as a dashing hero with a bushy tail.

The poem was originally given the titles 'Grazing Cattle' and 'Hunt and Grazing Cattle', suggesting that this is indeed a composition in which the hunt is not the focus, although it clearly is the most significant feature, as it storms its way through, disrupting the peace of the landscape with its alien sounds and forceful movements. Somehow she manages to balance this intrusion with the many and varied ingredients of the countryside through which it passes. The hunt breaks in upon the calm of the first eight lines with the distant cry with which the first long section begins, and from then on noise abounds, whether it be from animals or men. Remarkable, side by side with that, is the use she makes of silence – 'not a rustle, not a sigh', 'not a sound'- and barely perceptible noises, like that made by a berry falling, the cry of fright of the fly in the spider's web, a beetle scurrying through the plants, or the panting of the hounds, so different from the yapping and yawning she describes a few lines later.

Equally remarkable and effective are the descriptions of very different movements: the characteristic movement of the fox, slipping down the bank, gliding through the rushes and pattering on its way; the cattle thumping along the field and staggering around the heath; the sick heifer swaying wearily up. This is unmistakable Droste-Hülshoff the keen observer, with her matchless ability to express what she sees and hears and feels in powerful language. When she interrupts her account of the hunt and concentrates briefly on the chief huntsman, she does so with something close to humour, as she describes the paraphernalia that relates to his grisly office, before actually identifying him at the end of the five lines and then going on to describe the zeal with which he carries out his task. As at the end of 'The Shepherds' Fire' she introduces a different tempo, with what is presumably her own version of a chant of victory, perhaps based on authentic verses she may have heard, in which the crude shouts of glee contrast sharply with the swift yet steady rhythm which has characterised the description of the hunt itself, with its procession of men and beasts through a largely indifferent landscape.

The Hunt

The air has laid itself down to rest,
stretched itself out comfortably in the moss.
Not a rustle to disturb the plants,
not a sigh to awaken the blades of grass.
Only a cloud dreams from time to time,
down from the pale horizon,
where the pine forest extends
its dark candelabra over the bank.

Then, listen! A shout, a distant sound:
"Hallo! hoho!" so long drawn out
one thinks the noises make waves
in the field of gorse, and then again
"Hallo! hoho!" – a hesitant echo in the thicket-
everything silent!
You can hear the shrill cry of fright of the fly
in the spider's web, the sound of a berry falling;
you can hear the beetle scurrying through the plants,
and then the cling-clang of an army of cranes passing

on their airy way, and a sound
like the distant croaking of toads - cling, clang!
A chiming along the edge of the forest –
Whoosh! The fox slips down the bank,
gliding through the spearlike rushes
and pattering on his way.
And out of the thicket, white as snowflakes,
the living bells come panting along behind,
turning cartwheels on the steep embankment.
They shoot up from the ground like eels,
and on, on! fox and hound.
The swaying juniper whispers,
the rushes make a rustling noise, the heath is crackling
and scatters moths around the pack.
They yap and yawn after their prey,
spurting foam out of their mouths and noses.
The fox is still ahead,
trotting steadily along, dragging his bushy tail.
He leaves a dark streak in the dew
and scornfully shows his heels.
But soon he raises his bush again,
and, just as the fish darts in the pond,
he sets off over weeds and hair-grass,
throwing up gravel and dust as he races off,
and after him the pack with their swollen throats,
rustling like leaves in winter.
You can hear their jaws cracking
as they snap at the air with their bared teeth.
So they sweep round to the pine forest,
and then out of the thicket
the chiming of the hounds rings out.

What is that breaking out of the undergrowth in the fields?
It's tramping the ground at a clumsy gallop.
Ha! A herd of roaring cattle! at their head a bull
and after them comes a stray dog barking away.
They come thumping along the field with heavy movements,
their horns lowered, their tails held horizontal,
and stagger around a few more times

before taking up their positions on the heath.
Now at last they come to a standstill and look backwards again with a grumble,
measuring up the thicket with their glazed eyes,
then lowering their heads,
and crunching softly, as their teeth pluck at the thyme.
They snort at the yellow dust **f1)** irritably,
their udders brushing the juniper bushes,
and whip their tails at the cloud of buzzing insects and flies.
Thus, slowly shaking their filled bellies,
they go on grazing as far as the pool on the heath.

A shot rings out - hallo!- a second shot - hoho!
The herd is startled and their snorting crinkles
the surface of the pool,
then stretching out their necks, as the whirlpool roars
at the plug of the dam,
they draw up the water into their throats, and puff.
The sick heifer sways wearily up:
she shudders, shakes herself with a hollow cough,
and then: a shot, and then: a cry of triumph!

With his little green cap over his ear,
his half-moon **f2)** on a leather strap,
without a gun or a bag,
comes trotting swiftly out of the clearing - the chief huntsman,
right into the middle of the heath.
He swings his horn and clenches his fist,
then sets about it, and a thousand foxes
are not blasted to death so noisily
as today there blasts across the grass.

"The rascal is dead, the rascal is dead!
Let's bury the rascal!
If the dogs don't get him,
The ravens will eat him up.
Hoho! Hallo!"

Then there's a thundering up from all sides.
The hounds break out of brushwood and pine-forest,
and they can be seen throughout the land

howling and yelling in confused circles around the huntsman,
so that it muffles the noise of the fanfare,
but still the Gloria resounds louder and louder,
and the cry of victory roars through the gorse:

"Hang the rascal! Hang the rascal!
Hang him up on the willow tree!
I'll have the skin and you the tallow,
then we'll both be laughing.
Hang him, hang him!
the rascal, the rascal!"

f1) The pollen from the junipers.
f2) His hunting horn.

The next two poems belong to the same group, written in far-off Meersburg in early 1842 but likewise deeply rooted in the landscape and past of Droste-Hülshoff's native part of Germany. Both 'The Marl-Pit' and 'The Dolmen' link the terrain so familiar to her from her walks in the area around the Rüschhaus where she spent so much time alone, or later with Levin Schücking, in deep contemplation and observation which she must have saved in her memory until the time was right for her to express it in poetry. They have in common, too, the connection of the real, the present time, with ages past. Like 'The Hunt' they occupy a very important place in the *Heidebilder* and contribute to her reputation as a poet of great originality and depth. That this was not a reputation established in her lifetime is attributable to several features: the unusual, 'unpoetic' nature of some of her material, and the absence of obviously lyrical qualities. Yet if they lack something that can be described as 'melody', they nevertheless possess what has been described by a prominent critic, Clemens Heselhaus, as 'sound' (*Klang*), and contain some superb cadences which a translation which deliberately eschews any attempt at rhyme or even to emulate metre, can but hope to suggest.

Above all, what distinguishes her poems is the deep beauty of her language and her ability to convey rare yet strangely familiar human observations and responses with subtlety and strength. Such qualities, evident throughout her work, are no less present in these lengthy examples than in the more delicate poems for which she sometimes selects material more frequent in lyric poetry. Certainly the subject matter of both these poems is unusual, the first a marl-pit of the kind found in Westphalia and the second a megalithic tomb, similarly something she may have actually come across, or at least heard about. We know from the young Levin Schücking's account of his first visit that she collected fossils, unsurprisingly in an age when this was a popular hobby and given her lively interest in the natural world. Both these poems have at their base the kind of walk she may have taken in the countryside around the Rüschhaus, although in both cases she takes on the person of a man, something not unusual in her when she places herself in the role of observer and narrator or commentator. In both cases her knowledge and keen interest in the past join with her very active imagination to create poems of quite remarkable quality, and in both there is the added dimension of her own objective understanding of the place of imagination in colouring what she experiences, or suggests she experiences. Thus it is no chance that both poems end with a humorous twist, a sudden coming down to earth which, as in 'The Steppe', a very different poem though it is, leaves one with the question: what of all this is real, and what imagined?

These are poems rich in detail and extraordinary in her own age, or any other. The scope covered by both poems is enormous, even though her starting-point, and indeed the point at which each concludes, is a local and a personal one. Between those two points in each, she ranges far in time and place, with the connection always her fertile, brilliant imagination. There is no evidence that she had detailed scientific knowledge, nor even a particularly close interest in some of the thinking of her age, but she had an intelligent, inquisitive mind, and it is inconceivable that she was not aware of what was being discussed in informed circles. 'The Marl-Pit' ends with the brief encounter between the shepherd knitting his socks and mocking the 'modern' theories of evolution in this age before Darwin had put forward his theories in print, and the speaker, who has just emerged from his dreamlike experiences below the surface of the ground and produces the piece of slate by way of evidence to refute the biblical account. The old man, steeped in his own values and beliefs, is unlikely to be persuaded, even if he is reading, rather surprisingly, an established text-book of the day as he sits there guarding his flock. The speaker knows that he is mocking him and mocking modern ideas which challenge his firmly held views, and Droste-Hülshoff is touching lightly, but only very lightly, on an issue of her day which will set scientific thought in opposition to religious beliefs. Her own view is not expressed, but one may reasonably assume that she foresaw the conflict pending between the intellectual thinking of her day and the religious values of her pious family. That, however, is really not the point of the poem, which has traversed many centuries as she describes the imagined speaker prompted to some extraordinary thoughts in his search for fossils on the Westphalian heathland.

There is a different kind of transformation in 'The Dolmen', where she describes the accident of coming upon one of the megalithic tombs which existed, and indeed still exist, across Europe. The experience is a moving one, at that special time she cherishes, when day and night are held in balance and the mysterious light changes the world through which the speaker/she is walking in deep thought. Even the persona is ambivalent: it seems to be the poet herself who speaks initially, sunk in cares and brooding on ideas that elude expression. Is it too fanciful to suggest that she is recalling the drafts she worked on before the releasing power of the Meersburg winter allowed her to put them into a final form? She does not follow up this point, for the focus of the poem is the strange structure of stone that suddenly appears ahead and prompts a myriad of new thoughts. By the time the end arrives, when the changing light and the oncoming storm have brought idea upon idea - of supernatural beings, witches and gods, of runes and spells - a lamp and an umbrella pronounce the reality. A servant addresses him with the prosaic information that it is raining. The megalithic tomb that has filled the poem with such flights of fancy is no more than a crude grave in dusty ground.

However, brief accounts of what seems to be happening in these poems cannot possibly do justice to their extraordinary impact. They are both packed with detail of the kind that one recognizes from her other poetry, and indeed to some extent from her narrative writings. As the ground opens up at the beginning of 'The Marl-Pit' to reveal the brightly coloured fossils, she produces a series of images, of the stall set up by Nature to display her wares, the comparison with the leopard skin, the partridge, then the quail. This succession immediately gives way, however, to the precise identification of what these are, then how they came to be there, with the references to Genesis. Again, this is replaced by a different thought, for these are called 'foundlings' (the same word exists in German to describe erratic stones and orphaned children), and so she can pursue the image, with the idea that these stones were wrenched from their mother's breast and laid in a strange cradle, in an orphanage. Even that idea is taken further, with the rows of cells in this institution inhabited by children of different colours, for the fossils were swept there from all corners of the earth.

Climbing into the marl-pit to escape the cold wind, the speaker allies himself to the fossils, for he feels himself estranged from the world he knows, 'a foundling in the ruined cosmos'. The phrase is significant, for the whole point is that he has become separated from what he knows and has been transported into another world where he can imagine that he is in a dusty grave, 'like a corpse in the catacombs', with a wasp turned into a death-watch beetle and reminding him of his own death. From there it is not far in his fantasy to imagine that he is a mummy and that the creature he has heard is the scarab, the beetle sacred to Ancient Egypt and traditionally placed in the coffin to protect the dead. Small wonder, then, that when a ball of wool drops down into his lap, he thinks it must be a ball of byssus, the fine thread used to make the mummy's shroud.

This accumulation of fantastic thoughts cannot continue once he raises himself out of the pit and sees the sky and the misty sun, and, most of all, the familiar sight of Westphalian sheep. Most of all, the thoroughly Christian sound of the shepherd whistling 'Ave Maria' challenges his thoughts of pagan times and rituals long ago. When this changes to a little song, almost certainly Droste-Hülshoff's own composition but incorporating the traditional words and phrases of existing ditties, the transformation is complete: the simple shepherd, so much at one with his sheep, is going about his ordinary business, and all thoughts of Genesis and Leviathan and Egyptian tombs are banished. Thus the poem can end with a new thought, not followed up, but clearly related to the imagined experience that precedes it, and, in the most subtle way possible, Droste-Hülshoff has opened up an idea of enormous importance but one which she has no intention of pursuing. If the shepherd would not have thought that the stranger he has encountered was crazy, he undoubtedly does think just that, and Droste-Hülshoff must know that the issue she has touched upon will provoke much ridicule and controversy.

The Marl-Pit

Plunge your spade three spans into the sand
and you will see stones projecting from the cut,
blue, yellow and vermilion stones, as if Nature had set up
her jumble stall in preparation for an auction.
No leopard skin was ever so brightly spotted,
no partridge, no quail ever so chequered
as the rubble, blazing with colour like polished stones,
crumbles out of the soil at the touch of a hand,
or the scraping of the toe of a shoe.
How angrily does the black gneiss stare at you.
Balls of milky white spar roll down,
and around the mica burst silver flames,
pieces of speckled porphyry, big and small,
crystallized ochre and flint:
the soil produced only few of them,
this one saw the shore, and that one the mountain-top.
The angry wave, Leviathan with its gigantic shovel,
frightened them over this way,
when it passed foaming across Sinai.
The sluices of heaven stood open for thirty days,
mountains melted like candied sugar,

at the time when the Ark was poised on Arafat,
and a stranger, abundant Nature,
a new life, welled up out of new substances.
They are called 'foundlings' because they were
snatched from the breast, their mother's breast,
and an unknown hand laid them,
unaware, in a strange cradle, like a foundling-child.
Oh, what an orphanage this heath is,
which with its brown garment conceals
Moors, Pale-faces and Redskins from me,
all shaped the same!
How endless are the rows of cells!

I had climbed deep down, into the marl-pit,
for the wind was bitterly cold,
and I was sitting sideways on in the hollow chamber,
listening dreamily to the harping of the air.
There were sounds as if of ghostly echoes
disappearing melodiously in the ravaged universe,
and with a hissing sound, as if from chasms in the swamp
when it sinks down into itself, bubbling away.
Above my head a rustling, and sounds of activity,
as if someone were scraping sparks in ashes.
I pulled out foundlings one by one
and listened, listened with my ears alert.

In front me and round about me only the grey marl;
I could not see what was overhead, yet Nature
seemed to me like a wasteland, and an image
rose up of an earth, rotten and burnt red,
and I myself seemed like a spark
still trembling even so in the dead ashes,
a foundling in the ruined cosmos.
The cloud parted and the wind dropped.
I did not dare to poke my head out of the hollow,
In order not to see the horrors of the devastation,
how new things were welling up and old things disintegrating.
Was I the first human being, or the last?

Ha, on this slate slab are jelly-fish:
it seems as if they were still pushing out their rays

when they were hurled from the bosom of the sea,
and the mountain fell down to crush them.
Certain it is that the old world has passed away,
and here am I inside it, a fossil, a mammoth's bone.
And wearily, wearily, I sank down upon the edge
of my dusty grave, and the soil was trickling
on my hair and clothing. I turned as grey
as a corpse in the catacombs,
and at my feet I heard a soft creaking,
a rattling, crumbling sound, a whirring.
It was the death-watch beetle, who was just
burying a new corpse in the coffin.
With its feet, its little wings,
a wasp was pointing the way for me out of this world.
And now my dreaming had taken a new direction,
and the sand had turned me into a mummy,
my linen dust, my face ashen,
and the scarab was not lacking either.

What, corpses above me? At that very moment
a ball of byssus rolled into my lap.
No! It's wool! really lamb's wool,
and suddenly my dreams let go of me.
I yawned, stretched, started up out of the hollow.
The red ball of the sun was in the sky,
murky with mist, a bright cornelian,
and sheep were grazing on the raised heath.
Close above me I could see the shepherd sitting:
he twines his wool and his needles flash
as, deep in thought, he knits his socks.
He did not glance down at me
but began to whistle 'Ave Maria'
as softly and as sleepily as a passing breeze.
He looks at his sheep with such affinity
that one knows not whether he is sheep or man.
Then a clearing of the throat and slowly from his lips
he thrusts his song into the strands of wool:

"There is a little fish in a deep lake,
and I look at it to see if it is going to leap in the air.

If I wander across the green heath as far as the cool Rhine
all my thoughts are with my sweetheart.
Just as the moon gazes into the water,
and just as the sun shines golden in the forest,
so my love is hidden deep inside me
and all my thoughts are with you, my child.

If anyone said I wanted to go away,
that I have a sweetheart somewhere else,
do not trust that false tongue, whatever it tells you.
All my thoughts are with you and you alone."

I had climbed up and was standing on the edge (of the pit),
right in front of the shepherd, and I handed him the ball of wool.
He stuck it on his hat and went on knitting,
his white smock floating like a nun's veil.
A book was lying in the moss. I picked it up:
"Bertuch's History of Nature **f)**; are you reading this?"
At that his lips curled into a smile:
"He's lying, sir. But that's precisely the joke.
All about snakes and bears that have been turned to stone,
when, as it says in Genesis, the floodgates opened.
If it were not meant as entertainment, it would have been a bad thing to do.
After all, we know that all the animals drowned."
I handed him the slab of slate: "Look,
That was an animal". At that he raised his eyebrows
and slyly went on laughing at me.
He would not have thought that I was crazy.

f) Friedrich Justin Bertuch (1747-1822), writer and publisher, whose works were undoubtedly familiar to Droste-Hülshoff, particularly his 12-volume illustrated encyclopaedia for children, much of it devoted to natural history.

The Dolmen

At that time of the parting between night and day,
when the heath lay like a sick old man
and its groaning stirred the mossy carpet,
weak sparks flashed like electricity

in the dishevelled hair,
and, a dark spectre, the layers of cloud spread over it.

It was at this hour of dawn that I crept out,
alone with my cares,
not thinking much about events outside.
I walked deep in thought and did not notice
the rippling lights, or the light of the glow-worm,
nor see when the moon rose.

The way was straight, devoid of bridge or any hindrance,
and so I dreamt on and just as a bad book,
a penny magazine f1), torments us from station to station on a journey,
I gnawed at stuff discarded ten times over
and kept on harping on a worn-out tune.

Drafts ripened out of drafts,
but, just as the snake snatches at its own tail,
I always found myself at the same place.
Then suddenly a huge stag-beetle
hit me in the eye: I was startled
and lay on the ground, above me the rippling heath.

A funny place I had chosen for myself to rest!
Right and left stones rose up,
huge blocks, raw loaves of porphyry.
The edifice towered above my head,
plaits of long hair stroked my brow,
and at my feet the gorse shoots waved about.

I knew at once - it was a megalithic tomb -
and pressed my forehead down more firmly,
sucking eagerly at the sweetness of the horror,
until it seized me with its icy claws,
until the tempo of my blood increased
and hammered away like a glacial spring
beneath my fleecy coat.

The roof f2) over me, sunk down and crooked,
on which the moonlight rested, pale and mourning,

like a widow at her husband's grave.
Lumps of coal from the shepherds' fire
peered so like a fiery corpse through the thyme,
that I quickly pushed them down with my staff.
All of a sudden a lapwing hurtled shrilly out of the moss.
I burst out laughing, yet my imagination
was bearing me without restraint far away over ditch and wooden bar.
I listened to the wind so attentively,
as if it were bringing news from the land of spirits
and all the time I was staring at the roof.

Ha! Which sinews moved this stone?
Who sank these age-old blocks into the ground
when mourning for the dead rang out across the heath?
Who was the witch who, in the evening light,
transformed the valley with her runes and spells,
with her golden hair flowing in the wind?

That way is the East, that way, three shoes into the ground,
is the urn, and inside it
a savage heart, crumbled into flakes of ash.
Here the dream of sacrificial glade resides,
and above the stone the stern gods grimly
shake their clouds of curls.

What, did I pronounce a magic spell? There on the dyke,
it's rising up, spreading itself like a surge of waves,
a giant's body, massive and growing ever taller.
Now it's going forward with long strides.
Look! how it glided through the top of the oak tree,
and through its limbs the trembling moonlight shimmers.

Come here! come down! Your time is up!
I'm waiting for you, consecrated in the holy bath,
the smell of church still in my clothes.
Then it rises up, angrily it curls into a ball,
and slowly, a dark cloud, it swims above my head,
along the heathland.

A cry, a light bobbing up and down: something is swaying past me,
and "Sir, it is raining" says my servant,
calming stretching the umbrella over my head.
Once more I looked down at the stones.
Ah, God, it was only a crude grave after all,
covering up poor, parched dust!

f1) The idea of the popular magazine originated in England, and by 1833 it was appearing also in Germany, a throwaway publication intended for entertainment.

f2) Some examples of these erections were formed of upright stones with a horizontal stone balanced across them.

Levin Schücking left Meersburg in February 1842, to take up another post and, eventually, to marry. They were never to be so close again, and after his departure Droste-Hülshoff missed his company greatly and felt that she had lost the power to write with the speed and intensity she attributed to his influence. However, she remained in Meersburg for the summer of 1842, returning to the Rüschhaus in September and remaining there for over a year. During those months, however unlikely she may have thought this to be, she worked steadily and productively, though no longer with the enthusiasm that had characterised the winter in Meersburg, when she was intent on showing Levin that she could achieve her target.

It was, however, an important time for her career. 'The Jew's Beech' (*Die Judenbuche)*, the *Novelle* so central to her reputation, appeared in serial form published by Cotta, and she also completed the long poem 'Der Spiritus familiaris des Roßtäuschers' ('The Home Spirit of the Horse-dealer'), a strange work which hovers between epic and ballad, based on a legend related by the Brothers Grimm and telling the story of the battle for a man's soul when he becomes possessed by the evil spirit which has entered his home. The work has much in common with 'The Jew's Beech', in its evocation of dark forces, and the preoccupation with twisted motivation and warped morality, but the end, when it eventually comes, is not the grim fate of Friedrich Mergel but the gentler one of redemption. Once again, Droste-Hülshoff had seized on an unlikely choice of theme for a middle-aged lady of gentle birth, but again she carried it through with vigour and characteristic disregard for what might be expected of her. Her work on 'The Spiritual Year' was by now completed, at least for the time being, although she was to return to it again and again and, in any case, insist that it was not to be published until after her death.

In the summer of 1842 she also put together a series of sketches on the landscape and customs of Westphalia, which appeared anonymously in 1845. Moreover, she was working towards the 1844 edition of her work, a much more satisfactory compilation than the random effort of 1838. This does not sound like a woman reduced to inactivity by the departure of a lover, and indeed she was entering into a new phase of her creative life, and, particularly, for our purpose here, into a period of vitality and change in the area closest to her heart, the lyric. Thus the poems selected to follow here, and to show the work she produced until close to her final illness and the end of her life, are different in subtle ways from those already considered, yet, as throughout her work, there are many common features, and above all they are linked by the mark of her originality and her poetic genius. The selection also shows, once more, the range of her lyric in theme and style. Although many examples must necessarily be omitted, this is a representative selection, and it includes some of her greatest poems.

The Deserted House

Deep down in the ravine there is a house,
fallen into decay after the death of the forester.
There I often take my rest,
hidden among the weeds and young shoots.
It is a wilderness in which the light of day
only half penetrates the heavy eyelids.
The shadowy hedge of greying branches
presses densely round the deep chasm of the rocks.

Through my dreams I hear the black flies
buzzing as they reel about in the crevice,
moving gently through the wood like sighs.
In the shrubs crazy beetles drone.
When the sunset pushes its way forward
on the lather of the seeping slates,
its seems as if a miserable eye,
an eye red with weeping, were hanging over it.

The rafters, swollen with moss,
push up jumbled clumps of hay
and a spider has set up its tent
in the window-frame.
There, like a leaf of fragile blossom,
hangs the wing of a shimmering dragonfly,
and the golden mirror of its outer shell
rises headless up against the sill.

Where the lanky shoots tap
against the jutting structure of the ragged foliage
and carnation buds still creep along
on the wild overgrown hedge among the moss,
the dark moisture has seeped through
the dripping brickwork,
creeps round the box-tree in weary loops
and sinks down upon the clump of fennel.

From time to time a playful butterfly
has become trapped in the gorge

and for a moment remains suspended
on a group of narcissi.
If a pigeon comes flying through the glade,
its cooing falls silent on the edge of the ravine,
and one can only hear the whirring of its wings,
and see its shadow on the stonework.

And on the hearth where year in, year out
the snow has come flying down the chimney
are the old ashes damp and toughened,
covered in bell-shaped toadstools.
On the timber that supports the walls
hang the remains of a tousled piece of hemp
for spinning a rope,
like rotten hair, and inside that
a swallow's nest left over from last year.

And from a hook on the balcony
there hangs a string of bells on a buckle and a lead,
and clumsily embroidered in wool
on the leash, the name 'Diana'.
They left a little whistle here, too,
when they closed the pine coffin.
They buried the man and shot
the faithful old animal.

While I am sitting like this, alone among the bushes,
with the mouse squeaking in the leaves,
a squirrel chuntering its way from branch to branch,
and toads and crickets making their noises in the swamp,
a shudder runs through me,
as though I can still hear the sound of the bells,
and Diana barking in the forest,
and the dead man whistling still.

This poem, written in the summer of 1843 when Droste-Hülshoff was still in the Rüschhaus, almost certainly relates to a place she knew near Meersburg. It was known as 'das Többele', the ravine in the forest in the first line. This is not a common word in modern

German, but Grimm knows it; he defines it as a 'Waldschlucht' and lists a small number of instances of its usage, though mostly from little later than the Middle Ages. It is more than likely that it was not in Droste-Hülshoff's vocabulary at all, but that she picked it up, as she often did, while she was in that very southerly part of Germany, close to the Swiss border. More than likely this place was the destination of one of the picturesque walks she went on in the company of the Lassberg family, who were always anxious to entertain their visitor, particularly in the early days, when she was still able to walk some distance. This, of course, is surmise, and it is not really important, but it supplies a location for the deserted house.

This is not like the house in the heath of the earlier poem, which was obviously in Westphalia, and the two poems have no more than a passing likeness. Both cottages are isolated and surrounded by stillness, but here she is thinking, not of the mystical transformation of the place into the scene of the birth of Christ but of the one-time inhabitants, now long dead, the forester and his faithful dog. The poem needs little commentary, especially to anyone familiar with Droste-Hülshoff. Indeed, it is quintessentially Droste-Hülshoff, with its command of detail and the accumulation of sights and sounds. Beginning outside with the emphasis on the derelict state of the abandoned house, she accentuates its personality, tired and old, suffused in the red light of the sunset, which does not give it a glow but makes it look as though the eyes beneath the heavy eyelids were red with weeping. There are signs of life – a spider, a butterfly, a pigeon – but more striking is the realization that the dragonfly is dead and that it is its corpse which hangs there, shimmering in the gold and brilliant colours which were its hallmark.

Death plays a different role in this poem, however. It is not the harrowing emptiness of so many of her poems, but the awareness of the absence of life. The ashes in the fireplace are old and damp, toughened with time and covered with the toadstools which symbolize old age and decay. There is no fire burning there, for everything belongs to the past; the hemp that could have been made into a rope, the swallow's nest left over from last year. Nothing expresses this link with the past more poignantly than the single item left behind, the dog's lead, with the name embroidered on it. This was an animal that once roamed in that wood with a devoted master, and it takes no leap of the imagination to hear the barking of the dog and the whistling of the man amidst the sounds that still are there, of the mouse, the squirrel, the toads and the crickets, which continue in the present that goes on to add their sounds to the prevailing silence.

'The Deserted House' was a product of those months after the 'Meersburg winter', when Droste-Hülshoff seems to have been gathering confidence in her poetic range. It is extraordinarily simple, so different from those two long poems which are placed immediately before it in this selection. Its impact depends on the way she summons up something very human: a house once lived in but long abandoned through the demands of time. There is none of the extravagant imagery of 'The Marl-Pit' or 'The Dolmen', nor their wild flights of fancy. The past plays an important role, but it is a very different one. She writes with immense understanding of a situation which touches everyone, and the same is true of the next poem, in which she traces the progress of a sleepless night, each passing hour marked by the striking of the clock. Again the poem seems to need little in the way of commentary, for any reader will respond to the changing atmosphere she evokes. There is life outside, but it is the life of the night, and the creatures are heading towards their rest, except for the polecat, whose domain is precisely the night. Yet after the lulling of the opening strophes, another sensation intervenes, for the night holds a threat, the threat of darkness and of the unfamiliar. Things well known in daylight take on a new quality, and it is a disturbing quality. The eyes play tricks and distort, noises represent new experiences.

This state of 'sleeping wakefulness' produces a heightened sensitivity, and it is impossible to say, as she puts it, whether this is a blessing or a curse For a time it seems as though the sensation is all negative, expressed in the mention of weeping and of lamentation. Even the song of the nightingale, familiar to the romantic poet, has a different significance, 'like the soul released in dream'. Moonlight fills the room and distorts familiar objects, casting shadows and creating phantom images Now one of these phantom images turns into a child, a pretty, innocent, laughing child, but, in the language of Droste-Hülshoff, a symbol of something else: of childhood and the passing of time, or even of death perhaps. Like all other moments in this poem, this moment passes, however, and the hour changes again. Whatever the child has symbolised is gone, and with the coming of the dawn come new events, the stirring of the world outside, the crowing of the cock, the waking dog and the creaking of the stable door suggesting that someone is up and about. A new transformation occurs with the break of day, and with the first light reality reasserts itself, in the forest and on the heath outside, and through the sounds that mean things are happening, and that these are the normal things of life, focused in the noise of a scythe and the noise of hunting horns.

Anyone who has ever lain awake at night will recognize what Droste-Hülshoff is describing, and everyone will have his or her own response to it. She is not plumbing the depths of human experience, as she does at times, but presenting her reader in the simplest way with the material to comprehend the journey from the dark and lonely night to the emergence of a new and hopeful day.

On this occasion, the imagery is relatively sparse, but two examples stand out: her description of the moon as a silver gondola floating upwards 'drifting into nothingness on the blue steel of the pathway', and, in the last strophe, the impact of day breaking over the misty heath with the dramatic line 'life spurts upwards from a foaming chalice'.

Sleepless Night

How did the sun sink down, brilliant and heavy,
and then out of the scorched waves
how did the hosts of swirling mists
summon forward the starless night!
I hear the sound of distant footsteps.
The clock strikes ten.

All living things have not yet fallen asleep.
The last doors of the bedchambers creak shut.
The fitchet **f)** presses itself cautiously
against the bulge of the gutter
and slips along the rafters of the gable.
The heifer, drunk with sleep, nods off mumbling,
and from far away in the stable comes a booming sound
as the horse paws the ground,
snorting wearily until, lulled by the poppy,
his motionless flanks drop limply down.

Through the open slit in my window
drifts the heavy scent of lilac,
and against the misted grey window-pane
brushes the confusion of its swirling branches.
I am weary, weary as Nature! –
The clock strikes eleven.

Oh, wondrous state of sleeping wakefulness!
Are you a blessing or a curse to tender nerves?
It is a night, kissed awake by the dew,
and I feel the darkness, cool, like fine rain
sliding down my cheeks. The curtain frame
seems to be moving, rocking,
and the coat of arms on the plaster of the ceiling
is gently
floating and wriggling like a polypus.

How the blood jerks through my brain!
From the attic comes a creaking sound,
something is rustling in the desk and moving sharply,
as though a key were being turned,
and listen: the clock has woken up.
It's midnight.

Was that the sound of spirits, the soft, slight
tinkling sound of a glass barely touched?
And then again. like restrained weeping, the drawn-out sound of
lamentation,
rises up out of the lilac,
muted, sweeter now, as though wet with tears,
and struggling blissfully, the contorted movements of embarrassed love.
Oh, nightingale, this is no waking song,
merely the forward movement of the soul released in dream.

And now the mumbling sound of falling stonework,
the rotten fragments dropping from the tower.
The owl lets out its rasping noise and coughs.
A sudden breath of wind fills the branches
and the tree-tops in the glade.
The clock strikes one.

And down below the mounting clouds are swirling.
Like a lamp from an ancient barrow
the silver gondola of the moon floats upwards,
trembling into nothingness on the blue steel of the pathway.
On each lilac leaf a little spark of light is glowing
and, sharply outlined in the pale light,
the shape of the window is cast upon my bed,
enveloped in the shuddering leaves.

Now I should like to sleep, sleep straight away,
to fall asleep beneath the breath of the moon,
the whispering branches playing round me,
sparks in my blood, a spark in the bushes,
and in my ear a melody.
The clock strikes two.

And the sweet sound, the gentle laughter,
grows more distinct, and something begins to make its way
across the ceiling, like daguerreotype images
climbing upwards, fleeing like arrows.
It seems to me as if I can see bright curls falling,
and eyes glowing like fireflies
and then becoming moist, turning blue and gentle,
and at my feet there sits a pretty child.

The child looks up, eager and innocent,
its soul pouring out of its eyes,
and now it raises its hand playfully,
then pulls it back, and laughs.
And listen! The first cock-crow!
The clock strikes three.

How startled I was - oh, sweet sight,
you have vanished, floating away with the darkness.
The harsh grey twilight wells up,
the sparkle of the dew on the lilac Is extinguished.
the silver shield of the moon is rusted over.
In the forest there are anxious mutterings,
and my swallow on the edge of the frieze
is chirping softly, chirping away in the deep dream.

The flocks of doves are shyly circling,
as though intoxicated, round the courtyard,
and once again the cry of the cock resounds,
and the dog stirs on its straw bed,
and slowly the door of the stable creaks.
The clock strikes four.

Then the eastern sky is in flames –oh, morning glow!
It is rising, rising, and with the first rays of light
forest and heathland are flooded with the sound of song.
Life spurts upwards from a foaming chalice.
There comes the sound of a scythe, the brood of falcons flutters.
Close by in the forest the hunting horns are clashing,
and like a glacier the land of dreams
dissolves on the fiery horizon.

f) fitchet: an older, less familiar name for a polecat, selected here simply because it is older and less familiar.

'The Sleepwalker' dates from the same time as 'Sleepless Night', the spring of 1844. As far as the setting is concerned, the two poems have much in common, but 'The Sleepwalker' tells a story that recalls *Die Judenbuche* and the long ballad about the horse-dealer mentioned above. All three works, in their very different ways, show Droste-Hülshoff's obsession with the idea of guilt and the dark burden that rests on the central character in each. The story of the sleepwalker, the old man who lives in a grand house with all the trappings of wealth and engages in spine-chilling activities at full moon, is told only very gradually and not in detail, but by the time the poem ends we know enough to understand that this man has reaped the grim reward for his selfish acts and his contempt for fellow human beings, even his wife and child. The final line passes a laconic judgement which by now is fully understood: no one could envy him his terrible existence, except the central victim of his dreadful flaw, the greed which led him to betray the thief in exchange for money. That man ended on the gallows, and who can say whether his fate was not preferable to the old man's?

From the beginning, this awful tale of avarice is told against the background of the twilight which, for Droste-Hülshoff, so often prompts thoughts of mystery, even of the supernatural. Yet this old man belongs in the real world, or at least the world which he has made his reality. This is no ghostly apparition; in an ordinary sense he is no robber lurking at dusk. He is apparently leading a comfortable life, and only the rumours that have gathered about him suggest that the truth is different. These rumours, once raised, are dismissed, for no one really knows the truth. Thus the speaker/onlooker/the poet herself builds up the story, while seeming to throw doubt on it: 'they say' things, but who are 'they'? And what will people not say when the basis of the rumours is the existence of untold wealth?

This is how the story goes, but, even as he/she dismisses it – 'who believes all that?' – the foundation is firmly laid for the tangible evidence that constitutes the middle of the poem. The man engages in strange behaviour when the moon is full, counting his piles of gold by lamplight, terrified that someone is going to rob him. He wraps himself in his shroud, for this is indeed a living death he is enduring. When a cry resounds, it is as if someone were attacking his soul, and yet every indication is that he has already sold his soul by his awful deeds. We have already been told that the story goes that he handed a wretched thief over for execution in exchange for a taler, but local gossip has spoken, we have heard, of a wife and child who died long ago and were said to have been maltreated by him.

Because we have already been told this, it comes as no surprise that his other activity on those moonlit nights is an even stranger one, when he goes to a room in the house and seems to be dispensing food and medicine to whoever his crazed mind believes is lying in the bed there, and in the cradle next to it. The blue flame that suddenly appears warns the onlooker to get away from this scene of horror, and speaks perhaps of eternal penance. Judgement rests with God, and it would be a bold man who would dare to curse the sleepwalker.

This is another poem which shows Droste-Hülshoff's brilliant capacity for evoking suspense and building up an atmosphere. It is well paired with the preceding poem, where a different kind of suspense was achieved, the human being yearning for sleep throughout a night punctuated by the striking of the clock which marks the changing quality of the night. It is also appropriate to point out how, in both 'Sleepless Night' and 'The Sleepwalker', rhyme and metre play an important part. In the former, the alternating strophes mark the steady passing of the night, the first in each case six short lines rhyming ab, ab, cc, the second eight longer lines rhyming in a more complex, irregular way that denotes the changing mood from one hour to the next. 'The Sleepwalker' is composed of eight strophes, each comprising eight long lines: in this way Droste-Hülshoff manages to convey the sense of narrative and the inexorable progress of events.

This is a very much simplified way of analysing the structure of the poems, and, as has been said, there has been no attempt to emulate the structure in these translations, but it seems only right to draw attention to this other important aspect of her poetic skill, inevitably sacrificed here for reasons which may be criticised, but it is hoped this can be justified in the attempt to be true to the overall impact of the poems.

The Sleepwalker

Can you see the tiled roof over there in the grove?
Twilight is closing in, let us go quickly,
Soon the full moon will be rising on the edge of the moor
and then it is not a good idea to linger in these parts.
No ghostly apparition is floating up there among the pine trees.
No robber is lurking in that shed.
It is a bourgeois house, a bourgeois way of life.
An old man lives there, servants live inside.

The master is old, no one knows how old.
He does not choose to disclose it in the parish records.
His wife died many years ago,
A child died, too, but that is ages past.
They say he would not have a doctor come to her,
that he tortured his sick child with poor food,
but what will they not say to condemn people
when there is a mountain of gold?

Once he was poor, lived wretchedly,
in fact more wretchedly than other people.
And then, the story goes, he handed someone
over to the gallows for a taler.
They say the thief was young and wan with hunger,
his mother sick, but who believes all that?
Envy pursues the rich man. Look at those hovels over there!
That is where poverty resides, but their wealth stayed with him.

You can see him busying himself in the church,
and no one should criticise him for his habits,
but since his bodily strength has deserted him,
the old man succumbs to an evil affliction.
Whenever the full moon is shining,
he wraps himself, sleeping, in his shroud
and climbs out of his bed, fanning the little stub of his candle.
A servant follows him, watching where he is going.

Then out of that hut the workman watches
him counting for hours on end at the window,

filing the gold, making marks with his pen,
and all of a sudden making a grab, as though for the throat of a thief.
Then indeed a cry sounds out,
as if someone were attacking his very soul,
until his arms sink as though struck down by a storm
and he goes trembling on with his little lamp.

His next walk takes him to the room
where there is a little bed standing next to a bigger one.
Then he rocks the cradle this way and that,
as if he were shaking a bottle of fine wine,
and he pours and pours, as if he might never empty it,
and crams and crams as though he were forcing food into the bedclothes,
and seems to be trying to take hold of a pulse,
bent over, as if he were listening to the wheezing of weak breath.

Next he is standing by the other bed,
seems to be bending over and dribbling medicine in.
He tosses a cover over
and seems to be pulling a screen across.
Then in a flash he has reached the pane of glass,
the window from which in the darkness the gallows can be seen.
The servant leaps; you can hear a muffled whimpering sound.
The window clinks, and the room is dark.

Go quickly, more quickly! Look there at the window.
Look how there is a gentle glow and little trembling sparks.
Now a little blue flame starts up: away, just get away!
It seems to me as if a storm is filling the air all about.
Do not look back! You bold man, do not curse him!
Leave him alone with God and justice.
Do you think any curse could add to his sufferings?
Ah, let the thief on the gallows envy him!

To follow that poem with 'The Dead Lark' is to recognize the sharp contrasts that characterise her poetry, but this is true of her whole *œuvre*, and perhaps never more so than in the poems she wrote between the departure of Levin Schücking in February 1842 and the closing phases of her creative life. This period takes in, of course, the visit of Levin with his bride in May 1844, and their final parting at the end of May. Her farewell to him is spoken in the poem 'Lebt wohl' (see above), but the valedictory tone is balanced by the new strength she shows, as she speaks of her 'wild muse' and affirms the place of her work in her life. When they parted, she gave to him an important group of ten poems which included 'Late Awakening', 'I, the Centre of the World', 'The Poet. The Poet's Happiness', Fare well!', 'Hold fast!' and 'The Dead Lark'. Her intention was that he should publish them in forthcoming volumes of *Das Morgenblatt*, and, true to his commitment, Levin did so in most cases later that year, although a small handful had to await his 1860 volume *Letzte Gaben* ('Last Gifts').

These poems follow now, and, in whatever order one reads them, they represent an extraordinary group, with no obviously unifying theme, but having in common the confident hold on content and command of language which seems to reinforce her sense that she has indeed arrived at a new stage of her creative development. They are surely marked by the inspiration of her 'wild muse', and this will remain the case with all the poems she produced until her last period of illness and frailty meant that she had to content herself with very slight 'occasional poems' dedicated to those around her in her dying days. There can be little doubt that Droste-Hülshoff, dogged by ill health since her early days, was conscious of the closeness of death, although there were brief periods when she felt rather better physically and in spirits. Certainly it is this awareness which fills 'The Dead Lark', which, with its lyrical and elegiac mood, is surely one of her most beautiful poems. As she watches the lark soaring high over the field of grain in the early morning light, she immediately speaks in terms of songs and poetry, and so the transition in thought is inevitable. She is herself the lark, struggling towards the day, and it is her song and the beating of her wings that she hears. The language of those first two strophes repeats itself: the sun, the gnat, the light are there in both. But then there is a sudden change, for the bird drops down, and it is dead. This was its final song, and its nest is not completed.

It is not fanciful to believe that she is thinking of what she will not complete in her life, soon to be cut short, for Droste-Hülshoff was never in any doubt that her reputation would follow long after her and, despite the slight murmurs of acclaim that were beginning to be heard as her work was gaining some recognition, that she would not be widely known in her lifetime. The poignancy of this reality is expressed in her tender address to the little corpse- 'poor cold remains'- and in our knowledge that her wish to be returned to her beloved homeland was not to be fulfilled.

The Dead Lark

I stood at the edge of your land,
In your green forest of grain,
and with the first rays of light
your song came swirling down.
You chirped towards the sun,
like a gnat towards the light.
Your song was like a shower of blossoms,
the beating of your wings like a poem.

Then it seemed to me as if I myself
were struggling towards the new day.
As if I were listening to my own singing
and the beating of my own wings.
The sun was spurting forth fiery sparks,

my face was burning with flames,
and I myself was reeling as though intoxicated,
like a gnat towards the light.

Then suddenly it dropped down, sank down,
like a dead cinder into the seed.
I saw the little limbs still jerking
and approached in fear.
Your last song had faded away.
You lay there, poor cold remains,
after you had fluttered your last in the rays of the sun
and sung out your final song close to your half-built next.

I should like to weep for you,
shed tears pressed from the heart by anguish,
for the brightness of my life will also fade away,
I sense it, sung to an end and burnt to nothingness.
Then you, my body, your poor remains,
for you only a grave in the green meadow
and only close, close to my own nest,
only in my silent homeland.

Among the poems she gave to Levin when he departed at the end of May was the following, 'Late Awakening', and it has the gentle, lyrical quality of 'The Dead Lark'. It is also deeply personal, although it raises certain issues which, while not changing its quality, do pose questions. In draft form it includes a subtitle which dedicates it to Amalie Hassenpflug, an old friend from earlier days in Münster with whom she maintained a friendship that seems to have deepened over the years. Occasionally it appears as if Amalie were more devoted to Annette than the other way round. Annette found herself out of sympathy with the other woman's overtly Romantic leanings and her tendency to suggest that Annette, who was far superior as a writer, should be pursuing a different direction, more in line with literary fashion. This, together with their geographical separation, led to substantial periods when they were not in close contact, although this does not appear to have deterred Amalie, who drew much closer during Annette's final years and formed a close friendship with the Lassberg twins; in fact she lived with them for the last five years of her own life until her death in 1871 and expressed the wish that she be buried next to Annette's grave in Meersburg. Unlike Droste-Hülshoff, whose explicit wish was to be buried in Westphalia, Amalie did achieve her desire, and the two old friends lie together in the cemetery in Meersburg.

Perhaps Droste-Hülshoff mellowed with the years, and certainly two poems of these years are explicitly addressed to Amalie Hassenpflug (see below). It is not inconceivable that she was addressing Amalie Hassenpflug in 'Late Awakening', which evokes memories of the years they shared in Rüschhaus, yet the last four strophes of the poem seem to point to the revelation she experienced when she came to know Levin Schücking. The confusion and isolation she has described vanished when she looked into his eyes, and the 'human image printed on to the edge of every wave' she recognized as the transforming effect of the special kind of love she felt between them. Of that we can surely have no doubt. When the poem opens up towards the end, allowing her to embrace all humankind and draw them into her own paradise, it is not unlikely that she is expressing a broadening of her own horizons that coincided with the new warmth that is evident in many of the poems of this period.

The poem remains the same, and the autobiographical basis should not be denied. If she dropped the dedication to Amalie, yet did not replace it with an explicit one to Levin Schücking, this may well have had another explanation. She was bidding farewell to the recently married Schückings, who had been her guests for several weeks, and out of courtesy to Louise Schücking she may have elected not to make it public to whom she was referring. After all, the poem 'Fare well!', which appeared at the same time, makes it clear that she knew their friendship was at an end, replaced by the higher sense of her vocation. It was Levin himself, in the role he increasingly assumed as her editor and commentator, who was much later able to supply information about the origin of poems, and the personal part he played in their genesis.

What the poem does make clear is that Droste-Hülshoff felt deeply isolated in her earlier life. She clearly loved her home, and many of the people associated with it, but the dichotomy in her personality, remarked upon by many people, existed on a very deep level and meant that the appearance of a contented and outgoing personality was carefully contrived to disguise the discomfort and confusion beneath. This we cannot doubt, from her many letters and the observations of those closest to her. It is even possible to point far back, to the poem 'Restlessness' (see p.3 above) for a frank expression of her state of mind, and to discern the gradual blossoming of a different personality, never quite at ease it is true, but more serene in the developing of her sense of direction as a poet, and the deeper understanding of herself as a person. This growth – and one can but guess how much more would have come in both respects - is expressed simply and sincerely in this poem, with the unambiguous declaration of its title.

Late Awakening

How secluded was my existence
when in the house hedged with green,

through the song of the larks and the young branches of the pine trees
I was still dreaming up into the azure blue.

When I could still recognize no sight other than
the sunlight through the trees,
called the rocks my brothers
and my sister my reflection in the pond.

I do not speak of those years
which dawning childhood gives to us.
No: my whole youth was
so covered in a haze and so abstracted.

To be sure, I saw friendly figures pass
fleeting on the horizon.
I could hold hot hands
and draw hot lips towards me.

I heard the thudding of their greeting,
their soft whispering about my house
and sent out only half a sigh,
swimming and half-broken.

I felt the fanning of their breath
and yet no flower was sweet.
I saw the angel of love smiling,
and yet I had no paradise.

It seemed to me that with the notes
each sound confused me,
that each hand that was offered to me
went wondrously astray in the darkness.

I remained shut up, shut in,
in the magic tower of my dreams.
The flashes of lightning were companions to me,
and the storm the voice of love.

I allowed a song to sound forth into the forest,
as never before in human ear,

and I allowed my tear to fall,
a hot tear, into the flower-strewn meadow.

And I had to ask all pathways:
do you know the birds and the rays of sun also?
And yet asked no one: where are you going?
Which breath fills your breath?

How all that has changed,
since I have looked into your eyes!
How now is a human image printed
on to the edge of every wave!

How do I now feel in all warm hands
for the faint pulses,
and sense the shy look in every gaze,
and the cry in every heavy breast!

And I should like to ask all the paths:
Where are you going? Where is the house
in which beat living hearts,
and living breath bursts forth?

I should like to light all the candles
and call to every weary being:
In my head my paradise is open.
Come in now, all of you, come in!

A little poem from just a few months before the visit of Levin and his bride, and the parting now more or less inevitable, is perhaps appropriately placed here, although it does not belong with the more substantial poems she gave to him when they parted. 'Little' it may be in terms of its length, but it seizes a subject central to her thinking and treats it in a thoroughly characteristic way. It belongs with other poems often described as 'poems of the dead' (*Totengedichte*), and reflects her feeling of being close, not to death itself, but to the dead: they are her natural companions, comforters and the source of advice and counsel.

In its simplicity and directness, its fearless grasp of a huge subject, it achieves a kind of grandeur. Not 'little' at all, in fact. It would be so easy to treat her subject in a sentimental or maudlin way, but of course she does not do so. She is extolling those who are silent in their graves but who harbour deep emotions beneath the silence. What lies within them is the bleeding heart and the turbulence of raging lava. The graves, or death itself, may seem to subdue life, and yet the life is there, to be awoken when the storm gives way to sunset.

From the title on, the antitheses are present: these are the 'unsung ones', their lament is silent, there is no drop of moisture in the air. Their sacredness cannot be expressed in song, and yet it is expressed, and what they speak of is that which can never decay, which never departs. This, ultimately is the message of the poem, not the consoling thought that the dead are with us always, but that, through death, they dispense the sureness that what they once were endures within the grave, the tomb, the hillock.

The Unsung Ones
May 1843

There are graves where the lament is silent
and only the heart bleeds from within,
where no drop of moisture rises into the tree-tops
and yet inside the lava floods.
There are graves that loom on our horizon
like a stormy night
and press down upon all life,
yet when the red of sunset wakes

they stir their golden wings
like gentle seraphims.

They are too sacred for a song,
and yet are powerful orators before all people.
They speak to you of that which never parted,
that never, ever, can decay.
Ah, whenever doubt oppresses you,
and you would like to taste the breath of heaven,
and look upon the seraph's wings,
then walk towards your father's grave,
towards your brother's tomb,
towards the hillock of your child.

To speak of a 'message' in a poem like this makes it sound pedantic, and Droste-Hülshoff is no pedant. Not even in 'The Spiritual Year', where one might expect an element of teaching, does she seek to impose her thinking, and it seems to emerge in that central work that she is herself too uncertain of her position on so many issues to speak emphatically to others. It is rather, as she wrote, that she wishes to speak for those who, like herself, are assailed by uncertainty and at times by despair.

However, among these late poems, some of which she gave to Levin Schücking in May 1844, are a few that advance some kind of lesson. Yet, because this is Droste-Hülshoff, this is not in any polemical manner, but as part of a deeply-held conviction.

Three of the four selected to follow here – 'Carpe diem!', 'Hold Fast!', and 'One like many, and many like one' appeared for the first time in the posthumous edition of 1860, while 'I, the Centre of the World', which Schücking had taken away with him from their final meeting in 1844, did appear there, but had already been published in the periodical *Morgenblatt* at the end of that year.

These dates are important, of course, for they contribute to the understanding of the growth of Droste-Hülshoff's reputation, in that a very new kind of poetry, less lyrical and more nearly didactic, was unknown to her public until after her death.

If one takes into account the dates of composition, however, one can but marvel anew at the extraordinary range of her poetry, and at her ability to take this range in her stride and write with such authority.

The four poems which follow and can broadly by described as 'didactic' address issues one can reasonably suppose were close to her heart. They are not strictly speaking moral issues, but guidance for living in harmony with oneself and the world and in that respect offering pointers to a serene and honest existence. Yet that gives the impression that her tone is that of the preacher, and that is also simply not the case. Rather do they seem to represent, in this woman who was always the observer and keenly interested in her fellow men, a broad philosophy which is characterised by understanding and tolerance. No more than in 'The Spiritual Year' does Droste-Hülshoff impose a doctrine or a code of behaviour, even though each of these four poems, in its own way, suggests an attitude of mind.

Droste-Hülshoff lived in an age of revolution, in society, politics and religion, and from her vantage point she must have viewed the world as a place of changing values, in which the traditional beliefs of her own secluded life could be turned upside down. Her many letters give no real insight into her thinking, concerned as they mostly are with domestic matters and the humdrum events of everyday life. Yet it is inconceivable that she remained untouched by what was going on about her, albeit at a distance, or that, intelligent and in some ways quite opinionated, she did not absorb some of the information that must have reached her in the prominent Lassberg family, and participate in some of the talk she heard. Yet, just as she remained extraordinarily aloof from literary trends, so she does not to any extent reflect this social upheaval in her writings. Hers is a much more personal approach, and a more general understanding of the context of her increasingly restricted life.

Yet, although some would see Biedermeier trends in her, and point to a comparison with the comfortable, homely way of life that pervades some of the work of her near-contemporary Eduard Mörike, this is very far from being the whole story in either of these great poets. Rather do both of them rise above the parochial and the intimate to heights of passion and grandeur, although in both cases these heights are contained within the subtlety of their expression.

It is significant that the first poem that follows here was given another title when it was first published in the 1860 edition. There it is called 'Stille Größe' ('Quiet Greatness'), although, when she had sent it to Levin Schücking in April 1844, there was no doubt that she called it by the name most usually given to it now, the rather cumbrous 'One like many, and many like one'. The phrase 'quiet greatness' is indelibly associated with a great name of the German Eighteenth Century, Johann Joachim Winckelmann, who, in his ground-breaking work on the importance of Greek painting and sculpture had spoken of 'noble simplicity and quiet greatness' (1754).

Quite why Schücking should have substituted this phrase when he came to publish the poem eighteen years after her death is unclear, but her own title is also difficult to comprehend. Puzzling, too, is the fact that the poem, unlike the others she sent him at the same time which included 'Moon-Rise' and '*Gemüt*' (see below), was held back for so long and not mentioned again. Possibly Schücking disliked its distinctly 'unlyrical' quality, though that hardly explains what must have been his very rare decision to change the title.

At its simplest, this is a poem about those who live and die heroic deaths and who seem to merit lamentation. Some of these she names, people who have in various ways deserved their recognition. The list is strange and seemingly random, from the unnamed Socrates, as he accepts his fate and takes the poisoned chalice, to historical figures like Götz von Berlichingen and Sir Thomas More, and then to the artist Corregio, and Cervantes, creator of Don Quijote. All, in their different ways, bowed to their fate, and all have received acclaim, but her acclaim, her grief, attaches to lesser figures, the many who, though blessed with the capacity to love, did not possess the gifts valued by the world.

When she speaks of these unsung heroes, Droste-Hülshoff delivers a thoroughly personal verdict, for they are rich in the way that matters to her; their wealth is in their dreams, and their secret treasure is what nourishes them. This poem is, in its essence, deeply personal, and it supplies a vital clue to her nature and her approach to her art. Perhaps this was what made Levin Schücking uneasy; the poem reveals too much of her true self. In other places she declares that she does not seek the acclaim of the world, the fame that others see as paramount; if fame comes to her only after a hundred years, then this is enough for her. Yet, at the same time, she cherishes her gift of poetry, knowing, as she discloses in 'The Poet', the high price that it exacts (see below). This is a proudly resolute Droste-Hülshoff, close to her death, and the poem seems to be defiantly revealing what she has assiduously kept hidden for so long.

A hymn of praise to her vocation, then, but a joyful affirmation of love, is what ultimately emerges from this strange and wonderful poem which would not see the light of day for so many years, but which, in her letter to Levin, she spoke of in the same breath as the puzzling '*Gemüt*' (see below), saying that they should not be placed adjacent to one another, because they were 'so alike'. Perhaps, after all, Levin knew exactly what he was doing when he gave it another, even more puzzling title, and perhaps 'quiet greatness' is his eloquent comment on his much respected, much loved friend.

One like many, and many like one

I do not lament the man who falls,
a milestone to the vanquished land,
who holds the goblet of his fate
and mixes with determined hand,
nor him who strides towards the storm
and knows that he will break the oak.
Who was so rich as Götz inside the tower
or More before the scaffold?

I do not lament the man who dies
consumed by the world and his own fire,
him whom the fruit from the tree corrupts
and whom the manna from heaven feeds;
not Corregio who, pale and sick,
brought copper hellers home,
nor Cervantes who, half-starved,
still laughed at his Sancho Panza.

These are the princes of misfortune,
the mighty ones in the distant blue .
They feel that their breath runs

round the earth and sets it alight,
that the harvest likes to sprout joyful and abundant
out of the clods of their graves,
and that the seed must fall into nothingness
when the cedar stretches out its branches.

Him I lament whose love is great
and whose gifts are poor and meagre,
him whom the reflection of those rays
consumes, as the fire consumes the parched moss,
him who feels the spark as it wanders aimlessly
within his veins and wreaks devastation,
and whom then the wave spits out,
a little heap of thin, grey ash.

Oh, there are legions of you,
you half-blessed ones,
into whose hearts genius shyly fled
and left the pipe-dream barren,
you who would like to soar wingless
with the breath of longing
but, like feeble mist,
sink back into the bowels of the earth.

I lament you not because you are small,
nor because you are poor and sick.
I know that on your finger is,
unknown to you, the magic ring.
Ah, you are rich and do not know it,
for only the land of dreams is rich.
Ah, you are strong and do not know it,
for only the hand of love is strong.

When you sit bowed before your desk,
or at your paltry easel,
the breath of heaven arises
in you, and inside you the cry of fear.
When trembling you stretch forth
your fevered arms to some ideal
and hardly stir the blade of the nearest furrow
for your daily bread,

then you are more than the poet
who sells his heart's blood,
more than the proud artist
who names the hetaera **f1)** as a saint.
What you keep secret is more lovely
than the passion of the poet ever nurtured.
What you have buried is more sacred
than ever paint and brush revealed.

Nature gave me a bold heart:
I do not readily lower my gaze.
Greatness does not press me down;
no strange hand pushes me back.
Never upon a stranger's brow has the radiant wreath of fame
distressed me, yet have I a hundred times
been shamed
before the brightness of such silent eyes.

Weeping springs from which the sun
rolls down beneath the magic spell of the waves;
glowing steps where the gold cannot be
distinguished from the cinders.
For you I weep because you're sad,
because your hearts are swollen with tears,
you blessed, unknowing ones, and because you love,
yet doubt the image of the godhead.

Watch, watch over your silent treasure!
Leave us the land bereft of sun,
leave us the empty stage
and in a corner die unrecognized.
One day you will know what lived in you,
and what in him who mocked at you,
one day when the shining god arises
and only the pillar of Memnon sings. **f2)**

f1) Hetaera: in Ancient Greece, a highly cultured courtesan
f2) The reference is to the two pillars in Thebes, huge figures which are said to emit the sound of singing at dawn.

For the poem which follows here, Droste-Hülshoff took as her basic inspiration the famous ode by Horace, which urges that one should take hold of the present day and not ponder on thoughts of the next. In itself it is not a profound idea, but in her hands it is coloured with other thoughts: of simple pleasures that will inevitably pass and be a source of regret later, and of the intermingling of joy and sadness in human experience. Over all hangs the awareness that such thoughts are common to all.

It is hardly surprising that Droste-Hülshoff, when she wrote this poem in the summer of 1845, was thinking of the passage of time and the need she felt to hang on to the joys she could still experience. More surprising is the knowledge that, years earlier, she had written to her friend Christoph Schlüter of the pain of the regret for times past and never to return, and in particular had mentioned the idea raised here in the third strophe, of the prisoner who, after many years of freedom and contentment, might crave to return to his cell and read again the scribbled words he had written during his captivity (letter dated 5 December 1834). She had said that she knew that, with his very different temperament, Schlüter was most unlikely to share such thoughts: this very special friend, so dear to her for all her adult life, did indeed find her brooding hard to accept, and she was absolutely right that he would not comprehend this thought which is embedded in one of her fairly long letters to him, in which she was actually telling him of her sadness at her separation from her sister who had departed for Switzerland following her marriage, leaving Annette wondering if they would ever meet again. The friendship with Schlüter was very special to her, and their difference in temperament never seemed to prevent her imparting to him her deepest thoughts and concerns. He appears to have understood her on a certain level, and what he did not understand he accepted.

This little link between the letter and the poem eleven years later is yet another instance of the way she stored up thoughts and experiences over many years, returning to them, when the time was right as she would have it.

The last three strophes of this poem treat another of her favourite subjects: the passage of time, the changes it brings with it, and, by implication, the losses inherent in all lifetimes. From the reflective mood of most of the poem, she moves into the familiar poignancy she could evoke at all stages of her career.

Carpe diem!

Seize the hour, no matter how pale it may be,
a sprig of moss, wet from the mist of the moor,
a colourless little flower fluttering on the heathland.
Ah! some time or other the soul will dream sweetly
of everything that belonged to it and that it left behind,
and many a sigh is uttered for suffering fled away.

Into everything it sinks drops of blood,
and without knowing sets even into hours behung with grey
pearls from the sacred, deepest coffer.
If often a vague longing rises up in you,
you will perchance look as though through a veil of cloud
for days long forgotten, yet once sensed.

Who, thinking of his childhood,
when words made him fall into despair,
would not wish to be a child and frightened?
Yes, the prisoner who wrote upon the wall,
does he after years of happiness not feel the urge
to gaze once more upon the ancient sayings?

To be sure, there are hours so hated,
weighing so heavy on our memories, that

we try to shrug their shadows off.
Then sometimes such an hour sends to us heaven's fury,
and mostly in it is a poisonous thorn,
the hidden maggot of our secret guilt.

And so let anyone still worthy of an upward glance
accept whatever pleasure may be granted to him,
the proud hour just as much as the hour in simple dress.
Let him drain every silent drop of dew,
and if the blue of the sky is not reflected in it,
even so the pious willow is surely whispering overhead.

Rejoice at the smile from your tiny child,
rejoice at his uncertain cry of jubilation,
when he stretches out his delighted limbs.
Even if the pride that fills you were ten times greater
when one day he stands before you as a young man,
he will still not give you back your smiling child.

Rejoice at your friend before he grows to be an old man
and experience has lined his bold forehead
and flowers from the grave flutter on his head.
Rejoice at the old man, follow him for a long time with your gaze:
perhaps it will not be long before you would give many a day
to see once more that grey head.

Oh, whoever seizes the hour tightly and in earnest,
and strokes the garland away from its pale hair,
on that person the hour bestows its richest gift.
Yet, fools that we are, we push it back:
before us hope, behind us happiness,
and our tomorrows murder our todays.

Friendship and love, of whatever kind and whatever intensity, mattered very deeply to Droste-Hülshoff, and that is where she begins the next poem in this section. However, the advocacy of loyalty, intense though it is, is only a part of her concern, for the poem is about steadfastness in a broader sense, and ultimately about the familiar theme of her vocation, and the need to be loyal to that. There are echoes of 'Carpe diem!' here, in the injunction to cling on to the precious moment, and the poem even looks forward a few months to another poem, which she may well have had in mind as she wrote this, for 'The Golems' seems to deplore the current state of the world around her (see below). Here she reminds the listener that one day he will have to justify his actions before the Golem, but actually it is herself she is addressing, her troubled self, the child of anguish, with the burden she knows she has received through her poetry, given to her by God. Thus it is not on a single friend that she urges loyalty and constancy, but on her own fate, and, more widely, as in 'The Golems', she is almost certainly also urging respect for the *status quo* in a world which threatened instability and change.

This should not imply that Droste-Hülshoff was reactionary in her attitudes, but as a sensitive, thinking human being she was undoubtedly apprehensive at the thought that values she cherished could be swept aside on a wave of revolution, and that at the heart of this lay a disregard for emotions, above all for constancy in human relationships. This is where the poem begins, with the warning of decay and the reckless substitution of the new for the established, and this is where, by implication, it ends, with the image of the compass given to all human beings. No one has yet wrenched this compass from his breast, and it is, ultimately, the only guide.

Hold fast!

Hold fast to the friend when once you have found him.
He'll leave no gifts for you to build new things
but, like the house in which someone has died,
he'll leave an impure heart where faithfulness decays.
Do you believe that the press of the hand is yours, the light
from your own eyes innocent and full of love?
If you press a second time, look once again:
the fruit is mottled and the mirror dull.

Hold fast to your word, oh! as fast as to your own soul.
No laurel grows so green and joyful
that it can hide the mark upon a brow
that could falter beneath the pressure of the word.
The poorest beggar with an honest heart
may approach you like a king,
and you, you tug the laurel downwards
and secretly you must make your confession.

Hold fast to your belief, let it suffice you!
Who would wish to exchange blood for a foreign ichor **f1)**
If you banish the cherub from your cradle,
you will hear his wing rustling out of every leaf,
and if your spirit is too strong, perhaps too blind,
to see the flaming sword in his hand,
then do not doubt that he will stand,
a weeping child, at your desolate final resting-place.

And then the gift, graciously bestowed upon you,
the precious moment sent by God,
oh, cling on to its source as you flee.
Prize every drop more highly than diamonds!
The future is still sleeping, yet it will wake some time for me,
when your will has lost its strength,
and when you weep heavy tears
into the Charybdis **f2)** of your dead hours.

But above all, hold fast the child of anguish,
your troubled self, endowed by God.

Oh, do not suck the blood from your heart
In order to bring a bastard soul to life,
so that when one day you tremble before the Golem **f3)**,
it does not step before you with soft lamentation,
saying "I was like this, too, and thus I was entrusted to you,
wretched one, why did you slay me?"

So steadfast, only steadfast, only take no step to one side.
Heaven has truly drawn up the paths.
A pure eye can see them from a distance,
and only the will has failed to recognise the path.
A compass was impressed in each of us,
and up to now no one has torn it from his breast.
He who looks towards the earth calls it honour,
and he who looks to heaven calls it conscience.

f1) In Greek mythology, ichor is the golden fluid that is the blood of the gods.
f2) Charybdis: the hazardous whirlpool in the Strait of Messina
f3) In medieval and Jewish folklore, the Golem is an artificially created being, fashioned from clay and lacking sensitivity and emotion.

'I, the Centre of the World' was another of the poems that Droste-Hülshoff passed to Levin Schücking when he left with his new wife, and it was another of those he published, as was her intention, in the periodical *Das Morgenblatt* later that year. What he admitted only later was that it was he who had once urged her to make herself 'the centre of the world', and thus that actually this poem was addressed to him.

In his *Lebensbild*, Schücking tells of an occasion when he had argued with her, saying that she should follow her own inclinations more and put herself into the centre, rather than always putting others first and considering their wellbeing before her own. Certainly there are many indications that, although she was aware of her own standing as a poet, even though recognition eluded her, she was constantly setting her own needs aside, and sometimes her work, in order to care for other people. Her letters often refer to sick relatives whom she was nursing, or a neighbour in need to whom she was offering help of some kind, and remarks by other people speak of acts of kindness and selflessness from her, even if it affected the progress of her writing.

This poem makes it clear that this role of nurturer came naturally to her, and that she saw it as an important one, and one from which she derived reward, but Schücking, perhaps always more conscious of her enormous potential and genuinely anxious to promote her reputation, could see that this aspect of her personality took up time and energy which, from his standpoint, should be better spent on the writing he so admired. This very personal response makes it clear that, in a world where (as 'The Golems' makes clear) she was conscious that all too often selfishness and heartlessness prevailed, her own values had to be her guide. What Levin had said to her she might dismiss as a jest, but actually she probably knew that he was in earnest when he urged her to promote herself, knowing that the world they lived in, and her own social context, militated against her receiving due recognition.

This very personal, tender poem presents an important side of Droste-Hülshoff, and it leaves no doubt about her priorities. When, in the middle of the second strophe, she cries 'Oh, to be happy, loved and happy!' she must surely be giving voice to an essential desire in herself, and one has to recall that she gave this poem to him as she bade him and his bride farewell. However, no more than in 'Fare well! (See above, p) does she allow self-pity to dominate her mood. When she speaks of the special joy of being beside a loved one during a lengthy illness and experiencing the incomparable moment when the patient emerges from sickness, we recognize that she has known this experience. What she refers to in the face of the loved one is not just relief, or gratitude, but the dawning comprehension that a relationship has changed. This is 'a newly awoken radiance of the soul' which transcends the emotion of a friend or a lover. One cannot doubt that she has known this and that this is her answer to Levin's 'jest'.

Fulfilment exists for her, not only in friendship and love, but, as the next strophe makes clear, in the satisfaction of achievement. The important thing is not material wealth but the means by which that wealth has been gained, and, as emerges very clearly from 'The Poet', Droste-Hülshoff knew very well the depth of suffering and sacrifice that was necessary to achieve her own goals. As she declared on a number of occasions, she was guided not by the pursuit of fame, but by her profound belief in a God-given calling. The repeated question 'have you ever…?' is not a reproof to Levin but the assurance that she has known things which cannot easily be summed up in the injunction to set out to makes oneself the centre of the world. The 'weeks and weeks of self-forgetting sorrow', or the recognition of the potential in a 'new alliance' have already made a person fulfilled, loved and loving, and rich. Such depths of emotion transform a person into the centre of his own world, unknown perhaps to the onlooker, but replenished again and again, just as the stream goes back repeatedly to its source. There is nothing of the homily in this poem. It is a frank declaration of confidence from this woman, alone and ailing, that what is within her is enough to sustain her, and even to bring her a special kind of joy.

I, the Centre of the World

Once you offered these words in jest:
"Let anyone who wishes to achieve riches, love and happiness
Make himself into the centre of the world,
into a circle where all the rays meet up."
What you said, my friend, was like the door of the temple,
on the outside the inscription and the crowds of people,
but through the cracks shines the light of the lamps,
and incense drifts out, and holy singing.

How could the spring of happiness ever flow out
of anything but one's own heart?
How could the anger of heaven pour forth from any bowl
other than that which is born of oneself?
Oh, to be happy, loved and happy! –
If only an angel could direct me on those paths!
There the curtain of the temple billows, delicate and pure,
and I can hear it like an echo gliding through the folds.

"Have you ever stood beside a sick-bed,
after weeks and weeks of self-forgetting sorrows,
and then raised your heavy eyelids in the morning
to fevered prayers of gratitude
and seen hovering about the face of the recovering one
a newly awoken radiance of his soul,
and a look of love towards you as
no friend, no lover, could offer?

"Have you ever held your pencil in your hand
and reckoned up with cheerful spirit
the pennies that you yourself have earned?
Did every coin seem to you to burst into flames like the gold
of the treasure for the foreign pool of sorrows
from which you have cunningly extorted your joys,
and did you, as you relished your riches,
let out a deep, deep breath into your breast?

"And in that moment when a right hand passes
with an impassioned blessing over a beloved head,

when it takes the heart from its own heart
in order to lay it joyfully upon the other heart,
have you ever known that moment and then stood,
with your arms folded silently and lovingly,
happily working out what fruits,
what precious fruits, that new alliance can bring forth?

"Then you are happy, you are loved and rich,
a rock on which all lightning strikes can break.
Then, no matter if your garland withers, illness and old age
turn you pale and furrow your brow:
you are the centre of your world,
that circle out of which spring rays of joy,
and no matter how much the banks of the stream may swell,
how should it not replenish its spring!"

The sense of her vocation is expressed in a number of her poems, but most emphatically in two which, though written a little earlier, were given to Schücking during the spring of 1844. Both were published by him, 'My Calling' in *Das Morgenblatt* later that year and then in the 1844 edition of her poems, but 'The Poet' not until 1860. It says much for Droste-Hülshoff's own view of 'My Calling' –and perhaps eventually for Schücking's, too – that it heads the list of the poems in the 1844 edition.

It is undoubtedly one of the most powerful statements of her belief in what she clearly sees as her sacred calling and it contains some of her most important pronouncements on the nature of this gift which is also a burden. The same is true of the poem which follows 'My Calling' in this selection and describes the poet as being set apart from the rest of humanity and paying for his priceless gift with his very soul. She leaves no doubt of her awareness of the price she must pay in terms of suffering and isolation.

In 'My Calling' one has the impression not only that she had come to an even more profound understanding of her art as a vocation than ever before, but that it had brought her also to a grandeur of expression rarely reached until now, in her struggle to define the special nature of what has been laid upon her from birth. Only now does she seem able to articulate the emotions that have stirred within her from her early youth, and the result is a poem of wide-ranging thought. So complex is it, in fact, that Levin Schücking wrote to her that he found it difficult to understand, to the point of its being incomprehensible. In particular he found the sixth and seventh strophes difficult, he told her, but her response to that was that no one else had problems with it. She tried to elucidate those two strophes for him, but whether he was convinced remains unknown, although it apparently did not stop him publishing the poem as it stood.

The poem prompted a reaction such as she had hitherto not received. Some critics praised the language for its power and originality, while others pointed to it as an unambiguous statement of her belief in her ordained purpose. They stressed also the conviction she often expressed, though never so cogently as here, that she did not seek short-lived fame, but believed that her role was first and foremost that of healer to her fellowmen: 'to bring back to righteousness the one who has gone astray, awaken the sleeping one, stir up dull senses, warm the cold one,' but to do so without arrogance. This quotation is taken from an anonymous review of the 1844 edition and it focused attention particularly on this poem, emphasising the power of her intellect and her spiritual strength. (See *Historisch-Kritische Ausgabe* 1,2 p. 931). It would seem that this poem achieved recognition for Droste-Hülshoff such as she had not experienced before, but whether those who praised it understood it any better than Levin Schücking did is open to question. It is a difficult poem, of that there can be no doubt, but there is guidance in the opening two strophes and in the final two, as well as in what she replied to Levin about strophes six and seven. The opening addresses the issue very simply and directly: "you ask me why I abandoned the peace and quiet of my accustomed environment, and you ask me this as though I have somehow forced my way into Parnassus, the very seat of poetry." The answer is just as direct: "I was given this as my birth-right, by God Himself, and it is both a privilege and a burden."

Interesting in relation to this first strophe is the change she made to the first line, which originally read "which drove me away from my spindle". It seems that she was thinking of the fact that she was born a woman, tied to traditional womanly activities, but that she then had second thoughts and saw the restrictions she felt as due, not merely to her gender (though this was undoubtedly an important factor) but to the wider context into which she had been born, the world in which she found herself, her class and upbringing and, almost certainly, aspects of her personality which may have invited prejudice. The second strophe ends with her recognition that the time is right, the hour has come when she must lay claim to her heritage and take up her task. The next five strophes are placed in the mouth of Time, the Hour, and only at the end does she, the Poet, speak again, addressing once more the unidentified plural 'you'. She is declaring herself before those who seek to ask the question: this is her solemn manifesto.

Meanwhile, it is the Hour, that abstract moment in time, which dictates her course of action. The first call is to her to awaken the dreamer, lulled to sleep by the side of the road by the vapours from the datura plant. That person who had been reduced to silence and inactivity must be awakened and his emotions, whether of joy or sorrow, stirred by the clarion call of poetry. As an extension to this are the next two strophes, with the reference to the mother and the cradle, returning to the idea of birthright and heritage. However, there is more, for the message is of the healing power of poetry, and the need to embrace this precious gift which brings pain as well as joy.

The next two strophes, which particularly puzzled Levin Schücking, do indeed seem to make a bewildering leap of thought, although the defiant Droste-Hülshoff assured him that everyone she had read the poem to had declared it among the best of all. Her explanation of these two strophes is simple, oversimplified perhaps, but it must serve as guidance. What she told him was that the first of the two referred to a married couple who had lost their love for one another, the second a man prematurely aged in his innermost being: in both cases what had got lost along the way was not the feeling for the state they were in but the susceptibility to it. (That, at least, appears to be her meaning.) What is being urged in both instances is a return to the beginning, a recapturing of what appears to have gone astray. The explanation, of course, is in line with so much of Droste-Hülshoff's deepest belief about the validity of the past and the power of memory. There is also in both strophes a familiar conviction that the source of all emotion remains to be invoked and that inspiration does not ultimately fail.

The blond child and the devoted mother are linked as the guardians of the precious gift, and so the 'office' of which she speaks is constant and inescapable. Then, as the poem ends, a new image enters, that of the flower in the desert, which can bring succour to the thirsting, for that is its unique role. The traditional inhabitants of the natural world, the lion and the snake, pay no heed to it, but the pilgrim, the searcher after his own goal, will recognize it and give it his blessing.

My Calling

"What was it that drove me out of my circle,
out of my peaceful chamber?"
You ask me that as if, like a thief,
I had broken into Parnassus.
Well listen then, hear, since you have asked:
I have been burdened at birth
with this privilege, as far as heaven dawns,
and with this power, by the Grace of God.

Now, when the dead light
forces its way forward on the decaying stump,
where the loveliest bank of flowers
sways over the lifeless swamp,
the spirit, a bloodless meteor,
bursts into flames and then dies away on the smouldering moor.
And now the Hour cries out: "Step forward,
man or woman, living soul!"

"Approach the dreamer, who has been
lulled to sleep by the side of the road
by the scent of the datura f),
and who, sliding slowly from the wall,
still stumbles towards the magic breath.
And wherever a mouth still knows how to smile
in a dream, an eye still how to weep,
let the sound of trumpets blare out,
and the west wind whisper gently in the glades.

"Come closer to where the exuberant senses
offer as love their tortuous struggle,

and through the breast of their own mother
might bring the arrow to its target,
where even shame flutters open,
a merry victory banner.
Then let out a harsh rattle: “Wake up, wake up,
you wretched one, and think of your cradle.”

“Think of the eye that watched over you,
that offered you yet another joy;
think of the hand that many a night
soothed your bed of pain for you;
think of the heart that alone is hurt
and alone is blessed because of you.
Then kneel down on the ground
and beg for your mother’s blessing.

“And when two once so earnestly desired beings
imagine themselves in a dream
as in captivity,
as though a priestly utterance has the power
to lift the most sacred spell,
then whisper softly: “Wake up, wake up!”
Look into your eyes, the sad eyes,
where memory is gradually dawning
and then: wake up! wake up, oh holy light!

‘And when trembling in sleep the pulses
still throb from the opiate,
and the dry eye would give its sunlight
for one drop of water,
then softly say: “Poor creature, feast
your eye upon the beauty of the ether,
embrace a blond child and think
of the first tear of inspiration!”’

Thus did Time call, and thus was my office
bestowed upon me by the Grace of God.
Thus was my calling passed to me as my heritage,
with eager spirit and warm life.
I do not ask if you know my name.

I do not ask to court brief fame.
But know this: where the Sahara desert burns,
in the sand, there stands a flower,

colourless and without a scent. It only knows
how to preserve the pure dew
and offer it gently to the thirsting one
in its chalice.
The snake slips shyly past,
casting glances like arrows from its eyes.
The proud lion rages by,
and only the pilgrim will bless it.

f) The datura, a beautiful plant, with many varieties, has over the centuries been regarded as sacred. It is known for its toxicity but also for its healing powers.

The next poem clearly belongs with the previous one in that it is one of the group usually described as 'poet-poems', but it is less a manifesto, a statement of resolution, than a declaration of the cost of her art, something about which she never seems to have had any doubt. Although it is offered here as a poem in two parts, but nevertheless one poem, there has been controversy from the beginning about whether they should be viewed as two separate poems. There is a change in metre between the two, and an accompanying change in tone.

Against that is the unifying theme, and the image of the rose growing among the thistles raised in the first part and constituting the principal image of the final strophe. The critical consensus seems now to favour the view that it is indeed intended as one poem given to Levin Schücking in May 1844, and based on discussions they had had during the winter of 1841-42. In the address to an unspecified 'you people' in the opening line there is an echo of her bitter dismissal in her much earlier 'Agony' of the ordinary people from whom she feels herself to be totally isolated (see above p.11). These are the people, as she wrote in 1820, at the time of her anguished crisis over the relationship with Heinrich Straube, who go about their humdrum activities while others, by implication herself, of higher sensibilities, must suffer. Perhaps there is less bitterness now, in this poem which specifically speaks of the suffering of the poet, to whom she attributes a higher calling, and, as in 'My Calling' the sacred gift of healing. She nevertheless contrasts those who laugh and enjoy themselves and engage in such mundane tasks as cultivating pot plants with the poet who must suffer for his art and endure the total lack of comprehension of those who have no idea of the price he must pay. It is easy wealth which comes to them, inherited with no effort, while the poet's achievement is the product of suffering beyond their understanding. There is still contempt in her dismissal of them, and the desire to make known how completely apart she feels and probably has always felt.

The Droste- Hülshoff who embraced her sacred task in 'My Calling' is absent, at least in the first part of the poem. However, the second part, with its second title, if that is indeed how she intended it, restores the sense of the privilege even the suffering affords. The invocation of Prometheus brings with it the familiar idea, and certainly familiar to Droste-Hülshoff and her readers through Goethe's poem (1774), of the poet as the new Prometheus, bringing fire from Zeus to humanity but paying for it with his life of torment, his liver consumed by a vulture but constantly growing again, while the reference to the 'princely tippler' and the diver sent down to retrieve the goblet will have stirred echoes of her great predecessors, Goethe and Schiller. It is, however, another image which dominates as the poem ends: the 'mystic rose of the thistle', in which the worm gnaws away and yet, in the process, heals. This is her destiny, and she has already answered her own question.

The Poet – the Poet's Happiness

1.

You people who laugh as you enjoy your banquet,
who look after your plants in their pots
and contentedly allow yourselves to inherit
such gold as is bequeathed to you,
you people look into the face of the poet,
marvelling that he can pluck roses
out of thistles and knows how to suck
coral and pearl from the flood welling up in his eyes,

that he reaches for the lightning
to light his torch,
and in stormy weather, when you are afraid,
knows how to find the right breath.
You stare at him half-enviously,
the intellectual Croesus of his day,
and do not know with what anguish
he must pay for his treasures.

You do not know that, like the damned,
only liquid fire can nourish him,
and that only the kingdom of the storm-riven cloud
can grant to him the breath of life,
that, while you hang your head in thought,
bloody tears are pressing forth from him,
and that only in the cracks of the sharpest thorn
is his flower able to unfold.

Do you think the lightning does not set him on fire?
Do you think the storm does not shake him?

Do you think his tears do not burn?
Do you think the thorns do not prick him?
Yes, he has fanned his lamp
which only causes the very marrow of his bones to seethe.
Yes, he fishes for pearls and jewels
which cost nothing – but his soul.

2.

Do not lure me, you ray from on high,
the vulture of Prometheus still lives.**f1)**
Silent, silent, you radiant lake:
the monsters are still watching
over the coffers of your treasure-trove. **f2)**
Put your hand down, my princely tippler! **f3)**
Down under there the rotten bones are whitening
of him who dived after the goblet. **f4)**

And you fluttering spray of tendrils,
you mystic rose of the thistle,
do not spread out those tendrils
to strangle me so gently and so softly.
Often I hear your little worm whispering,
as it lingers inside to heal you.
Ah, must I then be the rose,
gnawed away to heal others?

f1) Legend has it that, as punishment for stealing fire from Zeus to give to mankind, Prometheus was chained to a rock where, by day, his liver was consumed by an eagle. By night it was renewed, so that his torment was perpetual, until he was rescued by Hercules. The idea here is of the poet as the new Prometheus, and almost certainly Droste-Hülshoff was prompted by Goethe's poem (first published in 1789).

f2) Probably another literary allusion, this time to the treasure of the Nibelungen, jealously guarded by the dwarf Alberich. After all, Droste-Hülshoff was entertained night after night in Meersburg Castle by readings from her brother-in law, the proud possessor of the great Hohenems manuscript of the Nibelungenlied.

f3) See Goethe's poem 'Der König in Thule' (1774) which tells of the grief-stricken king ('the princely tippler' here) who, as his final gesture, hurled the golden goblet left to him by his beloved into the sea.

f4) In his poem 'Der Taucher' ('The Diver', 1797) Schiller had told of the page who perished in the attempt to retrieve the goblet thrown into the water by his master, the king: the waves never brought him back again.

The Word
(9 May 1845)

The word is like the winged arrow,
and if it has once flown from your bow,
whether in play or in earnest,
its speed must needs put fear into you.

It is like a little grain of corn slipped
from your hand. Who can find it again?
And yet it grows in the earth
and forces its roots across the land,

like the lost spark which is perhaps
extinguished on a damp day,
perhaps on a mild day glimmers in the hedgerow
or on a dry day swells into a sea of flames.

And they are really words which once
dropped so heavily into your bowl:
if not a single one of them is a mere nothing,
nevertheless you hope for each of them, or weep.

Ah, grant my God to the fearful man and the blind man
a ray of light from the meadow of heaven!
How is he to find his goal and his field?
How measure the breezes and the dew?

Almighty One, who has bestowed the word
and yet held back its future from us,
may it please you to rule over your gift,
and may it be guided by your breath!
Direct the arrow towards its target,

nourish the little grain of corn drunk with sleep!
Either extinguish the spark or fan it into life!
For only you know what will be for the best.

With her deep sense of her vocation as a poet, and the responsibility that it brings with it, it is not surprising that she should also be conscious of the significance of the word, and the responsibility to use it wisely. 'The Word', which is neither long nor, by her standards, complicated, expresses this awareness and urges wisdom in the employment of words, which have the capacity to traverse great distances and to exercise untold influence. On the one hand, it contains a moral lesson, but on the other, and perhaps more importantly, it is another expression of her belief in her role and her awareness of what this means.

That the poem was personally very important to her emerges from what we know of its origins and the way she adapted and changed it. The fact that she did so is not in itself surprising, since she returned to versions of poems, sometimes often and sometimes after a lapse of time, making small changes for the most part, but sometimes also substantial alterations. This is an interesting insight into her way of working, as is the fact, recorded by Levin Schücking from his own observation, that she could write at great speed and apparently quite spontaneously when the inspiration came to her. That said, it is also apparent that she stored up ideas for many months, even years in a few cases, until she felt moved to put them into words.

Of particular interest in the case of 'The Word' is that she appears to have written it in the first place in response to a request from the Fürstbischof of Breslau, Melchior von Diepenbrock (1798-1853), who asked her if she would send an autograph to his friend,

Count Heinrich Lamoral O'Donnell. The latter was from an ancient Irish family at that time resident in Vienna; among other public positions, in diplomacy and the military, he was noted as a collector of manuscripts, and it was presumably this interest which prompted the request. Although his connection with literature was no more than as an enthusiastic commentator, there was an interesting link with Droste-Hülshoff which may have moved her to respond in the way she did: we know that the Count had written with immense enthusiasm of the 1844 edition of her poetry, singling out 'My Calling' for particular praise and applauding the power of its language. He cited the lines 'let the sound of trumpets blare out/and the west-wind whisper gently in the glades' as particularly stirring and illuminating and 'such as have long not been heard in Germany'. Whether this fulsome praise was entirely warranted in this instance may not be indisputable, and his own claim to speak as an authoritative critic may be questioned, but his opinion almost certainly contributed to the increasing interest that was paid to Droste-Hülshoff in these last years of her life, following the publication of the 1844 edition.

Interesting, too, is the fact that Droste-Hülshoff added the date to her first version of the poem, which was then enclosed in the lengthy letter she wrote to Fürstbischof Melchior on 9 May 1845. In that letter she expands on the idea of the seriousness of her vocation and the need to guard one's words with the utmost care, weighing them ten times over. This, she said, must be under the guidance of God. She returned to the poem the following year, and at that time replaced the last two strophes with a single one, and removed the original address to the Almighty. This revised version, one of the last dated poems of her life, was affectionately dedicated to an unidentified Euphrosine, elsewhere mentioned, but only once and in passing, as a visitor to the Rüschhaus. With the overtly religious appeal to God removed, the poem remains a deeply felt statement of belief in her gift, reiterated movingly at the close of her life.

The two images which begin the poem ensure its impact. Both will have been familiar to Droste-Hülshoff's public. The proverb 'A spoken word is like a shot arrow' is listed in Wander's Dictionary of German Proverbs (published 1867-1880). *Luke* 8, 5-8 tells of the sower who went out to sow his seeds, some of which fell on stony ground and failed to thrive, and some among weeds, where they were choked, but others 'on good ground where they sprang up and bore fruit an hundredfold'. The message is 'He that hath ears to hear, let him hear'.

Droste-Hülshoff uses the Gospel text in 'The Fifth Sunday after Epiphany' of *Das Geistliche Jahr,* where it appears to be a favourite of hers, with its message of communication and herself as the soil into which the word of God falls and flourishes. When she takes up the proverb and the Gospel reference in the closing strophes, she emphasises her sense of the purpose of her calling. The poem is indeed her manifesto, expressed quite unambiguously. Embedded in long poems of great complexity at this stage of her creative life, it stands out for its directness and rare simplicity.

The two poems which follow in this selection could hardly be more different from the preceding one. They were written at about the same time as 'The Word', in the spring and late summer of 1845, and both were almost certainly intended to express her appreciation of her friendship with Amalie Hassenpflug, with whom she had become acquainted through her relatives in

Bökendorf some years earlier. They remained in touch, though only intermittently, and Droste-Hülshoff's frequent references to Amalie, most frequently referred to as Male or Malchen in letters to mutual acquaintances, often speak of her as not having written, of visits planned but never materializing. She seems to have found her difficult, quite exasperating in fact.

Nothing in the extant letters to other people suggests an especially warm relationship between them and certainly nothing that would account for the depth of feeling in these two poems. Letters which we know to have been written by Droste-Hülshoff to Amalie Hassenpflug and possibly vice versa are no longer extant, quite likely the object of the conscientious pruning of her sister's private correspondence by Jenny von Lassberg , or perhaps because they were not deemed to be important enough to be kept by either of the women. Two poems, 'Der Traum' ('The Dream') and 'Locke und Lied' ('Song and a Lock of Hair') were written in 1841-42 and originally dedicated to Amalie, though the dedication was subsequently removed, and we have already seen that the much more substantial poem of 1844, 'Late Awakening', though initially bearing a dedication to Amalie and speaking passionately of the awakening of love, contains in its final strophes what seems much more likely to be a declaration of the impact upon her of meeting Levin Schücking again. (See p. 198 above.) Thus we are left with two poems from the closing phases of her creative life which, though ostensibly linked to Amalie, are more general meditations on other issues close to her heart and mind as she faced the prospect of a lonely old age and, not too far away, the end of her life. Both speak of the capacity of Droste-Hülshoff for friendship and loyalty, and, as the core of her being, for deep commitment. Perhaps it is that of which she is speaking in both poems, of herself and her own heartfelt emotions, the capacity for love and devotion which actually, in many different ways, imbues her whole poetic *œuvre*. The clue, perhaps, is in the title of the second poem printed here: this is another manifestation of her calling.

The Portrait

1. They stand before your portrait and gaze
into the veiled light of your eyes,
examining lip, chin and eyebrows,
and then they declare: This is not you.
The forehead is too smooth, the cheek too full.
There is too much hair.
A sweet face, but unfamiliar.

Ah, if only they knew how a faithful
spirit retains the slightest features,
embeds a single movement, fleeting and shy,
like a jewel into the soul,
how a mere word, breathed with
the same sound, carries the fearful,
stirred-up heart even towards the enemy.

They would understand me better
if they were to see me stroke the dark glade
of your locks with my gentle finger,
as if I were opening them up to the new day,
spreading out the mass of flowers densely and more densely,
so that no speck of sun can harm
the delicate radiance of your eyes.

I will not look at that which is unfamiliar,
I do not wish to know where it burns,
whether on the lip or on the eyebrows,
that flame which does not know your heart.
I wish only to look into your eyes,

take in only that one pure look
which silently speaks my name:

that look which surrounded me like heaven itself,
when in the sombre evening time
we sat hand clasped in hand
and thought of death and eternity,
that look which turned piously away
from the setting of the sun,
to find me,
and smiling said: I am ready.

2. And if it were also true that the plough of the years
has driven furrows into your smooth brow,
that the shape of your lips
no longer traces lithely your anger and your love,
if the covering through which penetrates the sunlight,
divinely inspired, has now embraced you more closely,
to me you have always remained the same.

If your figure is less proud, less noble,
I know that within is the unbowed soul.
If your gaze is enveloped as though in mist,
I know that the cloud conceals a glowing light,
and the deep sound of your soft voice,
echoing away, ghostly like the song of the waves,
I feel that no word of love is lacking in it.

Oh, curse of old age, if only the better part
must give way with it to the divine image!
If a smile is less warm with love because
misery has left its mark upon it,
an eye only kindly when a tear slips from it
gentle and full of charm,
and rosy cheeks are more chaste than pale ones.

And even so, the shape, born of dust, capable of transformation,
holds us all in foolishness.
An ear which softly hears seems willing to us,
the bold victory fanfare of a new voice.

We all can see only the light of Pharos f),
we do not see the glow in the womb of the earth,
and no one thinks of the lamp upon the altar.
3. I know how to find a better portrait
than that which moves further away from you,
where your roots grow deeper into the ground
and your corn bows more ripely:
a better picture than this one in the frame,
when the years went and the years came,
and someone creeps along like his own shadow.

If on the shore I listen to hear
whether the lukewarm, sleeping waves lie beneath
the flowers, the blue mass of flowers,
the sombre repose alive to me,
in the depths I see the corals,
see the golden rippling of the little fishes
and gaze deep into your heart.

And again on the curve of the graves
I see the stave of the walls,
sucked down by a thousand tendrils
into the heart of the stone,
the green locks heavy with dew,
glow-worms in the flakes of the eyelids,
that is the way you love, across the grave.

And when at the fountain of recovery,
with the star and ribbon on the table in the hall,
at midday sick beggars sun themselves,
eagerly drink up the last drop
and busily wave their dishes,
then I must think of what you have given,
and of your warm and generous hand.

Oh, that spring, gentle and glowing,
a sparkling foam welling from your breast,
which knows nothing of snow-flakes or of ice,
fills its steppe with blessings.
With that can only be compared that which

> can never become sick, never grow old,
> and only Nature is your portrait.

> **f)** The tower built on the island of Pharos, the ancient lighthouse of Alexandria that became one of the Wonders of the Ancient World.

Surely, in the last resort, this is a poem about love and friendship, the capacity of one human being to know and love another, and about those things which are eternal and which survive beyond the grave. Put like that, one can see the perfect consistency of this very late poem with what Droste-Hülshoff has been saying all along, in letters and literary writings, and in her steadfast relationships throughout her life. It contains something of the ideal towards which she is groping in 'The Spiritual Year' and just occasionally glimpsing there.

If one then views this poem in the light of a bigger picture, it does not matter to whom it is formally dedicated, and in fact it probably gains from being divorced from a specific person. The closing strophe places it within that bigger picture: only Nature, the broader context of life, can express the emotions which have flowed from the inadequate portrait with which she started. These emotions are unchanging, constant through old age and death. The spectator contemplating the portrait of the opening lines sees the flaws and misrepresentations, but the poem has moved way beyond that and done what Annette von Droste-Hülshoff is so good at doing: contemplating the whole. If any part of this interpretation of 'The Portrait' comes close to an understanding of its essential meaning, then the next poem achieves a seamless transition to another intimately-related theme. Droste-Hülshoff has spoken again and again of the 'calling' she recognises as having been given to her at her birth, and her gift of poetry is precious to her. Yet in this poem she reverts to a much earlier issue, the role of woman in a society antagonistic to feminine independence, and the difficulty, impossibility even, that a woman should pursue the course that fate has offered to her. Standing as she now was, on the brink of recognition and confident as never before of the nature of her genius, she was nevertheless hampered by the attitudes of the time. Whoever the partner in this conversation is – and her identity is irrelevant, and perhaps she has no specific identity - she shares the same fate. What emerges clearly from comments in her letters, and particularly in one to C.B. Schlüter (December 1838) is the very great difference between herself and Amalie on literary matters, since Amalie, well-meaning and earnest though she was, was obsessed 'with a certain romantic school' which was totally alien to her own way of thinking. There is nothing in the intervening years that suggests a closer understanding between them, much as Amalie may have hoped for it.

On the other hand, of course, these two friends are parting, going their separate ways, the one to the warmth of the South, the other 'to sicken beneath snow and ice'. Perhaps what Annette is suggesting is the unbridgeable intellectual gap between them, which would argue for the original dedication to Amalie Hassenpflug, despite the sadness of the parting and the tenderness of the whole episode. The poem was originally given the title 'The Parting' ('Der Abschied'), for that, on one level, is what it describes: the parting at sunset between two close friends. It must have been Levin Schücking who, when he came to publish it in the *Rheinisches Jahrbuch* the year after she had written it, chose the broader, more abstract title.

The poem falls into two distinct parts. It begins with the description of the episode, with the two friends hand in hand by the pond in the evening light, a time favoured by Droste-Hülshoff as the background to powerful emotions and the words spoken between them. This cannot be called a conversation, since it is not clear whether one is speaking, then the other, or whether it is a composite of what was said. The content is the knowledge that they have no power to withstand the pressures which constrain them and force them in their respective directions, since fate and circumstances are at variance. The fault is theirs, lacking as they do the courage to stand up to social conventions. Their reaction is a mixture of grief and anger. Although there is no change in the metre, the tempo of the poem does change, with the sudden storm which breaks over them and forces them to take refuge beneath a lime tree. In this emergency situation there are no distinctions, although the little group of people huddling there are a motley bunch, each identified by a specific feature. There is just the slightest touch of humour in her description of them, thrown together in this way, beneath the protection of the great tree which has grown there by the Grace of God. All else must be forgotten now, as the two friends, so close yet destined to part, silently take their leave of one another.

So, one asks oneself what the poem is about? It is about many things: the restrictions placed on women in the society of the day, the place of the poet, isolated and in pain, the place of love and loyalty so valued by Droste-Hülshoff as she contemplated her future, the overriding power of nature in the Hand of the Almighty. It is about all these things, or perhaps any combination of them. What it shows is the capacity of the mature poet to express herself and to challenge understanding, very much as she will do in '*Gemüt*', and it raises the unanswerable question of where her path would have taken her.

Also a Calling

The evening redness had flowed away.
We were standing at the edge of the pond,
and I had my hand clasped around her cold little hand.
"Must we then really part?
Fate is dicing with the two of us,
and we are like a land without a lord.

Bound by no duty to the home and hearth,
each one believes only that we have been invented
precisely only for his needs,
the willing fifth wheel.
What use is it to us that we stand free
and look towards the hands of no-one?
Nevertheless the path is shown to us.

Where the dense trees give out their branches
and a thousand neighbouring boughs bow down
around the slender trunk,
the hiking-staff makes its way swiftly.
But over there, see the single lime tree:
everyone writes on its bark,
and everyone breaks off a little twig.

Oh, if only we had the courage to handle
the gifts which fortune has bestowed!
Who could prevent us? Who detain us?
Who could take care of our own hearth for us?
We labour under the ancient law
which says that he who makes himself into a servant
does not merit golden freedom.

Go forth, as you have been called to do,
into the heat and sweat of the Campagna,
and I will go into my northern parts,
to sicken beneath snow and ice.
We are not worthy of better days,
for let anyone who does not choose to fight endure,

and if someone does not know how to act, then let him suffer."
That was what was spoken by the pond,
in anger half and half in pain.
We would have liked to break the staff
over all the petty tyrannies,
but only when the rain clouds mounted
did we truly make our way with pleasure into anger.

While the individual drops were falling,
there was naphtha-oil in our defiance,
along with one of the games of Fate,
to our detriment and of use to no one.
But when the leaden gates released their contents
we did as other people did
and sought out the protection of the lime-tree, too.

Thus a little crowd was huddling close together,
shuddering beneath the roof of leaves.
The cloud was hurling flames of sulphur
and chasing after the lashing rain.
We could hear it bouncing on the leaves,
yet not a drop could penetrate
our leafy chamber.

In truth, it was a wretched little crowd
that escaped the storm here:
a gaunt Jew with bleached hair,
a blind man with his dog,
a school official in his scant frock-coat,
and then the little limping Johann
with his beggar's sack.

And at each crash
they all looked up at the tree-trunk,
hugged the little bundles against them
and smiling pressed close to one another.,
for the more hollowly the rain beat,
the more broadly did the tree spread
its green canopy against the storm.

How it did battle with all its might
to protect that which was entrusted to it!
How joyfully did it sound out
to answer the faith which had been built upon it!
I felt myself strangely captivated
and, embarrassed, with cheeks blazing,
I gazed into the crown

of the tree which, belonging to no one,
was standing on the heath,
bore no fruit on its branches,
nothing with which to feed the fire,
which had sprung up only at a sign from God,
a companion for the stranger's heart,
for the wanderer in the sand of the steppe.

I looked at my friend, and she at me,
and very likely we were thinking the same thing,
for her demeanour was sadder
and her beloved eyes were moist.
And yet we spoke not a word,
only broke a little twig from the tree,
and silently gave one another our hands.

'The Golems' is another reflective poem from about the same period. It seems to be prompted by the disquiet she was feeling about the state of her world, and the world in general. She was not happy with the direction Levin Schücking was taking in his political leanings in a world in a state of upheaval, although she had yet to experience what she saw as his betrayal of her personally when he published his attack on the aristocracy in his novel *Die Ritterbürtigen* ('The Gentility', see above p. 98): in any case, by now she had come to accept that their close relationship was at an end. In her poem 'Hold fast!' she urges allegiance, not only to tried and tested friends, but to established traditions (see p. 212 above).

In 'The Golems', written in the autumn of 1844, she expresses herself very forcefully about the loss of values she cherishes, seeing this above all as due to the arid perceptions of the day, which are based on materialism and cold calculation and not guided by finer sensibilities and emotional ties to the past. It is not that she wishes to dwell in the past, but that she grieves for what she sees as the emptiness and lack of passion of contemporary life. She uses the symbol of the Golem to make her point, the bloodless creature made by man from a lump of clay and devoid of heart and soul. Already in the fifth strophe of 'Hold fast!', written just a few months earlier, she had referred to this creature known to Hebrew legend and warned against submitting to its blandishments and surrendering one's own identity as a sentient being, a 'child of anguish…, endowed by God'.

The poem has begun with a very personal grief, for the changes wrought in people she has known in their youth, who have been distracted from their early promise and lost the fire and passion they once showed. Whether the woman in the first strophe and the man in the second are identifiable is not known and would almost certainly be a matter of surmise. It is interesting, however, that she wrote to her friend Elise Rüdiger a year before this poem of the depression that had overtaken her when she had been going through a pile of old papers and letters. She says it would be better if she had burnt them much earlier, because now they have brought her great sadness. "What has become of the friends of my youth?" she asks. The one half is totally absorbed in domestic matters, husband and children, she continues, while the others have become miserable old spinsters, no joy to gods or mankind, in whom there is no more poetry than in a dried-up plum (letter dated

5 September 1843). She would almost certainly not have expressed herself quite like this except to someone she regarded as a very close friend indeed, one of three left to her from the past, as she tells Elise, whom she certainly did not include in either of the two categories. What she emphasises is that people have become 'older and colder' , but in these letters they appear in all their freshness and youthful warmth.

Her letter offers a helpful guide to the understanding of the first strophe of 'The Golems', with the evocation of the sweet child, in touch with 'the magic land of fairy tales' reduced now to someone who is living in the real world. She concedes that the adult woman is 'brave and lovely' but the magic has gone, the angel has fled, or, in the words she used to Elise Rüdiger, there is no sign of poetry. As for the man of the second strophe, he is a good solid citizen, 'a proud burgher', but the fire of his youth is gone.

Lest she seem to be suggesting the opposite, she hastily assures her listeners that she is not advocating a life in the past, among the dead. It is not death she laments but the changes wrought by time and convention. What is left is emptiness: 'wandering, bloodless images/empty temples without the heat of sacrifice/yellow glades without the messengers of spring'. Thus she arrives at the significance of the title: those man-made creatures have no life, no passion, though they may look like human beings. They cannot have these precious qualities, because they have no heart and there is no light in their eyes, and those who follow the Golem betray their dreams and crush their loyalties, destroying values that have stood them in good stead. Even life and death are meaningless, and there is no heaven.

Thus she comes to a familiar theme: support and consolation

are to be found with the dead, and in turning to the dead and away from the truly lifeless Golems, the living can find a way forward through tears which at least are real.

Levin may not have recognized himself specifically in the description in the second strophe, but he probably suspected that the poem was, in part at least, a warning to him not to sacrifice his deepest emotions for the sake of expediency. Annette, who rarely minced her words, may well have spoken to him of the perils of following the crowd and seeking material advancement at all costs. This was a course against which she resolutely set her face. He, on the other hand, was an ambitious man and he had recently contracted a marriage with a woman he had never met but who was certainly well connected. If one takes that into account, the poem, written immediately after her emotional but stoical farewell to him, may possibly be seen as both intensely personal as well as expressing some firmly held views. His response to it is not recorded, but it appeared in the *Kölnische Zeitung* within weeks of its composition and, eventually, in 'Last Gifts' of 1860.

The Golems

If I had not known you as a sweet child,
with your seraph in your clear eyes
leading you into the magic land of fairy tales,
and felt the trembling pressure of your little hands,
I would surely look at you with pleasure,
and you would be to me a brave and lovely woman.
Ah, as it is, I must search beneath your brow
and always seek the angel fled away.

And you, with your words careful and far-reaching,
your wise smile and the lines in your forehead,
does no poor dream speak to you of that time,

when you could split the rocks with your brilliance?
You are a brave burgher, worthy of high honour,
a veritable hero on the middle way.
Only my swirling flames, my Vulcan –!
ah! if only the mountains could bring forth mice!

Woe to him who lives looking at the past,
who strives for pallid images and washed-out colours!
That which is broken does not turn his hair grey,
that which death has bent in its sweet beauty,
but those things, those monuments without the dead ones,
those wandering, bloodless images,
the empty temples without the heat of sacrifice,
the yellow glades without the messengers of spring.

There is a legend from the Orient,
of wise men who make shapes of lifeless clods –
beloved shapes which yearning knows –
and breathe life into them with magic spells.
The Golem wanders with familiar steps,
and speaks, and smiles with a familiar breath,
except that in his eyes there is no radiance
and deep within his bosom beats no heart.

And when ancient loyalty subjugates itself to him,
he breathes upon it with the horror of decay -
however anxiously memory may call or knock
there is in him no dreamer to awaken –
and he sees loyalty, deeply broken, vanish,
no matter how long and sacredly he has conserved it,
and what is not of life and not of death
cannot be found here, nor in heaven.

Oh, kneel in silence at the grave of your dead ones:
there you can weep gentle, pious tears,
and there the air whispers to you with her breath,
and the moon will shine its face upon you.
They are yours, yours with their broken eyes,
as they were yours when last they looked at you,
yet flee, flee from the Golems,
who suck up your tears only like glaciers.

In the summer of 1844 Droste-Hülshoff was back in Meersburg, having managed, with the proceeds from *Die Judenbuche* to buy the little house high in the vineyards overlooking Lake Constance, where she was to spend many weeks during her remaining years. Emotionally it cannot have been an easy time for her: in October 1843 Levin Schücking had married Louise von Gall, although Annette had yet to meet her when the couple visited her in Meersburg in May of 1844. Her career, on the other hand, was progressing well, and preparations were well in hand for the publication of the second volume of her poetry by the distinguished publisher Cotta. Meanwhile she was often in demand for individual poems to be published in journals. She was constantly writing, never again with the same intensity as during the winter she had spent with Levin in Meersburg two years earlier, but certainly engaged in writing some of her finest poems.

The news of Levin's engagement and then marriage had affected her deeply, of course, and she was both physically ill and very depressed. The more or less chance encounter with a twenty-year-old English girl, Philippa Pearsall, who was visiting Meersburg with her father from their temporary home Schloss Wartensee, near Rorschach on the opposite side of Lake Constance, must have been an unexpected ray of light. Philippa was talented musically and artistically and had read quite widely. Above all she was sensitive to the much older woman's needs, showing intelligent and genuine interest in her poems, particularly the religious ones. Since Philippa had come with her father to Switzerland on medical advice, it is not unlikely that her fragile health drew Droste-Hülshoff to her, and that Philippa was herself responsive to the by now evident frailty of her new acquaintance. Certainly Droste-Hülshoff writes once, somewhat surprisingly, to Louise Schücking but also and more often to her very close friend and frequent correspondent Elise Rüdiger, of the speed with which they formed a remarkable bond, and it is clear that the brief period she was able to spend in the company of the younger woman was very precious to her.

The two poems addressed to Philippa, the first in the spring of 1844 and the second to mark their parting at the end of August of that year, require very little more biographical information. They speak for themselves of a real tenderness, but also, poignantly, of Droste-Hülshoff's perception of what Philippa meant to her at this stage of her life. She must have seen in her something of her younger self, and combined with her delight in her youth and promise is the obvious sense that she is herself declining, expressed really without the sentimentality that might have been expected in lines like 'You are a precious vision/on the horizon of my life'.

There is, of course, a measure of sentimentality in both poems, but this is countered by the sincerity of the emotions and the knowledge we have that although Droste-Hülshoff was capable of deep love and loyalty, she did not often express it in this uninhibited way, above all with the sense that it was returned. It is this knowledge, together with the simplicity of the expression and the lyrical directness, that places these poems side by side with others that she was writing at the time and contributes to the whole picture of the woman and the poet. As far as we know they did not meet again, but she enclosed the poem in a long letter in which she promised to remain in touch. This she seems to have done, if only occasionally and through her sister Jenny, who had introduced them in the first place.

A final letter addressed to Philippa, who by early 1847 was staying in Augsburg, contained some small tokens - coins and autographs - and the kind of snippets of domestic news at which Droste-Hülshoff excelled. However by that time she was not able to write at great length, even if she had wanted to.

To Philippa

The new light is springing up in the East,
its golden fragrance playing on the waves,
and I see, like a delicate vision,
a distant sail billowing.
Ah, if only, like a seagull,
I could encircle it in joyful flight.
Ah, if only the kingdom of the air were mine,
mine the youthful, vibrant wings!

About you, Philippa, the light is playing;
the breath of morning has surrounded you.
You are a precious vision
on the horizon of my life.
When I see your flag so far in the distance,
with the air flooding round it so dreamily,
then I would so dearly like to forget
that my horizon has closed,

forget that my evening came,
my light faded away spark upon spark,
that time has long since taken my flag from me,
and that my sails have long since dropped.
Yet if they cannot stretch out fresh
and youthfully beside yours,
Philippa, I can love you
and accompany your journey with my blessing.

Farewell greeting

(To Philippa Pearsall, 25 August 1844)

Must I then on this day
call out my farewell into the distance?
That which time has graciously created for us,
does it run away like the beating of the waves?
Does for a few short hours
remain to me only the consolation
of seeing if I can find your roof,
your little window in the grey tower?

I cannot and I will not ever think
that this is perhaps the last time.
Do you remain when my own steps make their way
down to my homely valley?
Yet, if mountains and foreign meadows
divide us, northwards and southwards,
believe me: I am following your tracks
and bringing to you a devoted heart.

Although the two poems addressed to Philippa Pearsall, especially the second, contain an unambiguous farewell, they lack the sombre tone of valediction, because in both something else is present: the sense that the young woman represents the future and that the bond between them will sustain them as they go their separate ways. This is important if one is to view the whole of Droste-Hülshoff's *œuvre* from the perspective of her closing years. In the summer of 1844 she had less than four years to live, and her last months, her last two years even, contain no poetry of significance. Indeed it is this summer of 1844 which marks a peak of creativity, when she produced some poems of great power and confidence and attained a serenity never consistently reached before.

For the purpose of this volume, which aims to show the range and quality of some of her most important poems throughout her relatively short creative life, six poems from this time have been selected and they follow here. It is not easy to decide in what order they should be considered. A chronological order is not helpful, since four of the six were written within a few weeks in the course of that summer, and there is no suggestion of a development, or of an obvious link between them. By this time, individual poems stand alone, each remarkable in its own way. Nor can they be said to fall into categories, so great is her originality, particularly at this point. The last datable poem is 'Groaning Creation' which is usually believed to be the last 'real' poem she wrote: after that point (late summer 1846), she wrote only slight occasional poems, to celebrate events within the family, or individuals within her circle.

However, it would seem unfortunate, unjust even, to conclude the selection with a poem whose message is unmitigated pessimism. Droste-Hülshoff's range is too broad and her courage too great to end on that note, important though the poem is, and crucial to an understanding of her. To end with what is probably her penultimate poem, the great 'Gethsemane' is also misleading, suggesting that her message is first and foremost a religious one, although this would be an unbalanced view of her work as a whole.

What dominates in these six late poems is the magnificence of the language and the scope of her concept. She seems to rise to new heights of thought and expression and to transcend what she has achieved before. Themes recur from earlier stages of her life, but there is a new command of her material and, one senses, a new serenity in her execution. These are qualities which run through all six, and ultimately the order in which one places them is a matter of personal choice. The aim is to leave the reader with the sense of a crescendo, the culmination of a lifetime of achievement.

The first poem selected here to demonstrate the qualities of her mature lyric is 'In the Grass', a poem which shows her ecstasy in her union with nature, a state suggested at times in earlier poems, but perhaps never so completely as in this joyful surrender to all the emotions and with all the senses alert, from the first strophe, which is in fact a single sentence. The repetition of the word 'sweet' is important. The experience described is total absorption in joy which embraces sight and sound, scent and touch, but above all the feeling of rare happiness. 'Deep' is repeated, too, for this is no passing moment but a profound experience which floods over her, not just as gentle rain but as an all-embracing sensation which transforms a physical perception into a deep understanding of herself and her place in time and space.

The 'beloved voice' of the first strophe leads her into what emerges as the principal theme of the poem, or rather into several themes which cannot be separated from one another. She thinks of that which is past - 'dead love, dead pleasure, dead time' – but death does not have a negative connotation, for it represents 'all the treasures', albeit 'confused in the rubble'. At this time and in that place, in the rapture of this overwhelming moment, the passage of time represents a positive gathering-together of experiences and sensations, expressed, in the third and fourth strophes, in terms of light and colour. The fleeting hours are expressed in four similes, each of which captures the passing in a single, tangible comparison: the touch of a ray of light on the lake, the sound of a bird's song, the glimpse of a brightly-coloured beetle, but then the clasp of a hand.

If one looks again at this amazing third strophe, one can see the mass of detail, for each simile is given more significance: the lake is 'mourning' and one recalls the way she has spoken earlier in her life of her belief that it carries deep secrets from the past. The song of the bird comes to her from a height, dropping down – another simile - 'like pearls', and one remembers how in 'The Poet' pearls have represented the tragic destiny of the poet; the shimmering beetle scurries along a sunny path, oblivious to the fate it shares with all creation (see below, 'Groaning Creation', p. 259). Above all, the fevered hand-clasp lingers for one last time: this is a parting gesture.

However, in this beautiful late poem, which brings together so much that is familiar and expresses it with the serene acceptance of the sick poet at her magnificent best, Droste-Hülshoff concludes with hope and the dream of happiness. The song of the bird brings with it the thought not of the soul which must be the price paid, but of the soul rising into the blue. She seizes each slight ray of sunshine, and it is the hem of her dress that shimmers, not the passing beetle.

In the summer of 1844, with Levin gone with his bride and Philippa heading towards a future full of promise, Annette felt very alone, as some of her correspondence at this time betrays, though she seldom allowed herself the luxury of self-pity, except in passing comments to those closest to her. She was very soon to return for one last time to her beloved Rüschhaus before coming back to Meersburg. That prospect is surely what she has in mind when she imagines the warm hands of friends waiting, not to say goodbye but to greet her in her homeland, where the memories of the past reside but allow her still to dream of happiness.

In the Grass

Sweet rest, sweet ecstasy in the grass,
enveloped in the fragrance of the plants,
deep flood, deep, deep intoxicated flood,
when the cloud evaporates in the blueness,
when sweet laughter flutters down
on one's weary, swimming head,
and a beloved voice drops rustling down
like lime blossom onto a grave.

Then, when in one's breast the dead stir and stretch out,
each dead body,
softly, softly drawing breath,
the closed eyelids flickering,
dead love, dead pleasure, dead time;
all the treasures, confused in the rubble,
touch one another with a shy sound,
like little bells tossed by the wind.

You hours, more fleeting, like the kiss
of a ray of light on the mourning lake,
like the song of a passing bird
which drops from on high down to me like pearls,
like the flash of the shimmering beetle
as it scurries along the sunny path,
like the hot press of a hand
which lingers for one last time.

But heaven, just this one thing for me,
always: for the song of each free bird
in the blueness, a soul which goes with it,
only for each slight ray of sunshine
my hem shimmering in its many colours,
my press for each warm hand,
and my dream for every happiness.

The theme of homesickness is more explicit in the next poem chosen to convey the quality of her lyric of those last years. Written at about the same time as 'In the Grass', it bears in one of the manuscripts the more specific title 'Greetings to the Homeland', which is how Levin Schücking also entitled it when he came to publish it in the 'Last Gifts' of 1860, although, like 'In the Grass', it had also appeared in the *Kölnische Zeitung* in the autumn of 1844. By that time, Droste-Hülshoff was back in the Rüschhaus, where she remained until late 1846, when she set off again for Meersburg. Thus these two poems belong together, both evoking thoughts of the past and memories of loved ones back in her homeland.

The poignancy attaching to both poems is intensified by the knowledge that when she returned to Westphalia she found one of her dearest old friends very sick, in fact on the point of death. This was her old nurse, Marie Kathrin Plettendorf, the woman from the village summoned to nurse the newly-born Annette, who appeared unlikely to survive. She had stayed with the family into her old age, often Annette's sole companion in the Rüschhaus after the marriage of Jenny, when their mother was to-ing and fro-ing between Westphalia and Meersburg and spending long periods with her other daughter and her granddaughters. The bond between them was immense, not least because the old countrywoman was a mine of information and anecdotes about the countryside around them and fed Droste-Hülshoff's obsession with the history and lore of that region.

It was typical of Annette that she insisted on nursing her old friend, her '*Amme*' (nurse) as she always remained, and was deeply grieved at her death in February 1845, at which point Annette herself became ill both physically and emotionally, to recover very gradually and only ever partially. It must have been the thought of clasping her old friend's hand that she dreamt of when, in far-off Meersburg, she pondered a return to Rüschhaus, and there can be little doubt that, writing in Meersburg in that summer of 1844, she is referring to Marie Kathrin when she speaks here of the 'dearest soul who never forgets me', conjuring up the thought of the old lady sitting by the light of her lamp, as they must have done evening after evening, saying their night prayers together. The little vignette is characteristic of this poem, which verges on the sentimental much more than the more elevated 'In the Grass', as is the reference to the little bed she has left behind in the place she always regarded as her home.

Droste-Hülshoff certainly never felt entirely comfortable in the south. In spite of its beauty, the closeness to the Lassberg family and what must have been some treasured memories of her brief time with Levin Schücking, it was alien to her temperament, as she had made clear in that early poem in which she took her leave of Switzerland. There is a dark brooding in her nature which must have made her temperamentally unsuited to the place where she spent her final months and where she died.

In this poem it is night which provides the link between the two places so intimately associated with her. The time of day so favoured by her for the way it stirs her deepest thoughts can transform what she sees and hears, and even the sound of the waves on the shore of the lake can sound like horses' hooves, bringing her homeland towards her. Then the jumble of noises can be converted into the sound of voices and she can persuade herself that what she sees are shapes recognizable to her. This is familiar Droste-Hülshoff, with her ability to transform one landscape into another, or to imagine herself transported to a different time or a different place. In the third strophe she recalls the details of the landscape she knew so well and which she had used effectively in poems at a much earlier stage of her life. Less familiar, however, is the evocation of her youth, in her father's house, the Hülshoff estate where she spent her childhood and early adulthood.

She recalls the size of Schloss Hülshoff, its towers and vast halls, but, more importantly, she remembers that it was the scene of the storms of her life, storms which, one senses, never truly abated for this troubled soul. Yet, with typical stoicism, she speaks of having been 'vanquished and gained the victory', a telling irony which seems to give a very rare insight into the conflict which was central to her life, and indeed to her poetry.

The poem ends, not with the hopefulness which appears to be achieved at the end of 'In the Grass', but with a deep wistfulness. All seems to speak of parting and loss, emotions so familiar to her: the tracks which took her away from that loved place, the eyes of dear ones which followed her, the hearts still beating for her and the hands which waved goodbye. It is lines like these that lead to the climax of the poem, with an outburst of sorrow at the human lot of loneliness and bereavement. This is no longer a woman speaking of her own sadness, but a statement much broader which must touch at all hearts: the realization that a time has come when there is no one left to pray for one, and when one is even deprived of shared consolation. A poem like this one provides a clue to the stature of Droste-Hülshoff, showing how skilled she is at suggesting contrasting emotions, and speaking to the ordinary human being in us all.

Greetings

If in this foreign land
familiar night rises before me,
if from the shore there comes the sound as if of horses' hooves,
if twilight comes rolling towards me
like clouds of dust
from my beloved, powerful north,
and if I feel my hair
stroking the air's word laden with secrets –

then it seems to me as if I hear come riding
and clinking towards me from all sides
my homeland,
and I feel its kisses burning.
Then the gentle rumouring of the wind
becomes to me like muddled voices
and each vague shape in the darkness
like a figure most familiar.

And I must stretch out my arms
and breath out kisses, kisses,
enough to waken up the bodies,
those decaying ones, in the green house.
I must salute each tree-top in the forest,
and every piece of heathland, every stream,
and all the drops of moisture flowing there
and each little blade of grass that's still awake.

And you, my father's house, with your towers,
rocked to sleep by the silent pond,
where in the storms of my life
I have so often been vanquished and gained the victory:
you vast halls, with your leafy vaulting,
who saw me, young and happy,
where my sighs surge endlessly
and my footprints remain.

You damp wind from my heathland

which weeps like shamed lament,
you ray of sunshine which shines down so modestly
upon the plants of the heath,
you tracks which took me forth,
you eyes which followed after me,
you hearts which beat for me,
you hands which waved goodbye to me.

And greetings, greetings, roof where the
dearest soul never forgets me,
and now, by the light of her little lamp,
says for me an evening blessing,
and where, as the cock crows for the first time,
she passes her hand over her grey brow
and once more before she goes to sleep
slips up to the bed I've left behind.

I should like to embrace you all,
I feel you all about me.
I should like to pour myself into you,
like a spent stream into the sea.
Ah, if you only knew how red with sickness,
how feverishly the ether burns,
when no one prays for us
and no one knows our dead!

The last dated poem by Droste-Hülshoff is different from the two just considered and different from any of her other last poems. For one thing it lacks their lyrical quality, and for another it is a statement of her total aloneness, unalleviated by any light or hope. She was prompted to write it by correspondence she had recently conducted with her dear old friend, the theologian and professor of philosophy Christoph Bernhard Schlüter, with whom she remained in regular contact until the end of her life. He can hardly have anticipated the direction she would take when he drew her attention to the passage in *Romans* 8,18-23, when St Paul says: "For

I reckon that the sufferings of this present time are not worthy to be compared with the glory that shall be revealed to us. For the earnest expectation of the creature waiteth for the manifestation of the sons of God. For the creature was made subject to vanity, not willingly, but by reason of him who hath subjected the same in hope, because the creature itself also shall be delivered from the bondage of corruption into the glorious liberty of the children of God. For we know that the whole creation groaneth and travaileth in pain together until now. And not only they, but ourselves also, which have the first fruits of the Spirit, even we ourselves groan within ourselves, waiting for the adoption, to wit, the redemption of our body."

In the course of the correspondence in the spring and summer of 1846 between Droste-Hülshoff and Schlüter she had confided in him, probably her most trusted friend, that she was much saddened at the prospect of leaving the Rüschhaus, as she knew she would be shortly, since it was no longer practicable or safe for her to remain there alone. A move to her sister and her family had become inevitable, but she could hardly bear to think of what she would be leaving behind, her beloved home and most of all the countryside around and everything it contained in terms of natural beauty. Schlüter was doubtless trying to distract her and offer her comfort, but exactly how he thought these lines would do that is unclear.

Certainly, traditional Christian thinker and devoutly religious as he was, he can hardly have expected the response he received, although he knew that her thinking was rarely akin to his and that, as he had put it, her faith did not seem to give her the true happiness he would have liked for her. What he cannot have foreseen is that she would seize upon the words 'Kreatur' and 'ächzen' (or 'ängsten') to produce a poem of unmitigated gloom.

Had she read further, she would have known that the message of St Paul was one of hope, but of hope there is little sign in this poem which, we are led to believe, she wrote at one sitting, on a cold, damp day in the grounds of the Rüschhaus, in front of the little garden room. Alone by choice, and undoubtedly deeply aware of her frailty and even of her closeness to death, she is responsive, as she has been throughout her life, to the details of nature which have always sustained her, as much in union with it, surely, as in the exuberant 'In the Grass' of barely two years earlier. Yet she sees herself as 'God's sorely tested child', and her thoughts are only of the guilt which rests on mankind since the Fall, and of the responsibility of human beings for the sufferings of all living creatures. The earth is beautiful, she knows that, but beside that beauty is the overwhelming and inescapable negative of pain and anger, sin and shame, and decay.

Groaning Creation

August 1846

On a day when the wind was damp
and the rays of the sun shrouded in grey,
God's sorely-tested child was sitting
in a dejected state close to the little garden room.
Her heart was so weary and her breast felt so constricted,
her head so dull and heavy that
even around her mind the pressure
of her blood drew veils of mist.

Wind and birds her only companions
in this solitude of her own choosing;
a great sigh from nature,

and place and time soon vanished.
It seemed to her as though
she were sensing the tide of eternity
rushing past her,
and yet must hear each drop of blood and every heartbeat.

She sat and thought, and thought and sat.
The throaty cricket was singing in the grass,
and from a far-off field came the faint sound
of a scythe.
The timid wall-wasp flew anxiously
about her face until she pulled her dress
firmly to one side, and the
little creature's nest was uncovered.

And a beetle ran across the stonework,
terrified and quickly, as though it were fleeing,
and buried its little head, now deep in the moss,
now in the nooks and crannies.
A linnet fluttered past,
on the lookout for food,
and, at the sound of the bird's cry,
the insect hid itself with a sharp movement in her sleeve.

Thus it became clear to her that God's curse
lay not only upon
human kind but yearns upwards towards the heavens,
groaning for salvation,
with heavy, dull agony, in the frightened worm,
the timid deer, in the parched blade of grass in the meadow,
thirsting with its yellowed leaves,
in every single creature.

How with the curse which he brought
upon himself in paradise,
the Prince of the Earth **f)** destroyed his blessed kingdom
and caused his servants to pay the price;
how he forced death and decay,
agony and anger, through the pure veins,
and how nothing remained for him but guilt,
and the sharp thorn of conscience.

This sleeps with him and wakes with him
on every new day,
tears apart his dreams at night
and goes on bleeding through the day.
Ah, heavy pain, never softened
by the greatest pleasure nor the boldest pride,
when gently, gently, it gnaws and thuds
and bores its way inside him like maggots in wood.

Who is so pure that he is not aware
of an image within the depths of his soul
because of which he must beat his breast
and feel himself afraid and wounded?
And who so wicked that there is not
one word remaining which he cannot bear to hear
but which forces the blood up into his face
with fiery, fearful, profound shame?

And yet there is a burden
which no one feels and each one bears,
almost as dark as sin
and nurtured at the same breast.
He bears it like the pressure of a breeze,
sensed only by the sick body,
as unaware as the cavern is of the cliff,
or the fatally wounded man of the bier.

That is the guilt at the murder
of the beauty of the earth and its gracefulness,
the deep and heavy guilt at the oppressive blight
on the animal kingdom,
and at the fury which inspires it
and the deceit which tarnishes it,
and at the pain which torments it
and the mould which covers it.

f) Adam

The consolation so desperately lacking in 'Groaning Creation' is to be found in a poem of just a few months earlier, the beautiful 'Gethsemane', which one would like to think expresses the unquestioning faith sometimes glimpsed but rarely sustained in 'The Spiritual Year'. Droste-Hülshoff sent it to Levin Schücking in late August 1845, along with 'Also a Calling' and 'Carpe diem!', and 'Paradise Lost', a poem which, like 'Gethsemane', she designated a *Legende*. The two thus belong together in her understanding of the term, which denotes a poetic retelling of a biblical story. More than that, though, 'Gethsemane' belongs with the greatest poems of her closing years, in its majesty and beauty of poetic expression.

The poem takes its content from the accounts given in all four Gospels, of Christ's anguish in the Garden of Olives, a scene depicted in art and, interestingly, in an engraving which Droste-Hülshoff knew from her childhood in Schloss Hülshoff. To the details of the familiar scene of the suffering of Jesus, and His two appeals to God, "Father, if it is possible, let this hour pass me by" and "Father, Father, not my will but Thine be done", Droste-Hülshoff adds the scene, known only to Luke, of the angel coming to bring strength to Christ. Her own addition is the final image, of the lily, symbolic of purity and holiness, which supplies a powerful conclusion to a poem remarkable for its visual impact.

The visual qualities of this moving poem link it with so much of what is familiar from Droste-Hülshoff throughout her creative life, but never more so than in the descriptions of her last poems, notably 'In the Grass', '*Gemüt*' and arguably most of all in the brilliant 'Moon-Rise'. It is this quality which places 'Gethsemane' more firmly with these poems than with her 'religious' poetry, and it is a very important example of her mature work.

In 'Paradise Lost' too, the visual quality dominates, with the picture of the sleeping Eve, and particularly its culmination in the picture of great beauty which is still threatened by sin and death, and the last sight of her drained of colour and her breast wounded by the thorns. The lesson of the temptation in the Garden of Eden is balanced by the message of 'Gethsemane', and, consolingly if one recalls the starkness of 'Groaning Creation', the ultimate message is of love. The millions of hands outstretched towards the Cross speak of Love more clearly than anywhere else in Droste-Hülshoff, and they draw together the many expressions of love throughout her work.

Central to 'Gethsemane' is the description of the Cross against the darkening sky which she has captured so vividly in earlier poems, lyric and narrative. The silence which is 'more terrifying than the raging of the storm' expresses with a simplicity characteristic of this great poem the redemptive moment central to Christian thought. Above all, it is the humanity of the Saviour which pervades the whole, the man, with 'His spirit broken', 'perspiration turned to blood', come to provide the solace so searingly absent in 'Groaning Creation'.

Gethsemane

August 1845

When Christ was lying on His face in the grove of Gethsemane
with His eyes closed,
the air seemed only to be uttering sighs,
and a stream was murmuring its pain,
reflecting the pale full moon.
That was the hour when the angel was sent down, weeping,
from the throne of God,
in his hand the bitter chalice of suffering.

And in front of the Saviour the Cross rose up,
and upon it He saw His own body hanging,
torn in pieces, stretched out.
The sinews on His limbs pressed forward
in front of Him like ropes.
He saw the nails projecting, and the crown upon His head,
where a drop of blood fell from every thorn, and there came
the muted sound of thunder rumbling, as though in anger.
He heard the sound of dripping and a soft whimper slid,
tormented, desolate, down the upright wooden Cross.
Then did Christ sigh, and sweat poured forth from all His pores.

And the sky darkened, a dead sun floated
in the grey sea, and the anguish of the Head with the crown of thorns
could hardly now be seen, swaying to and fro
in the pangs of death.
At the foot of the Cross lay three figures.
He could see them lying there, grey, like clouds of mist.
He heard the movement
of their heavy breathing.
The folds of their garments fluttered gently.
Ah, what love was ever as fervent as His?
He knew them; He had known them well.
The human heart within His breast ablaze,
the perspiration surged more strongly.

The corpse of the sun vanished, leaving behind only black smoke,
and sunk within it the Cross and the soft sound of sighing.
A silence, more terrifying than the raging of the storm,
floated through the starless alleys of the firmament.
Not a breath of life any longer in the wide world,
a crater round about, burnt out and empty, and a hollow voice cried
from above "My God, my God, why hast Thou forsaken me?"
Then the pangs of death overtook the Saviour, and Christ wept,
His spirit broken. Then His perspiration turned to blood,
and trembling came forth from the mouth of the suffering One:
"Lord, if it is possible, let this hour pass me by."

A flash of lightning streaked across the night.
The Cross was floating in the light, radiant with the symbols
of the martyrdom, and He saw millions of hands stretched out,

clinging fearfully to the stem of the Cross. Ah, hands
great and small from the farthest reaches!
And round the crown there hovered millions
of souls as yet unborn, like sparks.
A light haze of smoke crept out of the ground, and from the graves
of the departed came the sound of pleading. Then,
with abundant Love, Christ raised Himself to His feet and cried:
"Father, Father, not my will but Thine be done!"

The moon floated silently in the blueness. A lily stood
before the Saviour in the dewy grass, and out of the calyx
of the lily stepped the angel and gave Him strength.

The poem '*Gemüt*' was written in the spring of 1844 and so belongs with other significant poems of this late period, many of which are included in this selection, particularly perhaps with the last one here, 'Moon-Rise' . It is a poem which conveys the kind of ecstasy evident in 'In the Grass', an emotion at which Droste-Hülshoff can excel on the rather rare occasions that she abandons herself to unbridled exuberance. It is full of images and colour and one may well ask oneself what it is about, or if it is indeed about anything. Rather does it seem to be the expression of an abstract. Somewhat playfully, Droste-Hülshoff appended a subtitle to the draft, 'de omnibus rebus, et alliquot aliis', followed by a translation into German, 'Von allen Dingen und einigen anderen' ('About all things and some others'). One is left asking what that means, but then the actual title poses the same question, and the question and any attempt to answer it go to the very heart of a brilliant but puzzling poem. The word *Gemüt* presents difficulties, of interpretation and, more crucially here, to anyone attempting to translate it into English. The modern dictionary offers many possibilities as diverse as, among others, 'mind', 'nature', 'disposition', 'soul', 'feeling', 'warm-heartedness'; yet none of them conveys the myriad of meanings inherent in Droste-Hülshoff's concept in an important poem which again concerns her sense of her role as a poet and defines her vocation in a way which is both highly abstract and quite specific.

In his invaluable and still very useful handbook *A Dictionary of German Synonyms*, (first published in 1953), R.B. Farrell writes that the word identifies 'the seat of certain types of feelings, particularly those which embrace the world with warmth and affection' and continues with the comment very relevant to this poem that it is 'sometimes conceived as the source of poetry, particularly of the romantic order' and, further, that the 'sanity, stability, equilibrium, excitement of the mind may be implied.' However, the word 'Verstand' (reason, intellect, understanding), so often a concept problematic to Droste-Hülshoff, who saw it as an arid quality detrimental to the pure faith she so desired, is barely feasible as a synonym. All this information serves to pinpoint the complexity of this already complicated poem, but it is not helpful in suggesting a way forward in translating the title. Any single English word would be inadequate to render the nuances of this title and its applicability to the whole poem, while a combination of the possible translations ('Mind and Spirit', 'Heart and Soul') would tilt it in a misleading direction and fail to do justice to the idea which is its essence. The decision arrived at in this volume – to leave it in German - may appear defeatist, and it has been reached with some reluctance, though ultimately without misgivings. It seems all the more justifiable because it conveys the multiplicity of meanings of the German word and, given the element of address in the final line of the first strophe, attains the quality of personification.

From the opening there is a mood of joyfulness. The simple statement of the green of the meadow, the blue of the sky widens, with the play of light on the dew producing a myriad of shimmering colours. This is a powerful opening, impressionistic in its impact. But then comes the question: what is the gift of this thing called *Gemüt*, the iris of the soul? The question raises the central theme of the poem, for at its heart is the creative urge, symbolised in the dewdrop, which can creep into the very pores of the earth. On one level the poem is about the sacred calling she has talked about so often; on the other it is about the nature of all things, as the subtitle suggests, and about the relationship between heaven and earth, and between Nature and the soul. Poetry is the key to this communion of all things, and it is the expression of ultimate joy. The poet has the ability to transform all things, as the fifth and sixth strophes suggest, with natural everyday features – leaves , moss, pieces of gravel, withered leaves, weeds and grass - being changed by the hand of the poet into precious metals and stones.

At sunset, when the light has faded, comes another transformation, when the light casts strange new shadows. Then the poet is at peace with his own creation, known neither to heaven nor earth but only to himself, that elusive product of his special gift. It is a rare poem, which seems to unite many themes, all barely tangible, but linked in the metaphor of the dewdrop, the guardian of the secrets of the soul. It is rare, too, in its baffling presentation of emotions and moods and seeming to go to the very heart of her conception of her art and the relationship between that and nature in all its variety. It invites a multitude of different interpretations, like the word *Gemüt* itself, and perhaps one is well advised to return to the Latin subtitle for guidance in groping towards an idea of what Droste-Hülshoff may have intended.

Gemüt

Green is the meadow, blue the sky,
yet the dew sparkles with a thousand hues.
The dew goes on hoping until the grave,
but fulfilment was accorded to heaven.
And say: what is then your gift,
Gemüt, you, Iris of the soul?

You drop of dew from the clouds, which crept
into the pores of our clump of earth,
so that it might accustom it to heaven
through its most lovely poem,
you, earthly sacred like a tear,
and heavenly sacred like the light!

Only a drop, a reflection,
yet absorbing all miracles,
whether a pearl cradled on a leaf
and playing at the foot of a bee,
or - sweet dream! – lying in the grass
and smiling at a greeting from the blade.

Ah, earth and heaven smile, too,
when, like a child and woken by the morning breeze,
you lift your gentle, moonlike, bashful gaze
towards the day,
waiting to see what the hand of the Mighty One
will bestow upon you in terms of light and fragrance.

Only smile, smile on and on:
the riches of the child will be yours too.
The leaves of the branch will become your hall,
the fleece of the moss your velvet,
and mussel fragments and gravel will be washed
into opals, sparkling metals, for you.

The reddish green of the withered leaf
presses a ruby on your brow;

weeds and grass adorn your reflection
with the golden glitter of chrysolite,
and even the trembling of the barren leaves
offers you brownish topaz.

And even, when the sunlight has been extinguished,
and now your most precious poem,
the mirage of your sea, is flickering,
a dream of light, about your orb,
and casting fragile silhouettes,
captive spirits, in the crystal,

then you sleep, sleep in your own prison,
allow your hidden power to prevail,
that which is not known to heaven, nor to the earth,
but only to your own creation,
that which has never been, and never will become,
the embryos in your breast.

Oh smile, smile on,
you dewdrop, Iris of the soul!
Let the forest rustle, in the turmoil
let the rows of stars send forth their sparkles!
You have the earth, you have the sky,
and your spirits over and above that.

The final poem chosen to represent the work of the late Annette von Droste-Hülshoff, and possibly to characterise her lyric *œuvre* as a whole, is the stately 'Moon-Rise', another product of that prolific spring and summer of 1844. It is arguably one of the greatest of all her poems, if not perhaps the greatest, but such judgements are obviously a matter of personal taste, and, subjective as they are, of little significance in any case. What is indisputable is that it contains much which is quintessentially Droste-Hülshoff, and it has been the object of a number of individual appreciations by distinguished experts on her.

The first person dominates from the first line and continues to the end: this is the poet observing a natural phenomenon and watching the transformation of the landscape in the rising moon. It is impossible to doubt the identity of the 'I' for it is a deeply personal poem which ends with one of Droste-Hülshoff's most intimate insights. The moon has its own radiance, unlike the fiery light of the sun, and it brings to the dying poet a gentle consolation, as precious as his song. The final strophe greets that risen moon with a special emotion, summed up in the tender image of the 'friend arriving late'. It comes with gifts from the past, bringing memories of youth, and these memories are reflections of a life, like the moon which has no brightness of its own but reflects the light of the sun. Now close to the end of her life, Droste-Hülshoff returns to thoughts that have echoed throughout her work, but this is not a poem weighed down with grief and nostalgia, but a gentle, comforting reflection on a natural process which has resonances in a human life. It may be, as Clemens Heselhaus has said, a 'poem of old age' (*Altersdichtung*) but it is an old age which seems at last to have found comfort and even healing.

The sedate movement of the poem, with its long lines often flowing one into the next, accords with the gradual process which is described. She describes, as only she can, the details of the landscape as she sees it from her perspective high up on her balcony overlooking the lake, and sees, as each strophe follows on, the transformation of those details in the changing light. Side by side with closely observed details – twigs and branches, moths amidst the leaves, the firefly glinting as it climbs – is an image of such tenderness that it evokes real emotion: 'a heart making its way towards the harbour'. Then, however, the nature of her image changes, as the Alps become 'a sombre ring of judges' which, two strophes later, will convert into 'gentle old men': the familiar theme of judgement and guilt is softened as the light transforms the mountain peaks. This softening allows a new and homely image, one used by Droste-Hülshoff in earlier poems: the little drops of moisture on the branches of the trees seem like a little room, and in that little room the light of a lamp is flickering. The immense features of the landscape are changing now to something much more intimate, and that in itself admits the comparison of this huge natural phenomenon with 'a friend arriving late'. There is no threat here, and even what had seemed to pose a threat in the strophe before with the reference to a forlorn life standing cowering there, and the wretched heart with its guilt and its anguish, can be softened and transcended.

One can only hope to convey the impression of the steady metre, and the sheer beauty of language, which is actually extraordinarily simple, but, given all the limitations of a translation, the poem manages to be a magnificent example of the lyric power of the mature Droste-Hülshoff and even – dare one hope? - to suggest the serenity she seems sometimes to attain.

Moon-Rise

I leaned against the trellis of the balcony
and waited, gentle light, for you.
High above me, like murky ice-crystal,
was floating, melted, the firmament's great hall.
The lake stretched out, shimmering softly –
pearls floating away into nothingness, or the tears of clouds?
I waited, gentle light, for you.

I stood high up, beside me the tops of linden trees,
and, far below me, twigs and branches, and their trunks.
Among the leaves hummed rows of moths,
I saw the firefly glinting as it climbed,
and blossoms swaying, as though half-asleep.
It seemed to me that here a heart was making its way towards the harbour,
a heart full to the brim of happiness and sorrow,
and images of blessed past.

The darkness rose, the shadows closing in –
and where were you, ah, where, my gentle light?
They were closing in like sinful thoughts.
The rippling firmament appeared to sway,
The sparks from the firefly had trembled away,
and the moths had long since sunk to the ground.
Only the mountain peaks stood stark and close at hand,
a sombre ring of judges, there in the darkness.

And branches hissed at my feet,
like whispered warnings, or death's salutation.
A humming sound rose up in the broad valley,
like the murmuring of the crowd before the tribunal.
It seemed to me as if something were being called to account,
as if a forlorn life were standing cowering there,
as if a wretched heart were standing there alone,
alone with its guilt and its anguish.

Then a silver veil descended upon the waves,
and slowly, pious light, you rose up.

You gently stroked the dark brow of the Alps
and the judges turned to gentle old men.
The jerking of the waves became a smiling gesture.
On every branch I saw drops of moisture glistening,
and every drop seemed like a little room,
in which was flickering the light from the lamp of home.

O moon, you seem to me like a friend arriving late,
who joins his youth with the wretched one,
entwining round his dying memories
the tender reflection of his life.
You are no sun which charms and dazzles,
which lives in streams of fire and ends in blood –
you are what to the dying singer is his poem,
a strange, but oh, a gentle light,

ANNOTATED BIBLIOGRAPHY

The following short bibliography is offered as guidance to readers who may wish to extend their knowledge of the life and work of Annette von Droste-Hülshoff. It makes no claim to comprehensiveness but has tried to take into account likely availability of books and in particular the needs of readers with little or no knowledge of German.

Editions

The translations in this volume have been based for the most part on the *Historisch-Kritische Ausgabe*, but other available editions have been used where appropriate.

Annette von Droste-Hülshoff. Historisch-Kritische Ausgabe. Werke. Briefwechsel, ed. Winfried Woesler, 14 vols. Tübingen: Niemeyer, 1978ff.

This is the most recent and most authoritative edition of the complete works and letters. It is likely to be available in university libraries.

Annette von Droste-Hülshoff. Werke in einem Band, ed. Clemens Heselhaus, Münich: Hanser 1948. This remains a very convenient single volume edition, with useful notes and introductions, re-edited and reprinted several times. It should also be available in libraries.

Annette von Droste-Hülshoff. Sämtliche Werke in zwei Bänden, ed. Bodo Plachta and Winfried Woesler. Frankfurt am Main and Leipzig: Insel Verlag, 2004. This two-volume edition, based to a large extent on the scholarly findings of the *Historisch-Kritische Ausgabe*, may be seen to have superseded the single volume immediately above. It is easily available and very pleasant to use, probably the most accessible and useful way for readers of German to approach the subject on a fairly detailed level.

Annette von Droste-Hülshoff. Poems. ed. Margaret Atkinson. Oxford: Oxford University Press, 1964. An unpretentious but very useful book, often available in libraries or to buy second hand, this contains many of the most important shorter poems, and the introductions and notes, in English, are incisive and expressed in a straightforward and sensitive way.

Letters

Anyone wishing to look at the copious correspondence of Droste-Hülshoff will probably consult the classic two-volume edition of her extant letters which is likely to be available through university libraries:

Annette von Droste-Hülshoff: Briefe. Gesamtausgabe.ed. Karl Schulte Kemminghausen. Eugen Diderichs Verlag: Jena 1944.

A single volume paperback edition of her collected letters is also most conveniently available in DTV, Max Niemeyer Verlag: Tübingen 1987. This is based on the *Historisch-Kritische Ausgabe*.

Some secondary literature

Beuys, Barbara, *Blamieren mag ich mich nicht. Das Leben der Annette von Droste-Hülshoff.* Frankfurt and Leipzig: Insel Verlag 1999. A detailed and wide-ranging account of Droste-Hülshoff's life and times, readable if sometimes a little overwhelming in its detail and coverage.

Gibbs, Marion E, 'Annette von Droste-Hülshoff: the poet of the ever-open wounds' in *Sappho in the Shadows*, ed. Anthony J. Harper and Margaret C. Ives, Bern etc: Peter Lang 2000, pp. 223 -262. An introductory account by the present author with some translations of poems.

Guthrie, John, *Annette von Droste-Hülshoff. A German Poet between Romanticism and Realism*. Oxford etc. Berg 1989. A straightforward account of her work and its relationship to the literary context, with brief but detailed references to individual works. Useful and likely to be available.

Mare, Margaret, *Annette von Droste-Hülshoff.* London: Methuen 1965. This probably remains the best introduction in English. It is readable and reliable and achieves admirable coverage, with some translations of poems into English.

Pickar, Gertrud Bauer, *Ambivalence Transcended. A Study of the Writings of Annette von Droste-Hülshoff*, Columbia: Camden House 1997. Not the easiest book to read, but full of information and opinions, embedded in many pages.

'Too manly is your spirit': Annette von Droste Hülshoff", Rice University Studies, 1978, pp.51-68. This is a much more accessible account of the personal and social restrictions facing Droste-Hülshoff and their impact on her work.

Prawer, S.S, *A Critical Analysis of Selected Poems from Klopstock to Rilke*. Routledge and Kegan Paul: London 1952. This is a beautifully written account of German poetry of the 18th, 19th and 20th centuries. Pp. 162-167 are devoted to an analysis of *Mondesaufgang*, but the whole volume is worth reading, over fifty years on, for its insights into the literary context.

Tymms, Marion, *God's Sorely-tested Child*, Memoirs: Cirencester 2012. The precursor of the current volume, this is devoted to 'The Spiritual Year', with a complete translation into English.

Some suggestions for further reading

Several names occur from much earlier generations of Germanists, and their books may be available in libraries: any reading of these would undoubtedly enhance the understanding of Droste-Hülshoff and her position in German literature.

Gundolf, Friedrich, *Annette von Droste-Hülshoff*, in *Romantiker. Neue Folge*. Berlin: H. Keller 1931

Heselhaus, Clemens, *Die Entdeckung des Seins in der Dichtung des neunzehnten Jahrhunderts*, Halle: Max Niemeyer Verlag 1943. Heselhaus is one of the foremost authorities on Droste-Hülshoff, and other books and articles, particularly in the publications of the Droste-Hülshoff Society, would be well worth seeking for the really interested reader of German.

Staiger, Emil, *Annette von Droste-Hülshoff*, Frauenfeld: Verlag Huber and Co. 1967.

Any available edition of the *Lebensbild* by Levin Schücking, whose own memoirs, entitled *Lebenserinnerungen*, are readily available in a facsimile edition, would add to the picture of the relationship between Schücking and Droste-Hülshoff and increase the understanding of a complex figure.

INDEX OF POEMS TRANSLATED

Agony	p.11
Also a Calling	p.238
By the Pond	pp.24-26
Carpe diem!	p.209
Farewell Greeting (To Philippa Pearsall, 25 August 1844)	p.248
Farewell to Switzerland	p.106
Farewell to Youth	p.115
Fare well (it cannot be otherwise)	p.96
Gemüt	p.268
Gethsemane	p.263
Greetings	p.256
Groaning Creation	p 259
Heartfelt	p.27
Hold fast!	p.212
I, the Centre of the World	p.216
In the Grass	p.252

In the Moss	p.132
Katharina Schücking	p.81
Late Awakening	p.198
Moon-Rise	p.272
My Calling	p.221
My Dead Ones	p.129
On Lake Constance	p.144
On the Tower	p.112
One like many and many like one	p.205
Restlessness	p.3
Sleepless Night	p.185
The Boy on the Moor	p.151
The Bench	p.122
The Dead Lark	p.194
The Deserted House	p.180
The Dolmen	p.176
The Golmens	p.243
The Heath-Man	p.153
The House on the Heath	p.160
The Hunt	p.164
The Inn on the Lake (To Levin Schücking)	p.91
The Marl-Pit	p.172
The Old Castle	p.145

The Poet-the Poet's Happiness p.225
The Pond pp.138-140
The Portrait p.233
The Reflection p.127
The Right Time p.28; p.108
The Säntis pp.21-24
The Sick Eagle p.111
The Shepherds' Fire p.157
The Sleep-Walker p.191
The Steppe p.135
The Unsung Ones p.200
The Yew Hedge p.118
The Word p.227
To a friend (No word and even if it were…) p.94
To a friend (For the second time…..) p.95
To Levin Schücking (Oh, do not ask…..) p.93
To Philippa p.247

German Titles of Poems translated

It is hoped that the following list will help readers wishing to refer to specific poems in the original.

Abschied von der Jugend p.115

Abschied von der Schweiz p.106

Abschiedsgruß p.248

Am Bodensee p.144

Am Turme p.112

Am Weiher pp.24-26

An einen Freund ("Kein Wort und wär' es…") p.94

An einen Freund ("Zum zweiten Male….") p.95

An Levin Schücking ("O frage nicht……..") p.93

An Philippa p.247

Auch ein Beruf p.238

Carpe diem! p.209

Das alte Schloß p.145

Das Bild p.232

Das Haus in der Heide p.160

Das Hirtenfeuer p.154

Das Ich der Mittelpunkt der Welt p.216

Das öde Haus p.180

Das Spiegelbild p.127

Das Wort p.227

Der Dichter- Dichters Glück p.225

Der Heidemann p.153

Der Hünenstein p.176

Der Knabe im Moor p.151

Der kranke Aar p.111

Der Nachtwandler p.191

Der Säntis pp.21-24

Der Weiher pp.138-140

Die ächzende Kreatur p.259

Die Bank p.122

Die Golems p.243

Die Jagd p. 164

Die Mergelgrube p.172

Die rechte Stunde p.28; p.108

Die Schenke am See p.91

Die Steppe p.135

Die Taxuswand p.118

Die tote Lerche p. 194

Die Unbesungenen p.200

Durchwachte Nacht p.185

Einer wie viele und viele wie einer p.205

Gemüt p.268

Gethsemane p. 263

Grüße p.256

Halt fest! p.212
Herzlich p.27
Im Grase p.252
Im Moose p.132
Katharina Schücking p.81
Lebt wohl! p.96
Mein Beruf p.221
Meine Toten p.129
Mondesaufgang p.271
Not p.11
Spätes Erwachen p.198
Unruhe p.3

Poems from 'The Spiritual Year' translated in this volume

On New Year's Day p.36

On the Feast of Epiphany p.38

On the First Sunday after Epiphany p.41

On the Third Sunday after Epiphany p.43

On the Feast of the Purification of the Virgin p.45

On Maundy Thursday p.49

On Good Friday p.50

On Easter Sunday p.53

On the First Sunday after Easter p.58

On the Third Sunday after Easter p.59

On the Fifth Sunday after Easter p.61

On Whit Sunday p.63

On the Fourth Sunday after Whitsun p.66

On the Sixth Sunday after Whitsun p. 67

On the Eleventh Sunday after Whitsun p.68

On the Nineteenth Sunday after Whitsun p.70

On All Saints' Day p.72

On All Souls' Day p.74

On Christmas Day p.75

On the Last Day of the Year p.77